Robert Webber

Is 9/11 a Call to Heal America?

2 Chronicles 7:14

Is 9/11 a Call to Heal America?

2 Chronicles 7:14

The Wonderful World of Worship on Bended Knee

Ralph W. Rowe, MD

RESOURCE *Publications* · Eugene, Oregon

IS 9/11 A CALL TO HEAL AMERICA?
The Wonderful World of Worship on Bended Knee

Wipf and Stock Publishers
199 West 8th Avenue, Suite 3
Eugene, Oregon 97401

www.wipfandstock.com

ISBN 13: 978-1-55635-679-7

Manufactured in the U.S.A.

Contents

1

Why Study "Kneeling in Worship"?

2 Chronicles 7:14

The Wonderful World of Worship on Bended Knee

SINCE THE TRAGIC TERRORIST attacks on September 11, 2001, various political and religious figures have made many remarks in regard to kneeling in prayer. Just three days after the attacks, President George W. Bush visited the smoldering mountain of rubble that was once the World Trade Center. He came to cheer the thousands of workers who were desperately searching for survivors. With a bullhorn in one hand and his other arm draped around a firefighter, he addressed the crowd. "I want you all to know that America today—that America today—is **on bended knee** in prayer for the people whose lives were lost here, for the workers who work here, and for the families who mourn."[1]

Just four days after 9/11, a headline in the Religion Section of *The Dallas Morning News* read, "**Crisis sends people to their knees.**" Several pictures showed people in churches **on their knees**. An adjoining column claimed that students, both locally and around the nation, planned to gather at the annual "See you at the Pole" prayer service to pray. Students in middle schools, high schools, and colleges gathered around the flagpole and pray—just eight days after the nation endured the terrorist attacks. The chosen theme for the occasion was, "Desperate for God."[2]

1. "President Bush Salutes Heroes in New York." One Page. Accessed November 26, 2007. Online: http://www.whitehouse.gov/news/releases/2001/09/20010914-9.html.

2. Delgado, Berta. "Crisis Sends People to Their Knees." *Dallas Morning News*, September 15, 2001, Religion Section: page 1G. Accessed at Abilene Christian University on 12/4/07.

Youth Ministry News reported that "a movement known as the '30-Second Kneel Down' is sweeping the nation as high school students boldly **kneel** in prayer for the teachers, students, and administrators of their schools. Testimonials indicate a very real and tangible impact in our nation's schools as some teens report witnessing opportunities as other students ask them why they are **kneeling**." The article's headline reads, "Over One Million High School Students Bring Prayer Back to Public Schools." The '30-Second Kneel Down' was started by Pennsylvania Youth Pastor Tom Sipling.[3] The Website: http://www.30kd.org/what.htm Accessed 2005.

Max Lucado's prayer that was circulated widely on the internet just after 9/11, began as follows: "Dear Lord, the enemy sought to bring us **to our knees** and succeeded. He had no idea, however, that we would **kneel** before you . . ."[4]

1) Is 9/11 a "kneel-down-call" to heal America?

Just five days after 9/11, the popular preacher David Dykes, correctly modeled the true meaning of the word "humble" from the passage in 2 Chronicles 7:14. On his televised Sunday morning broadcast from Tyler, Texas, he **kneeled** as he began the opening prayer taken directly from 2 Chronicles 7:14. He said, "Father, we have heard people say that 9/11 is a 'wake up call' for America, but we think this is a '**kneel-down**-call' to America. We need to get **on our knees** and **on our faces before** You and seek Your face. We know that only when we humble ourselves and pray, seek Your face, and turn from our wicked ways—only then—will You hear from heaven, forgive our sin, and heal our land." Dr. Dykes then preached a very helpful sermon called "Facing the Future without Fear." How wonderful it would be if all Christians were to grasp that 9/11 is a "**kneel down** call for America" and begin to practice what is needed in 2 Chronicles 7:14 so that God will "hear from heaven, forgive our sin, and heal our land."[5]

Joseph Garlington, in his book entitled *Worship: The Pattern of Things in Heaven*, has emphasized that the word "humble" in 2 Chronicles

3. Sipling, Tom. "What is the 30 Second Kneel Down?" Two Pages. Accessed 2005.

4. Lucado, Max. "Do It Again, Lord." Accessed November 7, 2007. Online: http://www.maxlucado.com/read/do.it.again.html.

5. Dykes, David. *Facing the Future without Fear*, Green Acres Baptist Church in Tyler, TX, September 16, 2001, Videocassette: 30 min.

7:14 literally means to **"bend the knee"** in humility. He began by quoting the verse that tells what God requires to heal our land: "If My people who are called by My name will humble themselves, and pray and seek My face, and turn from their wicked ways, then I will hear from heaven, and will forgive their sin and heal their land" (2 Chronicles 7:14, NKJV). He then explains that, "The word ***humble*** is actually *kana*', one of the four Hebrew words for *worship* in the OT. It means 'to **bend the knee**; hence to humiliate.'"[6]

Ten years prior to the attacks on September 11, 2001, the well known preacher Charles Stanley predicted that America was "going to be humiliated" in some way at some time, unless God intervened. He was concerned about America's moral decline, so he invited "more than 2000 politicians and other notables" to **kneel** at "the annual Leadership Luncheon in the main ballroom of the Washington Hilton in 1991. He preached from James 5:16, eloquently and fervently, about the need for America to humble itself before God. He allowed that some might not be physically able, but for the rest he said, 'Unless God does something in this nation, we are going to be humiliated in some fashion, at some time. I want to ask you if you'll join me **on my knees.**' Gradually, chairs began shuffling, and most of the crowd followed his lead."[7] In looking back on 9/11, Charles Stanley had both foresight and insight. Also, he was apparently convinced that **kneeling** in humility and returning to God as stated in 2 Chronicles 7:14 was needed to heal America.

In 2004, Charles Stanley used 2 Chronicles 7:14 as the solution to heal America when he wrote a very insightful and appropriate article called *"America at the Crossroads."* He began by asking, "Which way America?" Then he reviewed Supreme Court rulings that had "brought an onslaught against our faith." Our constitution says that our government will not establish a religion. Charles Stanley pointed out that in 1947, Justice Hugo Black incorrectly interpreted the "'no establishment of religion' clause as a mandate for a wall of separation between church and state. In the 1960's the Federal Supreme Court removed prayer and Scripture from schools, arguing that Bible reading 'could cause psychological damage to students.' The Ten Commandments were subsequently stripped from

6. Garlington, Joseph L. *Worship: The Pattern of Things in Heaven.* Shippensburg, PA: Destiny Image Publishers Inc., 1998, 8-10.

7. Merrill, Dean. "Whatever Happened to Kneeling?" *Christianity Today,* February 10, 1992, 24.

the public square with the statement, 'If the Ten Commandments were to have any effect at all, it would be to induce students to read them. They will meditate on them. If they meditate on them, they will respect and obey them, and that would be unconstitutional.'" Dr. Stanley then emphasizes that,"Everywhere we turn today, the existence of God is being erased from our midst without our consent. America's greatest enemy does not lie outside our borders; it lies within us. Our complacency is destroying us, and why don't believers speak up? It is time for the body of Christ to awaken from apathy and act responsibly."

Charles Stanley concluded by saying, "There is just one way to win this fight, and that is to engage the most powerful force available—Almighty God Himself." He points out that, "The Lord reveals His plan to rescue a people under judgment," and then he quoted 2 Chronicles 7:13–14. His powerful conclusion reads as follows: "Christian, become the person you say you are. Humble yourself. Pray. Seek His face. Turn from your wicked ways. God is faithful to do what He has said—and He has promised, 'then I will hear from heaven, forgive their sin, and will heal their land.'"[8]

President Ronald Reagan also referred to 2 Chronicles 7:14 as "A most wonderful verse for healing of the nations" when he spoke at the Annual National Prayer Breakfast in1983. After giving God and the Bible credit for the survival of our nation, he announced that he had agreed to serve as honorary chairman for the "Year of the Bible." He then acknowledged that America had faced many great challenges and had conquered them all. He said, "What carried us through was a willingness to seek power and protection from the One much greater than ourselves, to turn back to Him, and to trust in His mercy. Without His help, America will not go forward." While recognizing the importance of the Bible, he said his mother Nelle had marked a verse in his Bible and had written a note beside it. The verse was 2 Chronicles 7:14, and the faded note written by his mother read, "A most wonderful verse for healing of the nations." President Reagan then read the verse that she had marked: "If my people, which are called by my name, shall humble themselves, and pray, and seek my face, and turn from their wicked ways: then will I hear from heaven, and forgive their sin, and will heal their land."[9]

8. Stanley, Charles. "America at the Crossroads" *In Touch,* November 2004, 8–9

9. Reagan, Ronald. Page 2 of 2. Accessed June 27, 2001. Online: http://www.reagan.utexas.edu/archives/speeches/1983/20383a.htm.

Remember that the word "humble" in 2 Chronicles 7:14 is "*kana*," and means to **"bend the knee"** in humility. Zodhiates says it means, "**to bend the knee,** thus to humiliate."

What will happen if we fail to obey 2 Chronicles 7:14? Helen Steiner Rice says:

"Keep Our Nation in Thy Care"

For when a nation is too proud
To **kneel** to daily pray,
It will crumble into chaos,
And descend into decay.

—Helen Steiner Rice

President Ronald Reagan mentioned **kneeling** for our nation as he signed the National Day of Prayer Proclamation in 1987. He said, "Throughout our history, our leaders have always turned to prayer in times of crisis. All of us know how George Washington **knelt** in the snow at Valley Forge to ask for divine assistance when the fate of our nation hung in the balance."[10]

In fact, George Washington wrote a prayer for his troops to recite while **bowing the knees** at Valley Forge that petitioned God as follows: "Look down from heaven in pity and compassion upon me Thy servant, who humbly **prostrates myself** before Thee."[11]

Francis Frangipane tells how people are **kneeling** in prayer for God to "heal their cities." She says, "All across the world holy men and women are being fitted together into a living temple for the Lord. These believers are finding themselves **kneeling** in one another's buildings and praying at one another's side. Their common prayer is that the Almighty might unite them in Christ and . . . heal their cities."[12]

10. Reagan, Ronald. "website: http://scholar.google.com/scholar?hl=en&lr=&q=Reagan%27s+actual+speech+at+Prayer+breakfast+1987." 2 Pages. Accessed June 27, 2001. http://www.reagan.edutexas.edu/resource/speeches/122286b.htm.

11. Washington, George. "Website: http://www.heartlight.org/prayerforthenation/articles/200210/20021023_pftn-pray.html" Accessed October 23, 2002. 2 Pages.

12. Frangipane, Francis. *Twenty Lessons Learned While Walking with God.* Impact Christian Books, Inc. 332 Leffingwell Ave., Suite 101, Kirkwood, MO 63122 U: 1994, 15.

Michael Youssef who is a preacher in Atlanta Georgia points out that, "Reading the Bible is legal in Russian schools, but the Bible is illegal in American schools. That ought to put us **on our knees** for America."[13]

2) Is the kneeling gesture authorized in the New Testament?

The primary focus of this study is to determine if the Greek "worship" word *proskuneo* used in John 4:23–24 includes "**bowing the knees**" or "**kneeling**." In the NT, *proskuneo* is the most common Greek word translated as "worship", and in the New Testament, it occurs a total of 60 times. Also, an attempt will be made to document all of the worship events in the New Testament that include a form of **bowing the knees** or **kneeling**. I truly believe that all dedicated Christians would like to know for sure if **kneeling** is a gesture that our heavenly Father approves and desires in our worship or if it is just another prayer posture. This task will be undertaken using five (5) reliable sources of information or testimony—(a) the testimony of God—which is Scripture (1 Corinthians 2:1), (b) the testimony of Lexicons (or Greek dictionaries), (c) the testimony of Bible translators, (d) the testimony of history, and (e) the testimony of Bible scholars. These five testimonies will be discussed separately except for the testimony of history because many historical facts will be mentioned throughout this study. However, the Word of God is the "Final Supreme Court of Appeal."

In years past, and especially in the last decade, many preachers and Bible scholars have expressed approval of **kneeling** in the worship assembly. In fact, some outstanding Bible scholars have spoken out very strongly in favor of the **kneeling** gesture being restored in our worship to the Lord God Almighty. Even though many of these individuals will be quoted throughout this study, it seems appropriate that some of their insightful remarks be mentioned early on.

Also, during the rest of this study on **kneeling**, the words that indicate a form of **bowing the knees** or **kneeling** will continue to be bolded for ease of recognition. Join with me as we explore together—the *wonderful world of worship* ***on bended knee***.

3) Is kneeling just another prayer posture?

Is **kneeling** a gesture that God has actually ordained and desires in our worship to Him, or is it just another prayer posture? Also, can a

13. Youssef, Michael. "Leading the Way." *INSP* TV, September 21, 2003.

person pray in any posture? Can we pray while lying down, sitting, standing, walking, running, driving, swimming, etc? Is there any posture that a person should not pray in?

The Bible says to "Pray without ceasing" (1 Thess. 5:17). I take that to mean that we should continue praying regardless of the posture we are in. If we are to "Pray without ceasing," would that not include any and all postures? The following poem appears to clearly illustrate the answer:

THE PRAYER OF CYRUS BROWN

Last year I fell in Hodgkin's well head-first, said layman Cyrus Brown;
With both my heels a-stickin' up, my head a-pointin' down;
And I made a prayer right then and there; best prayer I ever said,
The prayingest prayer I ever prayed, a-standin' on my head.[14]

—*Sam Walter Foss*

Surely, we all have prayed in various postures. Mike Armour is a gifted Bible scholar and preacher who reminds us that, "scripture talks about a variety of postures for prayer because there are differing needs at different moments in our prayer life. There are times when we need to be **on our knees** in prayer because something happens within the spirit of a man or a woman **on their knees** . . . Scripture talks about people who **fell on their face** before the Lord in prayer, **prostrate** before Him. There is an appropriate time for that posture. You see, He did not require of us a particular posture for prayer because He understood the complexity of the world in which we live and the complexity of the circumstances we would face and the need to address our prayers from an environment that allows us to get perspective. And if that includes my need to hold my hands out and look up or to **fall flat on my face** before Him, I am not to feel that I have done something wrong in taking that posture in prayer."[15]

4) Is kneeling just a matter of culture?

Richard Pruitt has expressed it well claiming that, "an unfortunate casualty of the Protestant Reformation and western culture has been the practice of **kneeling (and bowing)** during times of worship and prayer. **Kneeling/bowing** should not be understood as a cultural matter. It is

14. Foss, Sam Walter. "The Prayer of Cyrus Brown." Accessed November 26, 2007, Online: Website: http://www.histable.com/THE%20PRAYER%20OF%20CYRUS%20BROWN.htm.

15. Armour, Mike. *Destructive Words*. Shiloh Road Church of Christ in Tyler, TX, August 29, 2003, Audiocassette.

about humility and the breaking down of pride. Simply put, contemporary believers (American Protestants included) are supposed to utilize **kneeling** during **worship** and prayer just as any other people group at any other time in history. I believe that we do not utilize **kneeling** enough in our times of prayer and worship and that there is something greater that we can experience in Christ as we place ourselves in a position of humility. May our hearts be open to the Holy Spirit as He guides us in this humble position of prayer and **worship**? Let us **kneel** before our God!"[16]

In *Experience God in Worship,* George Barna claims that Satan, the tempter, "sought to be worshiped by the Son of God (Matt. 4:1–11). As soon as Satan uttered the words '**bow down** and **worship** me' the contest was over. Surely it's no mistake that the first commandment is that we must not worship any other deity (Exodus 20:3–6). Among adults who regularly attend church services, one-half admit that they haven't experienced God's presence at any time during the past year. When asked to define what worship means, two out of three are unable to offer an appropriate definition or description of worship."[17]

5) What do Bible scholars say about the topic of kneeling?

Approximately three years after I began exploring the topic of "**kneeling**" in the Bible and documenting all the **kneeling** events in the NT, I began to question whether or not there was a real need to continue the study. I then talked with Henry Blackaby, the author of the popular book, *Experiencing God.* After I explained that I was studying **kneeling** and trying to document what the Bible had to say about **kneeling** in the New Testament, he gave me some strong words of encouragement. Henry Blackaby said that, "God has given you an assignment. **Kneeling** is the deepest expression of humility. When your body **kneels**, it helps your heart to do the same. If there was ever a generation that needed to **kneel**, this is the one. This is a self-centered generation who refuses to **kneel** to anyone and it is affecting the life of the Church. It is difficult to walk into the presence of God and not **kneel**. If we just strut into the presence of God and not **kneel**, that is arrogance, and He is not pleased."

16. Pruitt, Richard. "Casualty of the Protestant Reformation." 1 Page. Accessed May 15, 2000. Online: htpp://www.guam.net/home/richpruitt/page22.html.

17. Barna, George . . . [et al.]. *Experience God in Worship.* 2000, Group Publishing, Inc., Dept. P.O. Box 481, Loveland, CO 80539 13–15.

Hal Hougey, author of *The Quest for Understandable Hermeneutics* asks, "O God, what has happened to us? Are we incapable of emotion? Have we forgotten how to adore and glorify you? Are our knees so stiff from spiritual arthritis that we never **fall down** before you? God, forgive us!"[18]

Ralph Gilmore, a Bible scholar and chairman of the Interdisciplinary Studies at Freed-Hardeman University, summarizes his view by saying, "Perhaps one of the most significant missing elements in many of our assemblies is the awe that should be felt or the penitent **bending of the knees** in the presence of God."[19]

A popular and gifted young preacher named Jeff Christian has also drawn some very insightful conclusions. He exhorts us by saying, "I would assert that one of our biggest downfalls in modern Christianity is that sometimes we like to talk about God so much that we actually forget to encounter Him . . . To study prayer without actually **falling to our knees** . . . Yes, read your Bibles but then do what it says . . . Read the beautiful words 'give thanks to the Lord for He is good.' But then, after that you **fall to your knees** and you give thanks . . . It is time that we admit to ourselves as Christians, that it is one thing to study theology and an entire quantum leap to follow through and practice it. To Him be the glory forever. Amen."[20]

Jack Reese, Dean of the Graduate School of Theology at Abilene Christian University, spoke for many of us in 1994 when he said, "I don't know when it happened, but it happened sometime in this century—that in Churches of Christ we decided we don't need to **kneel** anymore. Maybe it's because other churches **knelt**, and we don't want to do what other churches do. There was a time last century and early in this century, as many of you well remember, when it was common in Churches of Christ for members to **kneel** in prayer and worship. Growing up in the 1950s, I remember times that Godly men and women would **kneel in worship**. It is sad to me that those days seem to be gone. Somehow, we can come to our assemblies and just kind of sit—you know, everyone comfortable, ev-

18. Hougey, Hal. *The Quest for Understandable Hermeneutics.* Published by Manna, A Division ot Pacific Publishing Co., 1754 Mendocino Dr., Concord, CA 94521 1997, 462.

19. Gilmore, Ralph. "The Meaning of Worship." *Gospel Advocate.* August 1995, 13–14.

20. Christian, Jeff. *Making Theology Practical.*, Abilene Christian University Lectureship, 1997, Audiocassette.

eryone feeling good, and everyone just kind of relaxed. We offer a prayer to God here, a song there, and a scripture there, and get on home to the game—and we miss the dynamics of the submission and surrender of our hearts. I believe there is a direct connection between **the knee** and the heart."[21]

Robert Webber, the well known author of *Worship is a Verb*, and editor of the *Complete Library of Christian Worship* says, "**Worship** has a body language all its own, so why have we forgotten it? Scriptures tell us '**every knee shall bow** and every tongue confess that Jesus is Lord' (Phil. 2:11). 'He is Lord' is the earliest Christian creed implying **bending the knee** So, the next time you gather to worship, **bow down**! . . . For good **worship,** the inner person must intend what the outer person is doing."[22]

A. W. Tozer has repeatedly discussed this issue in sermons as well as in his new book titled *Worship: The Missing Jewel.* He summarizes the solution to the worship problem in the following quote: "Worship, I say, rises or falls with our concept of God . . . and if there is one terrible disease in the Church of Christ, it is that we do not see God as great as He is. We ought to have again the old Biblical concept of God which makes God awesome and that makes men **lie face down** and cry, 'Holy, Holy, Holy, Lord God Almighty.' That would do more for the Church than everything or anything else."[23]

Jack Lewis, an experienced Bible professor and a highly respected authority on the meaning of Bible words, wisely points out the difficulty that can occur when **bowing the knees** is taken figuratively. He says, "One of the most common words in the New Testament for worship is p*roskynein*, and its basic meaning is to **prostrate oneself** in the presence of a superior. In a democracy, we do not **prostrate ourselves** before superiors, and that attitude carries over into our relationship with God. The idea of **prostration**, even when taken *figuratively* and emotionally, comes hard for us."[24]

21. Reese, Jack. Dean of the Graduate School of Theology at ACU. Sermon at Preston Road Church of Christ in Dallas, TX, January 2, 1994, Audiocassette.

22. Webber, Robert. "Every Knee Shall Bow." *Worship Leader*, Vol. 7, No. 3, May–June, 1998, 14.

23. Tozer, A. W. *Worship: The Missing Jewel.* Christian Publications Camp Hill, PA 1992, 22.

24. Lewis, Jack P. "Time for Worship." *Gospel Advocate*, April 1998, 34–35.

Dan Dozier is an outstanding author, preacher, and mortgage consultant, who also strongly encouraged me in this study of **kneeling** in **worship**. When speaking at various seminars on **worship,** and especially in his book titled *Come Let Us Adore Him*, he reminds us that the heart of worship is a genuine encounter with God. To help us better grasp the awesome worthiness of our God and His majestic Son, the insightful Dr. Dozier effectively selects the scenes of worship described in the book of Revelation as "pictures of the way that we were created to experience intimacy with God" (Revelation 4:5; 5:1–14; 19:1–10). For example, Dr. Dozier says, "the primary picture that I get of heaven is a place of joyful praise, a place where **every knee will bow** and every tongue confess that Jesus Christ is Lord to the praises of God's glory (Philippians 2:9–11)."

Dr. Dozier says he is convinced that he will **kneel** in heaven and does not want to wait until he gets there to start expressing his adoration and reverence in that manner. This practice, he asserts, is "found in scripture in the form of commands, necessary inferences, and examples." He challenges us to "search the scriptures again" because "both the Old Testament and New Testament provide an abundance of Biblical examples."[25]

6) Does the worship word *proskuneo* in John 4:24 include "bowing the knees?"

Stafford North, a highly regarded preacher, author, and University professor, has emphasized that **bowing the knees** is essential in order to be in harmony with the Greek word "*proskuneo*" that is translated as "**worship**" in John 4:24. In his article that was published in the May 2000 issue of the *Christian Chronicle*, he summarizes the "essentials" of worship as follows: "John 4:24 capsules the essentials of worship: (1) God is spirit, (2) those who **worship**, (3) must **worship** in spirit, and (4) in truth. The word '**worship**' means for me to **prostrate myself** before the object of my worship. I would do this only to send a very strong message of submission and reverence to my God."[26]

Frederick C. Kubicek says that the Greek word for "**worship**," *proskuneo*, was an "eye opener" for him because the term "is used to designate

25. Dozier, Daniel A. *Come Let Us Adore Him*. College Press Publishing Company, 223 W. Third St. Joplin, Missouri 64802—1994, 233–91.

26. North, Stafford. "Unlocking Our Hearts to God is Key to Making Our Worship Meaningful." *Christian Chronicle*, May 2000, 31.

the custom of **prostrating oneself"** and **"kissing of another's feet"** He goes on to ask, "Will you wait, or will you **bow your knee** to Him now?"[27]

7) What is the meaning of the Greek worship word *proskuneo*?

I agree with Stafford North that the Greek word "*proskuneo*" translated as "worship" in John 4:24 is an act that is always done while **bowing the knees**. Also, I am in agreement with Dan Dozier and others that **"kneeling"** is in harmony with Scripture. In further support of these two Bible scholars and all the other scholars mentioned, the following conclusions are presented based on several reliable resources including Scripture.

Of the 13 Greek words translated **"worship"** in the NT, *proskuneo* is the most common and occurs a total of 60 times. When *proskuneo* is used in the NT, the object is always someone who is truly or supposedly divine.[28] The Lexicons or Greek dictionaries say that *proskuneo* is a compound word from *pros*, which means "to" or "toward," and *kuneo*, which means to "kiss." Literally, *proskuneo* means to "kiss toward." The lips of the worshiper were placed "to" or "toward" the hand, the foot, or the foreground of the person or object worshiped. Also, N. Woodruff says that to "kiss toward" or "throwing a kiss" toward someone while **on bended knee** may simply mean "touching the hand to the lips and extending it in reverence and obeisance toward the person so honored."[29]

8) What is the "proskuneo puzzle" of worship?

For many, the word **"worship"** and the word *proskuneo* are disconnected pieces to an unsolved "puzzle." The "proskuneo puzzle" of **worship** can only be solved by following the "pattern" revealed in Scripture. When the correct two acts are placed in the correct sequence as recorded in Scripture, the "proskuneo puzzle" is unlocked and becomes the "*proskuneo* pattern" of **worship**. In Scripture, the act of **"bowing the knees"** always precedes the act of **worship** (*proskuneo*: kiss toward). The next section will show 13 explicit examples of the "*proskuneo* pattern" in the New Testament that unlock the mystery of the "*proskuneo* puzzle" of worship.

27. Kubicek, Frederick C. "Worship Him Now." Accessed January 15, 2001. Online: www.unlimitedglory.org/needful.

28. Greeven, Heinrich. *Theological Dictionary of NT.* Eerdmans, Wm. B. Pub Co. Grand Rapids, MI 1968, 759–66, 763.

29. Woodruff, N. Online: http//music.olivet.edu/nwoodruff/A-Definition-of-worship .htm. accessed January 15, '01.

As mentioned previously, the Greek word *proskuneo* translated as "**worship**" in the New Testament means "to kiss," "kiss toward," or throw a "kiss toward" someone in adoration, **worship**, or homage while **kneeling** or **prostrating before** him.[30] For example, in the following 13 New Testament occurrences, the two acts or gestures are explicitly mentioned (Matthew 2:11; 4:9; 18:26; Mark 15:19; Acts 10:25; 1 Corinthians 14:25; Revelation 4:10; 5:14; 7:11; 11:16; 19:4; 19:10; 22:8). To illustrate the explicit "pattern" that emerges and to show the sequence of the two acts that the 13 verses have in common, a brief summary of each verse is presented. For emphasis and ease in recognition, the two acts that make up the "*proskuneo* pattern" of **worship** are bolded.

9) The 13 Examples of the "proskuneo pattern" of Worship in the New Testament (KJV). (The solution to the "proskuneo puzzle" is demonstrated by Scripture). In fact, a "pattern" emerges in the second chapter of Matthew!

1. Matt. 2:11	The wise men "**fell down** and **worshiped**" (*proskuneo*: kissed toward) Jesus.
2. Matt. 4:9	Satan said to Jesus, "If you will **fall down** and **worship** (*proskuneo*: kiss toward) me."
3. Matt. 18:26	The wicked servant "**fell down** and **worshiped**" (*proskuneo*: kissed toward) a certain King.
4. Mark 15:19	The Roman soldiers: "**bowing the knees** they **worshiped**", (*proskuneo*: kissed toward) Jesus.
5. Acts 10:25	Cornelius "**Fell down** and **worshiped**" (*proskuneo*: kissed toward) Peter.
6. 1 Cor. 14:25	The outsider will "**fall** on his face and **worship**" (*proskuneo*: kiss toward) God.
7. Rev. 4:10	The elders "**fell down** and **worshiped**" (*proskuneo*: kissed toward) the "Lord God Almighty."

30. Ibid: Zodhiates, Spiros. and Warren Baker. *The Complete Word Study Old Testament,* AMG International, INC. D/B/A Iowa Falls, IA: 1994, 1233–34.

8. Rev 5:14	The 24 elders "**fell down** and **worshiped**" (*proskuneo*: kissed toward) Jesus, the lamb.
9. Rev 7:11	All the angels "**fell before** the throne on their faces and **worshiped**." (*proskuneo*: kissed toward) God.
10. Rev11:16	The 24 elders "**fell** upon their faces and **worshiped**" (*proskuneo*: kissed toward) God.
11. Rev 19:4	The elders and creatures "**fell down** and **worshiped**" (*proskuneo*: kissed toward) God.
12. Rev 19:10a	John approached the angel and "**fell at his feet** to **worship**" (*proskuneo*: kiss toward) him.
13. Rev 22:8	Again, John "**fell down** to **worship**" (*proskuneo*: kiss toward) before the feet of the angel.

10) Do each of these 13 examples demonstrate the "proskuneo pattern?"

On close examination, it becomes obvious that all of the 13 *proskuneo* **worship** events have two things in common. First, there are two specific outward acts in each of these 13 examples of *proskuneo* **worship**. Second, the act or gesture that is expressed by various forms of "**fall down**" or "**bowing the knees**" always precedes the act of **worship** (*proskuneo*: kiss toward) that is translated as "**worship**" or "**worshiped**." Thus, the **worship** act of *proskuneo* does not begin until the **knees bend**. Therefore, it appears that the consistency of finding these two acts together in the same sequence a total of 13 times in the New Testament suggests a "proskuneo pattern" of **worship**. This "pattern" found in Scripture should serve as a model for placing the two **worship** acts or gestures together in the proper sequence whenever and wherever they are found in Scripture. The Bible says, "Hold the pattern of sound words" (2 Tim. 1:13, ASV).

Richard C. Leonard, who was chosen by Robert Webber to write the "The New Testament Vocabulary of Worship," speaks of a "pattern" for worship that involves the exact two-act pattern that is found in Scripture. He says, "Setting the pattern for the worship of the creator are the twenty-four elders. They interject their commentary in the form of powerful declarations of praise, **falling down** to **worship** God (*proskuneo* Revelation 5:14; 11:16; 19:4)."[31]

11) Is the two-act "proskuneo pattern" in the NT in harmony with the OT?

Historically, the two acts that are present in each of these 13 accounts are in perfect harmony with the ancient two-act "*proskuneo* pattern" of **worship** that is found in the Old Testament. For example, in 1 Kings 19:18, the two acts that make up the "*proskuneo* pattern" of **worship** (the act of **"bowing the knees"** and the act of **"kissing"**) are explicitly recorded and translated into English. When Elijah became discouraged because he thought he was the only faithful one left, God reassured him by saying, "Yet, I have left me seven thousand in Israel, all the **knees which have not bowed** unto Baal, and **every mouth which hath not kissed** him" (1 Kings 19:18 KJV). The word translated **"kissed"** is a form the Hebrew word *nashaq* and literally means **"to kiss."**[32]

When the Hebrew Old Testament was translated into Greek in 285 B.C., also known as the Septuagint, the Greek word *proskuneo* was used to replace the Hebrew word *nashaq*. As previously shown, *proskuneo* is the Greek word translated **"worship"** in all 13 examples of the "*proskuneo* pattern" of **worship**. By comparing Scripture with Scripture, we confirm once again that God's word always harmonizes with itself when we use the words that God used. Also, the knowledge that the Greeks used *proskuneo* to translate the Hebrew word in the Old Testament that literally means **"to kiss,"** helps us to grasp the meaning of the **"worship"** word *proskuneo* in the New Testament. All agree that the best interpreter of Scripture is Scripture. A more detailed discussion of 1 Kings 19:18 will be addressed later in this study.

12) What is the most common Hebrew word translated "worship" in the OT?

The Old Testament Hebrew word translated most often as **"worship"** is "*Shachah*," which literally means to **"bow down"** or **"bow the knees,"** and occurs 170 times in the OT. The Hebrews apparently preferred using

31. Leonard, Richard C. "New Testament Vocabulary of Worship." In *The Biblical foundations of Christian Worship*, edited by Robert E. Webber, 15–23. Nashville, TN Star Song Publishing Group, 1993.

32. Ibid: Zodhiates, Spiros. and Warren Baker. *The Complete Word Study Old Testament*, AMG International, INC. D/B/A Iowa Falls, IA: 1994, 81.

the first act in the "*proskuneo* pattern" when referring to the two-act event, realizing that the second act of **worship** (*proskuneo*: kiss toward) was a necessary inference. When the Old Testament was translated into Greek in 285 BC in a version called the Septuagint, the Greeks used the word "*proskuneo,*" which is the second act in the "*proskuneo* pattern," instead of the Hebrew word "*shachah.*" The Greeks apparently knew that the first act of **bowing the knees** by **kneeling** or **falling prostrate** was also a necessary inference. Since the New Testament was written in Greek, their preference of using the second act in the two-act **worship** event to stand for the whole pattern was brought forward by the NT writers.

13) What is a synecdoche?

The inspired writers of the New Testament had access to both the Hebrew Old Testament and the Greek Old Testament. Therefore, these writers occasionally used the first act in the "*proskuneo* pattern" like the Hebrews were accustomed to using. At other times they used the second act in the pattern like the Greeks used most often. Still, sometimes they used both acts when referring to the "proskuneo pattern" of **worship**. Thus, each act in the two-act pattern is a part of speech called a synecdoche, which means that a part can be mentioned for the whole.

The following table shows a summary of the three (3) ways the "*proskuneo* pattern" of **worship** is referred to in the King James Version of the New Testament by the following six (6) writers: Matthew, Mark, Luke, John, Paul, and the writer of Hebrews.

14) The Three Ways the Writers in the NT refer to the Two-Act "Proskuneo Pattern" of Worship

This table is also a numerical summary of the 99 acts presented in the "Worship Chart."

THE THREE WAYS THE WRITERS IN THE NT REFER TO THE "PROSKUNEO PATTERN" OF WORSHIP

"The sum of thy word is truth" (Ps 119:160 NASV)

The THREE WAYS	MATTHEW in Gospel of Matthew	MARK in Gospel of Mark	LUKE in Gospel of Luke & Book of Acts	JOHN in Gospel of John & Revelation	PAUL In Romans, 1Corinthians, Ephesians, Phillipians, & Quoted in Acts 24:11	"The Sum" or Combination of All
By the FIRST ACT	Six (6)	Seven (7)	Sixteen (16)	Three (3)	Four (4)	Thirty-five (35)
By the SECOND ACT	Eleven (11)	Two (2)	Eight (8)	Twenty-seven (27)	One (1)	Forty-nine (49) plus Heb.x 2=(51)
By BOTH ACTS	Three (3)	One (1)	One (1)	Seven (7)	One (1)	Thirteen (13)
						TOTAL = 99

Another example of a two-act pattern of "worship" is the Lord's Supper. Luke writes in Acts 20:7 that the disciples came together upon the first day of the week "to break bread." Even though there is no mention of partaking of "the cup" or the "fruit of the vine," there is consensus that the verse is referring to the Lord's Supper. In his presentation on "God's Pattern for Worship," Wayne Jackson uses this exact verse to explain the concept of synecdoche in more detail. He begins by asking the question, "Why does the Bible mention that they merely came together upon the first day of the week to break bread? Where is the cup? Where is the fruit of the vine? Well, it is there encompassed in a figure of speech that we call a synecdoche. A synecdoche is a figure of speech whereby a part can stand for the whole, and the whole can stand for the part. The breaking of bread by means of this figure known as a synecdoche stands for the whole communion celebration ceremony. Both elements are included in that."[33]

Therefore, when either the first act or second act in the two-act "proskuneo pattern" are used alone in the New Testament, the other act or "part" is understood to be present in a figure of speech called a synecdoche, whereby a part can be mentioned for the whole.

An interesting illustration of a two-part "pattern" outside the NT that can be referred to in three ways is the "bow and arrow." For example, I recently stepped onto an elevator with two men who were talking about deer hunting. I overheard one man ask his friend, "What did you get your deer with?" The friend replied, "I got him with a bow." Then, I spoke up and said, "Did you shoot him with a bow or an arrow? And the man said, "I shot him with an arrow." Then he smiled and said, "I shot him with a bow, and an arrow!!" After that, we all chuckled.

15) Did the "*proskuneo* pattern" change *during* the First Century?

The 13 explicit examples of the "*proskuneo* pattern" in the New Testament verify that the ancient two-act "*proskuneo* pattern" did not change during the First Century. The first four of the 13 *proskuneo* **worship** examples occurred under the old law *before* the church was established, and the last nine examples occurred under the new law *after* the church was established. The same two-act "*proskuneo* pattern" that was practiced by the wise men in example #1 (Matt. 2:11) is the same two-act "*proskuneo* pattern" of **worship** that was practiced in example #13 by the

33. Jackson, Wayne. *God's Pattern for Worship.* Freed Hardeman University Lectureship, Henderson, TN, 1994, Audiocassette.

apostle John in the last chapter of Revelation (Revelation 22:8). The wise men **"fell down and worshiped"** (*proskuneo*: kissed toward) the Christ child, the Son of God, while "His star" shone overhead. Over 90 years later, the apostle John **"fell down to worship"** (*proskuneo*: kiss toward) before the feet of the angel.

When measured in years, the two-act "*proskuneo* pattern" of worship was performed by the wise men under the old law approximately 33 years *before* the New Testament church was established. However, the apostle John was performing the same two-act "*proskuneo* pattern" of worship under the new law approximately 60 years *after* the church was established. The ancient two-act "*proskuneo* pattern" of **worship** did not change during the writing of the New Testament.

Kenneth Chadwell is a devout Bible scholar, preacher, and practicing attorney who also encouraged me in this study on **kneeling**. He was asked by Freed-Hardeman University to present the topic, "New Testament Word Studies in **Worship**" at their 1994 lectureship on ***Worship** in Spirit and Truth.* After listening to the audiocassette of his presentation and reading the printed copy of his material in the Lectureship book, I decided to call and consult with him on the **"worship"** word *proskuneo*. He graciously listened while I reviewed the highlights of my study on **kneeling** in the New Testament and also the concept of the "proskuneo pattern." I asked if what I had shared sounded "Biblical." He said, "Yes, I think it is Biblical." When asked if he thought the **worship** word *proskuneo* had changed in meaning during the writing of the New Testament, he said, "I remember that some older gentlemen in the congregation where I grew up would frequently **kneel** down when they prayed. Even though *proskuneo* lost its outward meaning to some over time, does that mean it lost it's meaning in the New Testament? I don't think so." He then added, "I think Restoration is an ongoing process." (Personal communication: December, 1995).

16) Did the words in the "proskuneo pattern" change in meaning *after* the First Century?

First of all, God has taken an oath that He will never change the pattern: "**every knee shall bow** to me." He said in Isaiah 45:23: "I have sworn by Myself, The word has gone forth from My mouth in righteousness and will not turn back. That to Me **every knee will bow**, every tongue will swear allegiance" (NASV). Paul quoted this verse and added, "We shall

all stand before the judgment seat of Christ" and "give account" (Romans 14:10–12).

Also, we must always consider the original meaning of a word when interpreting Scripture. God's Holy Spirit inspired the Bible which was penned in Hebrew, Aramaic, and Greek. When Alexander the Great conquered the Middle East in 330 B.C. he imposed the Koine Greek language upon those he conquered. Thus, the New Testament was written in the Koine Greek language, which was the language of that period. However, the Koine Greek language was banned by Roman decree approximately 200 A.D and eventually became a dead language. That means in a very practical way that the words of the New Testament would never change in their meaning.[34]

In contrast, the English language continues to evolve. That is why a number of words in the KJV of 1611 no longer mean the same as they did in 1611. Dr.Jay Lockhart reminds us that, "Words have a way of evolving, but the Koine Greek language became a dead language and did not evolve. Do you suppose that God's providence was in that so that the words God used then would mean the same today as they did in the First Century? One of the lines drawn in the sand is the authority of scripture."[35]

Thus, if the meaning of the worship word *proskuneo* changed after the New Testament was written, it was changed by men and not by God. We must speak "the oracles of God" (I Peter 4:11). The next key question is as follows:

17) Did the congregations kneel in Worship in the early 'Restoration' Churches?

In his book, *Come, Let Us Adore Him,* Dan Dozier recorded how a New York congregation described its worship activities as practiced in March, 1818. Dabney Phillips also presented this information on "Worship in the early Restoration Churches" at Harding College Lectures in 1978. Alexander Campbell first documented this detailed information in Vol. V of *The Christian Baptist* in 1827. Notice that **kneeling** was the first 'act of **worship**' performed by the congregation.

34. http://en.wikipedia.org/wiki/Koine_Greek#History Title: "Koine Greek" 10 Pages-Accessed March 15, 1998. Online: www.gospelcom.net/lifetime/local/equipped/qa3/85.

35. Lockhart, Jay. *What's Right with the Church?* West Erwin Church of Christ, Tyler, TX, April 25, 1999, Audiocassette.

"The elders presided during the worship period. **Worship** opened by the congregation **kneeling** in prayer, which was led by an elder or one appointed by them. A portion of the Bible is read by one of the elders relative to the Lord's Supper. This is followed by another hymn. A passage of scripture is read for the collection of poor saints, and a prayer for proper use of the funds, and then the collection. Next, one chapter is read from the Old Testament and one in the New Testament, and time is allowed for comments from any of the brethren. Exhortations from the Bible are followed by the elders or brethren. There is a song, prayer, and separation."[36]

Alexander Campbell also recorded that a church of Christ in Manchester received a copy of those New York **worship** activities. The Manchester church responded and sent a summary of their **worship** proceedings to the church of Christ in New York dated September 1818. The sequence of the **worship** format sent was as follows:

1st We commence by our elder, who presides, selecting a suitable hymn, in singing of which we all stand up and join.

2nd We **all kneel down** when our elder, or one of the brethren named by him, offers up prayers, supplications.

3rd A portion of scripture is read both from the Old and New Testament.

4th Prayer, with a view to the fellowship, which follows.

5th We greet each other with a holy kiss.

6th We attend to the Lord's Supper . . .

7th A hymn suitable to the occasion is then sung.

8th The brethren are requested to teach and admonish one another—our elder addresses the church—another hymn is sung—prayer is made—and we separate (September 13, 1818).[37]

36. Dozier, Daniel A. Ibid: *Come Let Us Adore Him*. College Press Publishing Company, 223 W. Third St. Joplin, Missouri 64802—1994, 273–96.

37. Campbell, Alexander. "Attempt at the Restoration of the Ancient Order." *The Christian Baptist,* Vol. V No. 7, 1835, 389–414.

18) What did the leaders of the "Restoration Movement" say about kneeling?

Dan Dozier, in his book, *Come Let Us Adore Him*, points out that, "All the early restoration leaders agreed that people should pray **on their knees.**" He lists quotes on **kneeling** by Barton W. Stone, Walter Scott, and Alexander Campbell. He then asks, "Why did we stop? Could it be that we have become too sophisticated and proud to humble ourselves before God to get down **on our knees** in public **worship**? He said that Barton W. Stone was upset when he observed that in some congregations people were standing, some were **kneeling**, and some were just sitting. Stone concluded that some did not **kneel** for fear of "sullying their fine garments by **kneeling**." He said if the members would keep the floors clean, this "would be no problem."

Dan Dozier said Walter Scott felt that some who stood during prayer did not really believe in prayer for they were "gazing around upon all present as if they stood in a menagerie of wild beasts." He said "the early restoration leaders felt passionately about **kneeling** in **worship**." He also quoted Alexander Campbell who said, "**Kneeling** in prayer is always to be preferred, if it can be made convenient."[38]

It is also interesting that Walter Scott, in *The Gospel Restored*, commended Sir Frances Bacon by saying, "He was a man who, for his greatness of genius and compass of knowledge, did honor to his age and country. We find him **prostrating himself** before the great mercy-seat, and humbled under afflictions which at that time lay heavy upon him. We see him supported by the sense of his integrity, his zeal, his devotion, and his love to mankind . . ."[39]

Lynn Anderson is a widely known preacher and author, who has also done research on Alexander Campbell. He has written a very timely article entitled, "**Kneeling** in Prayer! Literally?" In the article he quotes Donald Kinder who said, "Alexander Campbell was convinced that body language was part of **worship**. Prayer posture meant something: He noted in 1835, 'To sit down and address God, as is very common at most family tables is most indecorous and disorderly. This, unless in cases of great physical debility, is not to glorify God with our bodies. Shall a man arise

38. Dozier, Daniel A. Ibid: *Come Let Us Adore Him*. College Press Publishing Company, 223 W. Third St. Joplin, Missouri 64802 1994, 286–88.

39. Scott, Walter. *The Gospel Restored*. Joplin: College Press Publishing Co., 1836, 105.

to address a respectable friend, and sit down to thank God! To stand erect, and lift up holy hands—or to **bow the knee** before the Lord Almighty—or to **prostrate oneself** upon the earth is sanctioned by the examples of the great, and wise and good of all dispensations."

Lynn Anderson also points out that, "(Campbell) complained that the current practice of sitting for prayers came from a degenerate, apostate age and had not been known to earlier believers. He returned to the topic in 1845, writing in his *Millenial Harbinger* that when people offered prayers in church, '**kneeling** should be preferred, when it could be made convenient. If not convenient, then standing was the required posture.' He viewed **kneeling** as a sign of submission, standing as a sign of reverence, and sitting as a sign of nothing."

Appropriately, Lynn Anderson opens the article by saying, "Sometimes the content of our hearts is better expressed in the posture of our bodies when we **worship** than in just the words we say. Generations of God's people who have come before us appreciated the importance of **worship** posture far better than many of us do in our day. Whether this is just another sign of our culture's lack of respect for important things, or important people, or if it is just a habit, our attention to **worship** posture has changed dramatically over the years." He concludes by asking, "Could our day have lost some of the sense of God's Majesty and Holiness expressed in the posture of worshippers in former times?—Something to think about, unless we just want to sit there 'as a sign of nothing.'"[40]

19) Are Bible scholars teaching that *proskuneo* includes bowing the knees?

David Young began his presentation on *Rethinking Worship* by first asking this question: "When preachers and teachers talk to you about '**worship**,' they tell you that the Greek word *proskuneo* means what? Or in the Hebrew it was *histahawah*. They say it means to **get down on your knees**. Well, if it means **get down on your knees**, it means **get down on your knees**'. It doesn't mean '**worship**'. It means **get down on your knees**. By the fact that we have limited '**worship**' to five acts, that we have even conceived of **worship** in terms of five acts, may have left us with such a flat concept that many people are thirsty for God and unable to find drink."[41]

40. Anderson, Lynn. "Kneeling in Prayer! Literally?" 2 Pages. Accessed June 20, 2001. Online: http://www.heartlight.org/articles/200105/20010530_kneeling.html.

41. Young, David. "Rethinking Worship." Jubilee Seminar, Nashville, TN, 1996, Audiocassette.

In his book called *The Wonder of Worship,* Ronald Allen points out that the primary Hebrew word translated as **worship** in the OT is the one used in Psalm 95:6–7: "O come, let us worship and **bow down**: let us **kneel** before the Lord, our Maker. For He is our God; and we are the people of His pasture, and the sheep of His hand." He further explains that, "Verse 6 actually includes three verbs that speak of **bowing down** to God. The first is the word under discussion (*hawa*), often translated **worship**. The second and third verbs, '**bow down**' and '**kneel**', simply carry on the idea of the first. They all present the same idea, but by using three different verbs the Psalmist emphasized his point more forcefully. Although **worship** proceeds from the heart, it extends to the body."[42] You will recall that the Greeks used the verb *proskuneo* instead of the Hebrew word translated as "**worship**" in the verse.

Ronald Allen then quotes Eugene Peterson who said, "**Worship** is the strategy by which we interrupt our preoccupation with ourselves and attend to the presence of God."[43] Allen concluded by saying, "How better to show this grand 'interruption' than by **kneeling before** His glory? How better to demonstrate our sense of God's presence than to **bow before** His majesty? And how wonderful that the verb in question is one that means 'to cause **oneself to bow down**' in humble adoration!"[44]

20) What about reading in the OT where people "bowed the head and worshiped?"

The phrase, "**Bowed the head and worshiped** (*shachah*)" occurs in the OT at least 15 times. However, the Hebrew word *shachah* translated as "**worship**" literally means "**to bow down**" or "**bow the knees.**" Spiros Zodhiates says that, *proskuneo* (NT) and *shachah* (OT) were "not used in the general sense of **worship** in the Bible, but specifically to **bow down, to prostrate oneself** as an act of respect before a superior being . . . See the equivalent, *proskuneo.*" Thus, the act of bowing the head was always followed by **bowing the knees.** That is, they bowed their heads on the way down. Also, when the OT was translated into Greek in 285 B.C.

42. Allen, Ronald B. *The Wonder of Worship.* Nashville: Word Publishing, 2001, 117–18.

43. Peterson, Eugene. is quoted by Ronald Allen in *The Wonder of Worship* pages 117–18.

44. Allen, Ronald B. Ibid: *The Wonder of Worship.* Nashville: Word Publishing, 2001, 117–18.

(the Septuagint), the Greeks replaced the word "*shachah*" with the word "*proskuneo,*" knowing that **bowing the knees**, which is the first act in the "*proskuneo* pattern," was there by necessary inference.[45]

21) What is the significance of kneeling—the first act in the "proskuneo pattern"?

You will recall that the first example of the two-act "proskuneo pattern" of **worship** in the NT is when the wise men "**fell down** and **worshiped**" (*proskuneo*: kissed toward) Jesus. The last example is when the apostle John "**fell down** to **worship**" (*proskuneo*: kiss toward) before the feet of the angel (Rev. 22:8). This section will focus on the first act in the pattern which requires **bowing the knees** by **kneeling** or **falling prostrate.**

Steve Flatt, currently President of Lipscomb University, says that he once "totally underestimated the value of posture in prayer." When giving the keynote address at the Area Wide Worship service held at Lipscomb in 2004, he said, "A moment ago you heard Philippians chapter two, verses 5 through 11. "**Every knee shall bow**" is our text for tonight. I confess that most of my life, I totally underestimated the value of posture in prayer and in praise. But I suggest to you that there is something about **hitting your knees** and **bowing before** God that teaches you a lesson about His sovereignty that you cannot receive any other way. If you have not been **on your knees** in a while, don't let this night pass without doing it. **Bow down** and **worship** Him. The wise men did. It reminds me that He is king and I am not." Dr. Flatt then shared an interesting story about the birth place of Jesus. He said, "Going back to the year 150 AD, Christians identified a place where Jesus was born. They built a church over it and called it the Church of the Nativity—the oldest church building in the world. Around the church they built a wall with a small opening for everybody to go through. They wanted to be sure that everyone that entered **stooped and bowed** before the king of kings . . . Tonight, as we focus on this great passage and this theme—"**Every Knee Shall Bow**" I just want to ask you, is Jesus your KING or not?"[46]

45. Ibid: Zodhiates, Spiros. and Baker, Warren. *The Complete Word Study Old Testament,* Iowa Falls, IA: AMG International, INC. D/B/A Iowa Falls, IA: 2372. 1994, 81.

46. Flatt, Steve. "Every Knee Shall Bow." Area Wide Worship, Lipscomb University, Nashville, TN, November 14, 2004, Audiocassette.

Lynn Anderson has asked, "Now what is the significance of **kneeling**? When we **kneel** we are physically saying to God that 'I have no right to stand in Your presence.' We are humbling ourselves. When you **fall on your knees** to beg someone, what you're saying is, 'I am **falling before** you and recognizing my humility before you.'"[47]

Ted Waller further emphasizes the purpose of **kneeling** in his book, *Worship: Bowing at the Feet of God*: "We must keep in mind the purpose of it all, letting the glory of the invisible God come into our awareness and **bowing before** Him. Without this there is no **worship**, even if the temple is magnificent and the ritual activities are totally correct."[48]

John Willis brings to our attention that, "Getting **on one's knees** or **kneeling** communicates three attitudes of the heart according to the Bible." He then quotes Bible verses to document these three things: "Petition" (Acts 7:60; Acts 20:36), "Obedience to a superior" (Matt. 17:14–15), and **"Worship."** As an example of **"worship"** he appropriately tells us, "Psalm 95:6 says: 'O come, let us worship and **bow down**, let us **kneel** before the Lord, our Maker!'" He concludes by saying, "**Kneeling** has a way of putting one in a proper frame of mind to come before God." Website accessed 2001, but the website is no longer available.

David Dykes said in his sermon, "Prayer that Moves Heaven", says that the act of **kneeling** indicates adoration and submission in recognition of someone's authority. He quoted from Ephesians 3:14 through 21 and said, "Paul is dictating this letter and right there in that prison cell on that rough stone floor, the apostle Paul **goes to his knees** and prays this prayer. You know, there is something special about **kneeling** when you pray. Sometimes the attitude of your heart is demonstrated by your body language. You may not be physically able to, and of course, we would understand that. **Kneeling** demonstrates a couple of things, and I think that is why Paul **knelt** when he prayed. One, **kneeling** demonstrates adoration. Two, **kneeling** demonstrates submission. We understand that **kneeling** recognizes someone's authority."

Dr. Dykes then points out some interesting requirements of Caesar, the Roman emperor: "In the Roman Empire where Paul lived, every person every year was required to **go to their knees** and say these words in

47. Anderson, Lynn. Ibid: Harding University Annual Preacher's Forum, Searcy, AR, April, 1994, Audiocassette.

48. Waller, Ted H. *Worship: Bowing at the Feet of God*, Nashville: 20th Century Christian, 1994, 21–22.

Greek, 'Caesar is Lord'. You say, 'Well, why did they throw those Christians to the lions? Why did they burn those Christians at the stake?' I'll tell you why: Because Christians refused to **bow their knees** to Caesar. They refused to **bow their knees** to anyone or anything except the Lord Jesus Christ. And when you **bow your knees**, you are showing that Jesus is in charge of your life."[49]

Earnest Gentile wrote the book, *Worship God*! He believes that the act of **Kneeling** does "four things: 1) *Gives you the right perspective.* **Kneeling** is a deliberate act of submission and openly avows God's superiority. It expresses humility and subjugation to the will of God. 2) *Encourages you to be more straightforward with God.* **Kneeling** helps worshipers be more honest and conversational with God. 3) *Enables you to concentrate better.* The less the mind is distracted the better the prayer. **Kneeling** before the Lord in sincerity and simplicity helps keep thoughts more clear. Spiritual things come into focus, and the will of God becomes more apparent. **Kneeling** helps calm the anxious mind. 4) *Empowers you to serve.* Archbishop Trench captures the change beautifully—We **kneel,** how weak! We rise, how full of power!"[50]

Ronald Allen says, "One day **every knee will bow** before the risen Christ, but, sadly, not all will **bow** in joy. But we have the opportunity now, in this life, to **worship** God. We can **cause ourselves to bow down** in reverent **worship**."[51]

Jim Goll wrote the book called *Kneeling on the Promises*. In the first chapter titled, **On Bended Knee**, he asks, "Why **kneeling**?" He then explains that, "**Kneeling** is a picture of dependency. **Kneeling** is a posture of humility and brokenness. **Kneeling** is a sign of reverence and honor. **Kneeling** is the act of worship that precedes petitioning. **Kneeling** is an outward expression of an inward work of grace. In fact Paul tells us, 'I **bow my knees** before the Father of our Lord Jesus Christ." Isn't that awesome? Sooner or later we are all going to **kneel**. Philippians 2:9-10 portrays this picture graphically."[52]

49. Dykes, David, Ibid: "Prayer that Moves Heaven." KLTV, Tyler, TX, April 23, 1995, Audiocassette.

50. Allen, Ronald B. Ibid: *The Wonder of Worship*. Nashville: Word Publishing, 2001, 119.

51. Gentile, Earnest B. Ibid: *Worship God*! Portland: City Bible publishing, 1994, 196.

52. Goll, Jim W. Ibid: *Kneeling on the Promises*. Grand Rapids: Chosen Books, 2000, 20.

James Burton Coffman states, "Many in all ages have **prostrated themselves before** God in **worship** and in prayers, and the admissibility of this as legitimate is plain enough in this verse (Commentary on I Corinthians 14:25)."[53]

Jack Reese uses the apostle Paul as our example. He says, "In Acts 20, Paul prays for the last time with the Ephesian elders and they pray, **down on their knees,** Paul and the elders in prayer. And in Acts 21, he makes his way to the city of Tyre and they go to the beach—men and women and children and Paul—**down on their knees** in prayer, because an appropriate response of **worship** is to surrender."[54]

John Carroll explains that, historically, **kneeling** or **falling down** indicates submission of someone who is conquered. In his book, *How to Worship Jesus Christ*, he says, "In the days when Revelation was written, when a king was conquered by the Roman legions, either he was brought to Rome to **prostrate himself at the Emperor's feet** or a massive image of Caesar was placed before him, and he was required to **fall down**, casting his crown at its feet. So John, in Revelation is revealing the first two essentials of **worship**. The first is **falling down**, the submission to the one worshiped. The second is the casting of the crown at the feet of the one **worshiped**. The first essential condition of true **worship** is total submission."[55]

These are just a few of the many quotes by Bible scholars on "**bowing the knees**" or "**kneeling**" that are recorded in this study. Most of the quotes will be found in the last section called The Testimony of Bible Scholars.

While pondering the purpose of **kneeling**, it vividly occurred to me that the greatest "battle" in the history of mankind was won while **on bended knee** in the Garden of Gethsemane. It was there that Jesus **kneeled** and surrendered His will to the Father and presented His living body for a sacrificial death upon the cross for our sins. By the time the soldiers came to the Garden with swords and spears, the "war of the wills" had already been won. The weapon that won the war over Satan was **worship on bended knee** in total submission to the Father's will. This

53. Coffman, James Burton.Ibid: *Commentary on 1 and 2 Corinthians.* R.B.Sweet Austin,TX 236.

54. Reese, Jack. Ibid: Preston Road Church of Christ, Dallas, TX, January 2, 1994, Audiocassette.

55. Carroll, John S. Ibid: *How to Worship Jesus Christ.* Chicago: Moody Press, 1984, 36–37.

was the weapon that Satan tried to buy from Jesus by offering Him "all of the kingdoms of the world" just before He began His ministry (Matthew 4:9–10). Jesus refused because He knew that **kneeling** in total submission to the Father's will wins wars over Satan and, therefore, is worth much MORE than "all the kingdoms of the world." We should always give God our best.

Question: What is the best posture for us to present our bodies to God "as a living sacrifice?" (Rom. 12:1).

22) What is the significance of the Kiss—the second act in the "proskuneo pattern?"

Before discussing the "**kiss**" in the "proskuneo pattern", a few interesting quotes on "**kiss**" will be presented. For ease in recognition, the word **kiss** will be bolded.

The world's longest **kiss** was held for 29 hours in New York on March 24 through 25 in 1998. The couple had to remain standing and not break contact.[56]

"The sound of a **kiss** is not so loud as that of a cannon, but its echo lasts a great deal longer."—Oliver Wendell Holmes

"An honest answer is like a **kiss** on the lips."—King Solomon, (Proverbs 24:26 NIV)

Kisses are the messengers of love.—Danish proverb

"Prayer is the moment when Heaven and earth **kiss** each other."—Old Jewish Proverb

A **kiss**: a thing of no use to one, but prized by two.—Robert Zuickey
Mothers know that a **kiss** can heal a broken heart.—Author unknown
Jesus said, "I ascend unto my Father, and your Father; and to my God, and your God" (John 20:17). The act of **kissing** is treating God as "Father", and

56. *Guinness Book of World Records.* Ibid: Publisher: Guinness Publishing LTD. Bantam Books, a division of Random House Inc.1540 Broadway, New York, New York 10036, May 2000 p. 70.

the act of **kneeling** is treating God as "God." Rick Atchley helped us see God as "Father" more clearly at a seminar in 1998 when he presented, "A View of the Father." Some very key points he made are as follows: "In the OT you don't find individuals calling God 'Father.' In the NT, you find the word Father over 350 times. Jesus' first words in the Bible were, 'I must be about my Father's business.' Jesus taught us this new way of looking at God. He taught us to pray, 'Our Father, who art in heaven.' The last thing He says on the cross is, 'Father, into Your hands I commit my spirit.' I think the whole message of the cross is that the Father wants to find His lost kids."[57]

The "proskuneo pattern" is further described by Andrea Hunter and Jeremy Riddle who wrote the words and music of "To Bow and to Kiss" in 2002 for Life Unto Life Music.

To bow and to kiss, to pour forth our love, the perfume of our adoration,
To wash with our tears the feet that were bruised,
to bless and to serve and to gaze on.
Jesus, my Savior, my life and my love, You are my treasure, my gift from above.
To bow and to kiss, to pour forth our love,
the perfume of our adoration,
to press to our lips the hands that were pierced,
to bless and to serve and to gaze on.
Jesus, my Savior, my life and my love, You are my treasure, my gift from above.

Jesus equated the "**kiss**" with much "love" (Luke 7:47). Jesus said unto Simon, "Thou gavest me no **kiss**, but this woman, since the time that I came in, hath not ceased to **kiss** my feet. Her sins, which are many, are forgiven; for she loved much: but to whom little is forgiven, the same loveth little" (Luke 7:45–47 KJV). Also, to **kiss** Jesus' feet, she must have **bowed the knees**.

David Thomas agrees. He said, "In Luke 7:37–50 there is a beautiful example of a woman who worshiped Jesus in a manner consistent with both the Hebrew and Greek meaning of the word 'worship.' **Worship** is

57. Atchley, Rick. "A View of the Father." A View from the Cross Celebration, Auburn, WV, 1998, Audiocassette.

the expression of a love relationship. **Worship** also requires open, public expression. Concealed love is to be questioned."[58]

God's word harmonizes with itself only when we use the words that God used. Examples are: Psalm 2:7–12: "This day have I begotten thee . . . **Kiss** the Son, lest he be angry." (Luke 7:40–47): "Woman . . . hath not ceased to **kiss** my feet . . . forgiven, for she loves much." Philippians 2:10 supplies the second act in the 2-act "proskuneo pattern": "at the name of Jesus **every knee should bow** and confess Jesus as Lord . . ."

"The sum of God's word is truth." (Psalm 119:160 NASV)

THE PROSKUNEO PATTERN OF WORSHIP

REFERENCE	FIRST ACT	SECOND ACT
(1) Psalm 2:12		Kiss
(2) Luke 7:40b,45,47		Kiss
(3) Philippians 2:10	Every knee should bow	
The Sum of All	Every knee should bow	(and) every mouth should Kiss (toward) Jesus

When *proskuneo* is translated literally rather than "**worship**," the exact meaning is communicated and confusion may be avoided. Another option would be to use footnotes or place the word *proskuneo* in parenthesis. The original text, when literally translated, is the very word of God because all scripture is inspired or God-breathed (2 Timothy 3:16). God breathed inspiration into the writers. Word selection was made by the spirit which enabled them to receive and communicate the word of God without error. "The true test of any word is to interchange it with the original word wherever used."[59]

a) Has the act of "confession" replaced the literal act of "kissing?"

The custom of **kissing** is still practiced by some Christians today. However, some churches **kneel** and "confess," but they do not **kiss**. It could be that they believe Proverbs 24:26 that says, "An honest answer is like a

58. Thomas, David. "Worship Him." 2 Pages. Accessed 2001. Online: www.accucomm .net/-worship/worship1.htm.

59. McCord, Hugo. *Spiritual Sword.* Published by Getwell Church of Christ, 1511 Getwell Rd. Memphis, TN. January 1994, 8.

kiss on the lips" (NIV). The writers of the NKJV remind us that, "Proverbs provides God's detailed instructions for His people to deal successfully with the practical affairs of everyday life." In many churches the act of "confession" has replaced the **kiss**. Here are some current examples:

George Yandell says, "Every Sunday we **kneel** and *confess* our sins. Visitors to Episcopal Churches often comment it's strange for all the worshipers to hit the deck and confess."[60]

Scott Weidler asks, "How can we **worship** without words? Postures can effectively reinforce words and actions. Lutherans **kneel** as a sign of humility to prepare for **worship,** when *confessing* sins, offering intercessory prayer, and when receiving Holy Communion."[61]

Vivien Rivera wrote, "**Kneeling** is an expression of submission, adoration and humility. It is a deep, expressive posture of penitence, thus the posture assumed by the penitent in confession."[62]

Les and Leslie Parrot chose King Solomon's famous quote for the theme of their book for couples entitled, *Like a **Kiss** on the Lips—Meditations on Proverbs for Couples.* The authors shared some very strong counsel from Proverbs to help married couples to be honest. The book emphasized that "Solomon in all his wisdom, equaled a **kiss** on the lips with an honest answer. Love cannot last without honesty. Honest answers create trust, the very bedrock of a relationship."[63] Does that not include God?

Mike Warner wisely used the terms "**bow**" and "confess" in his "Words of Life" article in the *Tyler Morning Telegraph* on February 27, 1998. Mike Warner said it well: "To be a Christian is to **bow before** Jesus Christ and *confess* Him as your Lord—Lord of your head, heart, and life. There IS no 'lesser form' of Christianity."[64] In a more recent "Words of Life" article on August 11, 2000, Mike Warner wrote of love that pleases God. He said, "The love commanded in the Bible seeks to honor and please and meet

60. Yandell, George. "Hallowed be Your Name" 2 Pages. Accessed 1999. Online: www.google.com/search?hl=en&ie=UTF-8&q=+e.

61. Weidler, Scott. "*Worship Without Words..*" 2 Pages. Accessed 2000. Online: www.elca.org/dcm/worship/qa/nonverbal.html.

62. Rivera, Vivian. "Confession by the Penitent." 1 Page Accessed 2001. Online: http://userpages.nkn.net/stjoseph/nuviv4.html.

63. Parrot, Les and Leslie Parrot. *Like a Kiss on the Lips,—Meditations on Proverbs for Couples.* Grand Rapids: Zondervan, 1984, 13.

64. Warner, Mike. "Words of Life." *Tyler Morning Telegraph* Sec. 4 February 27, 1998, 4.

the needs of another, even at the price of self-sacrifice. In order to love Jesus, one has to know what He wants. If you really love Him, you care enough to find out what He wants from you; you find out what will please Him. It's all there in the Word. He tells us what He wants from us. We just have to love Him enough to want to know how."[65]

Next: What is *proskuneo*? The Testimony of the Lexicons document that the word worship (*proskuneo*) includes bowing the knees.

As mentioned earlier, the "**worship**" word in John 4:23–24 is translated from the Greek word *proskuneo.* Spiros Zodhiates wrote *The Complete Word Study New Testament and The Complete Word Study Old Testament.* He says that *proskuneo* (NT) and *shachah* (OT) were not used in the Bible for **worship** in general. He emphasizes that, "*Shachah* was not used in the general sense of **worship**, but specifically to **bow down, to prostrate oneself** as an act of respect before a superior being." He concludes by saying, "See the equivalent *proskuneo*."[66]

Brian Kenyon reminds us that, "A first step in understanding true worship is to examine the words the Holy Spirit chose to use in teaching about the subject . . ."[67]

To determine the exact English definition or true meaning of the "**worship**" word *proskuneo*, the first resources consulted were the Lexicons (or Greek dictionaries). The following table shows a list of all the Lexicons reviewed along with a detailed display of the words that each Lexicon used in defining *proskuneo*. To facilitate comparison between the various Lexicons, the findings were placed in a table format. Notice that some Lexicons define *proskuneo* by the first act in the "*proskuneo* pattern" (Bridges & Weigle), and one Lexicon defines *proskuneo* using the second act in the pattern (Young's Concordance). However, the majority of Lexicons use both acts that make up the whole "proskuneo pattern" of **worship**, plus other words that describe the attitude and intent of the **worshiper**. When examining these Lexicons or Greek dictionaries, it seemed appropriate to begin by asking two key questions that have emerged

65. Warner, Mike. Ibid: "Words of Life." *Tyler Morning Telegraph* Sec. 4 August 11, 2000, 4.

66. Ibid: Zodhiates, Spiros. and Warren Baker. *The Complete Word Study Old Testament,* AMG International, INC. D/B/A Iowa Falls, IA: 1994, 81.

67. Kenyon, Brian. "True Worship: A Word Study," *Florida School of Preaching,* Vol. XIX, No. 9, April 1999, 1.

during this study: Question #1: What is the literal meaning of the Greek "**worship**" word *proskuneo*? And question #2: Do the Lexicons document or confirm the two-act "*proskuneo* pattern" of **worship**?

Next: The Testimony of The Lexicons (or Greek Dictionaries).

2

The Testimony of the Lexicons (Greek Dictionaries)

The Two-Act "Proskuneo Pattern" of Worship is Documented by the Lexicons

Most Lexicons define *proskuneo* in a manner that groups all words and phrases describing the inward attitude or intent together with the outward physical acts. This grouping is usually mixed together in no certain order. The table on the next page, however, attempts to separate the outward physical acts in the Lexicons from terms that describe the inward attitude or intent of the worshiper. Also, the terms that indicate outward acts in the "proskuneo pattern" are separated or "rightly divided" into the "first act" and "second act" in accordance with the two-act "proskuneo pattern" of worship as recorded in scripture. For example, in Matthew 2:11 the wise men **fell down** and **worshiped** (*proskuneo*: kissed toward) Jesus. Also, recall that God told Elijah was told the following by God himself:

"Yet I have left me seven thousand in Israel, all the **knees which have not bowed** unto Baal, and every mouth which hath not **kissed** (*proskuneo*-LXX) him" (1 Kings 19:18 KJV).

Testimony of the Lexicons (Greek Dictionaries)

	OUTWARD ACTS		INWARD
Reference	**FIRST ACT**	**SECOND ACT**	**ATTITUDE or INTENT**
*Bauer, Walter. *A Greek-English Lexicon of the NT*. 2ded. publisher: American Bible Society 1865 Broadway New York, NY 10023 1979, 723-4.	* (Fall down and) worship Prostrate oneself	Kissing the feet, the garment hem, the ground, etc.	Worship Do obeisance to Do reverence to Welcome respectfully
Bridges, Ronald and Weigle. Luther *King James Bible* *Word Book*. Thomas Nelson, Nashville,TN 1994. 387-388	To Kneel Or prostrate oneself		Honor Supplication Worship
Brown, Colin *The New International Dictionary of NT Theology*. Zondervan Publishing House 5300 Patterson Ave. SE Grand Rapids, MI 49530 1986, 2:876.	Fall down Prostrate oneself Adore on one's knees	To kiss Throwing a kiss to deity	Reverence Humility Worship Do obeisance to Adoration

	OUTWARD ACTS		INWARD
Reference	**FIRST ACT**	**SECOND ACT**	**ATTITUDE or INTENT**
Balz, Horst. & Schneider, Gerhard. *Exegetical Dictionary Of the NT.* Vol. 3 Publisher: Eerdmans, Wm. B. Pub. Co. Grand Rapids, MI 1993, 173-5.	Fall down Prostration		Worship Homage Reverence
Greeven, Heinrich. *Theological Dictionary of NT.* pub city: pub. Co. Eerdmans, Wm. B. Pub Co. Grand Rapids, MI 1968, 759-766.	Prostration Fall down Falling on the knees Falling on the face	To kiss reverently	Veneration Honor True adoration Worship
Louw, Johannes P. and Eugene A. Nida eds. *Greek-English Lexicon of the NT based on Semantic Domains.* American Pub. Co.1988, 1:541.	To prostrate oneself To bow down		Worship Express allegiance to Deity

Continued on page 38

	OUTWARD ACTS		INWARD
Reference	**FIRST ACT**	**SECOND ACT**	**ATTITUDE or INTENT**
Kittel, Gerhard and Gerhard Friedrich. *TDNT Abridged in one Vol.* by Bromiley, Geoffrey W. Wm. B. Eerdmans Pub. Co. 1985, 948-49.	To bow down	To kiss	Worship Veneration Unconditional subjection
Strong, James. *Strong's Exhaustive Concordance of the Bible.* Thomas Nelson, Nashville, TN 1990, 61.	Prostrate oneself	To kiss	Homage Do reverence to worship Adore
Thayer, Joseph Henry. *Thayer's Greek-Lexicon of the NT.* Zondervan Publishing House 1977, 548.	Prostrate oneself Fall upon the knees & touch —the ground with the forehead In the NT by Kneeling or prostration	To kiss the hand to (towards)	To express profound reverence To do homage To make obeisance To express respect To make supplication
Young, Robert. *Young's Analytical Concordance to the Bible.* Wm. B. Eerdmans Pub. Co. Grand Rapids, MI 1970, 1075.		To kiss (the hand) toward	Worship

	OUTWARD ACTS		INWARD
Reference	**FIRST ACT**	**SECOND ACT**	**ATTITUDE or INTENT**
Zodhiates, Spiros. *The Complete Word Study Dictionary of the NT*. Pub. AMG Publishers Chattanooga, TN 1992, 1233-34.	Kneeling or prostrating oneself To bow down To fall upon the knees and touch forehead to the ground	To (pros) kiss (kuneo) To kiss To kiss toward someone To throw a kiss toward someone	Adore To worship Do obeisance Do reverence
The Sum or Combination of All	Kneel or prostrate oneself	To (pros) kiss (kuneo) To kiss (hand, feet, ground, hem of garment reverently). or kiss toward someone or throw a kiss toward someone	(Fall down and) worship Reverence, Humility, Veneration Honor, do obeisance to, homage To adore, to express allegiance Unconditional subjection

Conclusion: The testimony of the lexicons document that the two-act "proskuneo pattern" of worship is present in the definition of *proskuneo.* Notice that Bauer, the first listed, gives the shortest definition of *proskuneo,* which is "(**Fall down** and) worship." According to that Greek-English Lexicon, the act of *proskuneo* is always preceded by **bowing the knees.** In fact, all of the Lexicons except Young's Concordance include a form of kneeling or prostration in the definition.

Next: What is proskuneo?—"Testimony of Bible Translators" Part I (Does the "worship" word *proskuneo* include "bowing the knees?")

3

What is proskuneo?

The Testimony of Bible Translators

Part I

As shown in the previous chapter, all of the Lexicons except one include a form of kneeling or prostration in the definition. As discussed earlier, the most common Greek word translated as a form of "worship" in the NT is the verb *proskuneo.* The term literally means, "to kiss," "to kiss toward," or "to throw a kiss toward" the object of worship. Here are the questions: Does the act of *proskuneo* include "bowing the knees?" What do the Bible translators say?

The Testimony of Bible Translators Document That *Proskuneo* Includes "Bowing the Knees"

Thirty (30) different Bible versions were examined regarding the translation of the Greek word *proskuneo* and are listed below (pages 42 and 43), along with their abbreviated codes. Only the 1611 King James Version and the 1901 American Standard Version translate the verb *proskuneo* as "worship" each time that it occurs for a total of 60 times. In contrast, all other twenty-eight (28) Bible versions translate the verb *proskuneo* as "kneel" or an equivalent of "bowing the knees" at least one or more times. This fact indicates that the more recent translators of the New Testament acknowledge the fact that the act of "bowing the knees" by kneeling or falling prostrate is present or included in the *proskuneo* worship event.

For example, the 1898 Young's Literal Translation (YLT) translates *proskuneo* as "bow" for a total of 47 times. However, the 2001 Analytical-Literal Translation of the New Testament (ALT) acknowledges that bowing the knees is present in the *proskuneo* worship event for a total of 59 times out of 60. (The "No. of times" in each Bible version was hand counted; therefore, the phrase "or more" was added in the "No. of times" column).

Does *proskuneo* include bowing the knees? What do the translators say?

30 Bible Codes	THE 30 BIBLE VERSIONS	The No. of times *proskuneo* is translated as "kneel" (or an equivalent)
1) ABUV	The New Testament of Our Lord and Savior Jesus Christ, American Bible Union Version (John A. Broudes L., et al.)	One (1) or more
2) ALT	Analytical-Literal Translation of the New Testament of the Holy Bible	Fifty-nine (59)
3) AMP	Amplified New Testament	Twelve (12) or more
4) ASV	American Standard Version	Zero (o)
5) Ber	The Berkeley Version of the New Testament (Gerrit Vurkuyl)	Five (5) or more
6) CEV	The Contemporary English Version	Five (5) or more
7) ESV	The English Standard Version	Seven (7) or more
8) Gspd	The New Testament: An American Translation (Edgar J. Goodspeed)	One (1) or more
9) ISB	The International Student Bible for Catholics	Five (5) or more
10) JB	The Jerusalem Bible	Thirteen (13) or more
11) KJV	King James' Version	Zero (0)
12) KNOX	The New Testament of the Monsignor Ronald Knox	Three (3) or more

13) LB	The Living Bible	Four (4) or more
14) MNTT	McCord's New Testament Translation of the Everlasting Gospel	Eight (8) or more
15) Mof	The New Testament: A New Translation (James Moffatt)	Five (5) or more
16) NASB	The New American Standard Bible: New Testament	Eight (8) or more
17) NEB	The New English Bible: New Testament	Twelve (12) or more
18) NIV	New International Version	Seven (7) or more
19) NKJV	New King James Version	One (1) or more
20) NLT	New Living Translation	Seven (7) or more
21) Nor	The New Testament: A New Translation (Olaf M. Norlie)	One (1) or more
22) Phi	The New Testament in Modern English (J. B. Phillips)	Nine (9) or more
23) Rhm	The Emphasized New Testament: A New Translation (J. B. Rotherham)	Seven (7) or more
24) RSV	The Revised Standard Version	Six (6) or more
25) TCNT	The Twentieth Century New Testament	Six (6) or more
26) TEV	Today's English Version	Eleven (11) or more
27) TM	The Message-The New Testament in Contemporary Language	Eight (8) or more
28) TNT	The New Testament: A New Easy-to-Read Version (World Bible Translation Center)	Six (6) or more
29) Wey	The New Testament in Modern Speech (Richard Francis Weymouth)	Five (5) or more
30) YLT	Young's Literal Translation of the Holy Bible (Robert Young)	Forty-seven (47) or more

Conclusion: The Testimony of the Translators document that *proskuneo* includes **bowing the knees.**

NEXT: What is *proskuneo*?—"Testimony of the Bible Translators" Part II. The next section will show examples of seventeen (17) different Bible Versions and how they translate the Greek word *proskuneo* in seven (7) different Bible verses. These examples will further document that the more recent translators recognize that the act of **bowing the knees** by kneeling or falling prostrate is present by definition in the meaning of the Greek word *proskuneo*. For comparison purposes, the presentation will again be summarized in a table format.

What is proskuneo?

The Testimony of Bible Translators

Part II

Some Explicit Examples

Examples of Bible Versions that Translate Proskuneo as the First Act in the Two-act "Proskuneo Pattern" of Worship

Seventeen (17) different Bible versions are listed on the next page along with seven (7) scripture references as examples to show that the more recent Bible Versions translate *proskuneo* as a form of "Kneel" or "bowing the knees," one or more times instead of "worship." For comparison, the KJV is listed first.

Proskuneo	*Proskuneo*	*Proskuneo*	*Proskuneo*	*Proskuneo*	*Proskuneo*	*Proskuneo*	*Proskuneo*
Bible Codes	Matt 8:2	Matt 9:18	Matt 15:25	Matt 20:20	Mark 5:6	Heb 11:21	Rev 3:9
1) KJV	Worshiped	Worshiped	Worshiped	Worshiped	Worshiped	Worshiped	Worship
2) NIV	Knelt	Knelt	Knelt	Kneeling	Fell on his knees	Worshiped	Fall down
3) RSV	Knelt	Knelt	Knelt	Kneeling	worshiped	Bowing in worship	Bow down
4) TEV	Knelt	Knelt	Fell at his feet	Bowed before	Fell on his knees	Worshiped	Bow down
5) PME	Knelt	Bowing low	Knelt	Knelt	Knelt	Bowed in prayer	Bow down
6) MNTT	Kneeled	Kneeled	Bowed Before him	Fell at his feet	Fell Before him	worshiped	Bow at your feet
7) ALT	Prostrating himself	Prostrating himself	Prostrated himself	Prostrating herself	Prostrated himself	worshiped	Prostrate
8) NASV	Bowed down	Bowed down	Bow down before	Bowing down	Bowed down	Worshiped	Bow down

Proskuneo	*Proskuneo*	*Proskuneo*	*Proskuneo*	*Proskuneo*	*Proskuneo*	*Proskuneo*	*Proskuneo*
Bible Codes	**Matt 8:2**	**Matt 9:18**	**Matt 15:25**	**Matt 20:20**	**Mark 5:6**	**Heb 11:21**	**Rev 3:9**
9) JB	Bowed low	Bowed low	Kneeling	Bowed low	Fell at his feet	Bowing to Pray	Fall at Your feet
10) YLT	Bowing to him	Bowing to him	Bowing to him	Bowing	Bowed before him	Did bow down	Bow before
11) NEB	Bowed low	Bowed low	Fell at his feet	Bowed low	Flung himself down	Worshiped	Fall down at your feet
12) CEV	Kneeled	Kneeled	Kneeled	Kneeled	Kneeled	Worshiped	Kneel down
13) ESV	Knelt	Knelt	Knelt	Kneeling	Fell down before him	Bowing in worship	Bow down before
14) TM	Went to his knees	Bowed	Went to his knees	Knelt	Bowed in worship	Bowed Worship-fully	Acknow-ledge
15) NLT	Knelt	Knelt	Worshiped	Knelt	Fell down Before him	Bowed in worship	Bow down
16) Mof	Knelt	Knelt	Knelt	Praying	Knelt	Bending in prayer	Do homage
17) TNT	Bowed down	Bowed down	Bowed before	Bowed before	Bowed down	Worshiped	Bow at your feet

NEXT: The Parallel Accounts—"Testimony of Scripture" Part I—will show that the two-act "proskuneo pattern" of worship is documented in the parallel accounts of the *proskuneo* worship events and is what the apostles taught and practiced. Also, Matthew, Mark, Luke, John, Paul, and Jesus taught the two-act "proskuneo pattern."

4

The Testimony of Scripture

Part I

*The Parallel Accounts Document the "*Proskuneo *Pattern" of Worship*

Comparing what two or more writers said about the same proskuneo **worship** *event*

WHY USE THE KJV? Church doctrine was apparently taken from the KJV during the Restoration movement and the later part of the Reformation. The ancient custom of **bowing the knees** to **worship** (*proskuneo*: kiss toward) someone who is divine or thought to be divine is a Scriptural event that has a Scriptural pattern. The two-act "*proskuneo* pattern" can be documented in both the OT and the NT.

Comparing and Harmonizing the Parallel Accounts of the *proskuneo* Worship Events

A.T. Robertson, who wrote *A Harmony of the Gospels*, which is a popular book that is used in many of our Bible Colleges, proclaims the following: "One who has never read a harmony will be amazed at the flood of light that flashes from parallel and progressive records."[1] Therefore, harmonizing and comparing these parallel accounts of the two-act "*proskuneo* pattern" of worship, should shed new light on many questions.

1. Robertson, A. T. *A Harmony of Gospels*. Harper & Row, San Francisco, CA 1922, viii.

Each of the following 10 parallel accounts compare what two or more inspired writers said about the same **worship** event regarding the acts performed. The account of each writer contains one or both acts in the "*proskuneo* pattern" of worship. Therefore, the selection of the parallel accounts was limited to those worship events that always begin with the worshiper **"bowing the knees,"** which is the first act in the "*proskuneo* pattern." For review, the second act in the pattern is *proskuneo*, a Greek word that is always translated "worship" in the KJV. The word literally means that the worshiper "kissed," or "kissed toward," or threw a "kiss toward" the object of worship. In the New Testament, a variety of expressions are used to indicate that the worshiper "bowed the knees." Examples of these expressions include "kneeled," "fell down," "fell at his feet," "fell on his face," "fell before," "bowing the knees," etc.

By comparing the parallel accounts of two or more inspired writers, it can be documented that the two-act "*proskuneo* pattern" of worship is always referred to in one of three ways: by the first act, by the second act, or by both acts. Also, harmonizing these parallel accounts will show that the inspired writers supplement each other without contradiction by using acts that are always in harmony with the two-act "*proskuneo* pattern." These 10 parallel accounts fully demonstrate that God's Word always harmonizes with itself when we use the words that God used.

When the Greek word *proskuneo* is translated literally into any other language including English, we have the word of God. For example, the parallel accounts of the same *proskuneo* **worship** events by different inspired writers can only be harmonized by using the literal translation of God's Greek word *proskuneo*. By doing so, God's word always harmonizes with itself. "Literally" means using the English equivalents of the words that God used. It is "Speaking the oracles of God" (1 Pet. 4:11). For example, God Himself said to Elijah in 1 Kings 19:18, "Yet, I have left me seven thousand in Israel, all the **knees which have not bowed** unto Baal, and every mouth which hath not **kissed** him" (K.J.V). Other Bible versions say **"kissed"** as well. When the Greeks translated this verse into the Greek language (the Septuagint) in 270 A.D., they used the Greek word *proskuneo* in place of the Hebrew word for **"kissed"** (*nashaq*). Therefore, in the following presentation of the parallel accounts, the **"worship"** word *proskuneo* is translated literally as **"kissed"** or **"kissed toward"** to know what the worshiper actually did and to answer certain questions. For example, in parallel account # 1, why does Matthew say that Satan requested both acts in the two-act "*proskuneo* pattern" of worship whereas Luke says that Satan requested the second act only? The answer to this question is discussed following parallel account #1.

~

Parallel Account #1
(Matt. 4:9; Luke 4:7)

Comparing What Matthew Said with What Luke Said

Satan Tempted Jesus to Kneel and Worship (*Proskuneo*) Him

(1) Matthew 4:9	(2) Luke 4:7
And saith unto him, All these things will I give to thee, if thou wilt **fall down** and **worship** (*proskuneo*: **kiss toward**) me.	If thou therefore wilt **worship** (*proskuneo*: **kiss toward**) me, all shall be thine.

In recording the acts that Satan requested, notice that Matthew said that Satan requested both acts in "*proskuneo* pattern" of worship whereas Luke said that Satan requested the *second act only,* which is worship (*proskuneo*: kiss toward). Why does Luke omit **"fall down,"** which is the first act in the two-act *"proskuneo* pattern?"

First of all, if both accounts can be true, then an omission is not a contradiction. Surely, both accounts are true because God's word is inspired, inerrant, infallible, and without contradiction. Luke knew, therefore, that the act of "falling down" or "kneeling" was understood to be present in his account by necessary inference because the act of worship (*proskuneo:* kiss toward) is always done while **bowing the knees.**

In regard to the two-act "*proskuneo* pattern" of worship, the whole of anything is the sum of its parts. Therefore, the "part" or "act" of **bowing the knees** is understood to be present in Luke's account in a figure of speech called a synecdoche, which means a part can be mentioned for the whole. If the act of **bowing the knees** is not understood to be present in Luke's account, then there is a contradiction between the two accounts. Thus, these two parallel accounts of the same *proskuneo* "worship" proposal document that the New Testament writers sometimes used the *second act only* when referring to the two-act "*proskuneo* pattern" of worship. Further documentation is shown in the following summation chart.

"The sum of thy word is truth . . ." (Ps. 119:160 NASV)

THE PROSKUNEO PATTERN OF WORSHIP

REFERENCE	FIRST ACT	SECOND ACT
(1) Matthew 4:9	fall down and (kneel and)	worship (*proskuneo*: kiss toward) me
(2) Luke 4:7	(kneel and)	worship (*proskuneo*: kiss toward) me
The Sum or Combination of all:	kneel and	worship (*proskuneo*: kiss toward) me

J. W. McGarvey's *Fourfold Gospel* combines the two accounts into one as follows: ". . . **fall down** and **worship** before me."[2] In 1914, J. W. McGarvey and Philip Y. Pendleton harmonized the four gospels in a book called *The Fourfold Gospel.*

Conclusion: The sum of God's word documents that the "*proskuneo* pattern" is understood to be present in both accounts of the inspired writers. Why is the term "kneel" used in the summation chart in place of the term fall down? As stated previously, a variety of expressions are used by the NT writers to indicate that the worshiper bowed the knees. Although these expressions include "**kneeled,**" "**fell down,**" "**fell on his face,**" "**fell at his feet,**" "**bowing the knees,**" etc., the Holy Spirit has authorized the use of the term "**kneel**" as an option to the expression "**fell.**" For example, parallel account #2 is presented next which shows that scripture uses "**kneeling**" as an option to "**fell on his face.**" In addition, the newer translations use the term "kneel" or an equivalent expression at least one or more times in translating the Greek word *proskuneo.* For uniformity and consistency, therefore, the term "**kneel**" was selected for use in the summation charts

2. McGarvey, J. W. Ibid: The *Fourfold Gospel.* The Standard publishing Co. Cincinnati, OH 1914, 99.

in an effort to lessen confusion and to better communicate the worship gesture to our present culture.

Next: Why does Mark's account appear first in the following five (5) parallel accounts? A.T. Robertson says, "It is now known that Matthew and Luke made use of Mark for the framework of their Gospels. This change simplifies amazingly the unfolding of the narrative."[3] Therefore, Mark's account is placed first in the next five parallel accounts.

Parallel Account #2
(Mark 1:40; Matt. 8:2; Luke 5:12)

Comparing What Three Different Inspired Writers Said About What the Worshiper Did

A Leper Kneeled And Worshiped (*Proskuneo*) Jesus

In these three parallel accounts of the same *proskuneo* "worship" event, Mark says that the leper came "**kneeling,**" whereas Matthew says that the leper "**worshiped**" (*proskuneo*: kissed toward) Jesus, and Luke says that the leper "**fell** on his face" (or fell prostrate—which means that he **kneeled** and touched his forehead to the ground). These three parallel accounts of the same *proskuneo* "worship" event of the leper document that the New Testament writers sometimes used the *first act only* and sometimes the *second act only* when referring to the two-act "*proskuneo* pattern" of worship. Therefore, the inspired writers supplement each other without contradiction as shown in the summation chart that follows the parallel accounts.

3. Ibid., vii.

(1) Mark 1:40	(2) Matthew 8:2	(3) Luke 5:12
And there came a leper to him, beseeching him, and **kneeling** (*gonupeteo*) down to him, and saying unto him, if thou wilt, thou canst make me clean.	And behold there came a leper and **worshiped** (*Proskuneo*: **kissed toward**) him saying, Lord, If thou wilt, thou canst make me clean.	And it came to pass, when he was in a certain city, behold a man full of leprosy: who seeing Jesus **fell** (*pipto*) **on his face**, and besought him, saying, Lord, If thou wilt, thou canst make me clean.

"The sum of thy word is truth . . ." (Ps. 119:160 NASV)

THE PROSKUNEO PATTERN OF WORSHIP

REFERENCE	FIRST ACT	SECOND ACT
(1) Mark 1:40	kneeling (gonupeteo)	
(2) Matthew 8:2		worshiped (*proskuneo*: kiss toward)
(3) Luke 5:12	fell (*pipto*) on his face (kneeled)	
The Sum or combination of all	Kneeled (gonupeteo)	worshiped (*proskuneo*: kiss toward)

J. W. McGarvey's 1914 *Fourfold Gospel* combines the three accounts as follows: "**kneeling** down to him, he **fell on his face** and **worshiped** him."[4]

Conclusion: The sum of God's word documents that the "*proskuneo* pattern" is understood to be present in each of the three accounts. That means that either of the two acts in the pattern can be used alone to stand for the whole "*proskuneo* pattern" of worship. Apparently, touching the forehead to the ground was an option in the first century, and is certainly an option in this century.

4. Ibid., 178.

Parallel Account # 3
(Mark 5:22; Matt. 9:18; Luke 8:41)

Jairus Kneeled And Worshiped (*Proskuneo*) Jesus

In the following three parallel accounts of the same *proskuneo* "worship" event, Mark says that Jairus "**fell** (*pipto*) **at his feet,**" whereas Luke says he "**fell** (*pipto*) **down**" at Jesus' feet, and Matthew says that he **worshiped** (proskuneo: kissed toward) him.

(1) Mark 5:22	(2) Matthew 9:18	(3) Luke 8:41
And, behold, there cometh one of the rulers of the synagogue, Jairus by name; and when he saw him, he **fell** (*pipto*) **at his feet.**	While he spake these things unto him, behold there came a certain ruler, and **worshiped** (*proskuneo*: **kissed toward**) him, saying, "My daughter is even now dead." But come and lay thy hand upon her and she shall live.	And behold there came a man named Jairus, and he was a ruler of the synagogue; and he **fell** (*pipto*) **down** at Jesus' feet and besought him that he would come into his house:

The three inspired writers supplement each other in perfect harmony as can be seen in the summation chart below.

"The sum of thy word is truth . . ." (Ps. 119:160 NASV)

THE PROSKUNEO PATTERN OF WORSHIP

REFERENCE	FIRST ACT	SECOND ACT
(1) Mark 5:22	fell (*pipto*) at his feet (kneeled)	
(2) Matthew 9:18		worshiped (*proskuneo*: kissed toward)
(3) Luke 8:41	fell (*pipto*) down at Jesus' feet (kneeled)	
The Sum or Combination of all:	kneeled (and)	worshiped (*proskuneo*: kissed toward)

J. W. McGarvey's *Fourfold Gospel* combines the three accounts as follows: "he **fell [falleth] down** at Jesus' feet, and **worshiped** him."[5]

Conclusion: The sum of God's word documents that the New Testament writers sometimes used the *first act only* and sometimes used the *second act only* when referring to the whole "*proskuneo* pattern" of worship.

Parallel Account #4
(Mark 7:25; Matthew 15:25)

A Woman Of Canaan Kneeled And Worshiped (*Proskuneo*) Jesus

In these two parallel accounts of the same *proskuneo* "worship" event, Mark says that the woman of Canaan "**fell at his feet,**" whereas Matthew says that "she **worshiped** (*proskuneo*: kissed toward) Jesus."

(1) Mark 7:25	(2) Matthew 15:25
For a certain woman, whose young daughter had an unclean spirit, heard of him, and came and **fell** (*pipto*) **at his feet.**	Then came she and **worshiped** (*proskuneo*: **kissed toward**) him, saying, Lord, help me.

"The sum of thy word is truth . . ." (Ps. 119:160 NASV)

THE PROSKUNEO PATTERN OF WORSHIP

REFERENCE	FIRST ACT	SECOND ACT
(1) Mark 7:25	fell at his feet (kneeled)	
(2) Matthew 15:25		worshiped (*proskuneo*: kissed toward)
The Sum or Combination of all:	kneeled (and)	worshiped (*proskuneo*: kissed toward)

5. Ibid., 852.

J. W. Mc Garvey's *Fourfold Gospel* combined the two accounts as follows: "She came and **fell down** at his feet and **worshiped** him."[6] In context, the manner in which the woman **"kissed"** (*proskuneo*) his hand, apparently reminded Jesus of a puppy. With great insight, Mary Martini grasped the concept of the **"kiss"** well in this verse and wrote the following: "She sought Him out and **fell at His feet**. She came and **worshiped** Him saying: 'Lord help me!' The word **'worship'** as used here is interesting. Apparently, she **prostrated** herself in front of Him. Notice the irony of the literal meaning of the word worship, according to Strong's Concordance: 'to **kiss** like a dog licking his master's hand.' The next exchange of words is among the most fascinating in the Bible. Jesus said, 'Let the children be filled first, for it is not good to take the children's bread and throw it to the little dogs' ... With quick wit and reason she replied: 'Yes, Lord, yet even the little dogs under the table eat from the children's crumbs.'"[7]

Parallel Example #5
(Mark 15:19; Matt. 27:29)

The Soldiers Kneeled and Worshiped (*Proskuneo*) Jesus

(In Pretense and Mockery—not "In Truth")

These two parallel accounts of the same *proskuneo* "worship" event document that the New Testament writers sometimes used the *first act only* when referring to the two-act "*proskuneo* pattern" of worship. In recording the acts performed by the soldiers, notice that Mark used both acts in the "*proskuneo* pattern," whereas Matthew used the *first act only* when referring to the two-act event. However, an omission is not a contradiction, and Matthew knew that the second act was present in his account by necessary inference because the two acts are *inseparable* in the "*proskuneo* pattern" of worship.

6. Ibid., 401.

7. Mary Martini. "Women in the Book of Mark." *The Restorer*, July/August 1999.

(1) Mark 15:19	(2) Matt. 27:29
And they smote him on the head with a reed, and did spit upon him, and **bowing their knees** (*gonupeteo*) **worshiped** (*proskuneo*: **kissed toward**) him.	And when they had platted a crown of thorns, they put it upon his head, and a reed in his right hand: and they **bowed the knee** (*gonupeteo*) before him, and mocked him, saying, "Hail, King of the Jews!"

"The sum of thy word is truth . . ." (Ps. 119:160 NASV)

THE PROSKUNEO PATTERN OF WORSHIP

REFERENCE	FIRST ACT	SECOND ACT
Mark 15:19	bowing their knees (kneeled)	worshiped (*proskuneo*: kissed toward)
Matthew 27:29	bowed the knee (kneeled)	
The Sum or Combination of all:	kneeled (and)	worshiped (*proskuneo*: kissed toward)

J. W. McGarvey combined the accounts as follows: "**bowing the knees** they **worshiped** him."[8]

Conclusion: The sum of God's word documents that the soldiers "worshiped" Jesus outwardly by "kneeling" and "kissing toward" (*proskuneo*) him in harmony with the "proskuneo pattern." However, we also know that inwardly, or in "attitude," that the two gestures were done "in pretense" and mockery; not "in truth."

8. McGarvey, J. W. The *Fourfold Gospel.* The Standard publishing Co. Cincinnati, OH, 1914, 719.

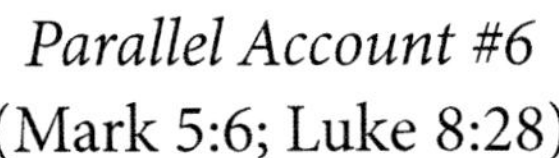

Parallel Account #6
(Mark 5:6; Luke 8:28)

Legion Kneeled and Worshiped (*Proskuneo*) Jesus

In these two parallel accounts of the same *proskuneo* "worship" event, notice that Mark used the *second act only*, whereas Luke used the *first act only* when referring to the two-act "*proskuneo* pattern" of worship.

(1) Mark 5:6	(2) Luke 8:28
But when he saw Jesus afar off, he ran and **worshipped** (*proskuneo*: **kissed toward**) him.	When he saw Jesus, he cried out, and **fell down** (*pipto*) before him, and with a loud voice said, "what have I to do with thee, Jesus, thou Son of God most high? I beseech thee, torment me not."

"The sum of thy word is truth . . ." (Ps. 119:160 NASV)

THE PROSKUNEQ PATTERN OF WORSHIP

REFERENCE	FIRST ACT	SECOND ACT
(1) Mark 5:6		worshiped (*proskuneo*: kissed toward)
(2) Luke 8:28	fell down before (kneeled)	
The Sum or Combination of all:	kneeled (and)	worshiped (*proskuneo*: kissed toward)

J. W. McGarvey's *Fourfold Gospel* combined the two accounts as follows: "**fell down** before him, and **worshiped** him."[9]

Conclusion: The sum of God's word documents that legion kneeled and worshiped (*proskuneo*: kissed toward) Jesus in perfect harmony with the "*proskuneo* pattern." Also, there is documentation that the New Testament

9. Ibid., 345.

writers sometimes used the *first act only* and sometimes the *second act only* when referring to the two-act "*proskuneo* pattern" of worship

~

Parallel Account #7
(I Kings 19:18; Romans 11:4)

God Reserved 7,000 Men Who Refused to Bow the Knee to Baal and Whose Mouths Had Not Kissed Him

These two parallel accounts of the same *proskuneo* "worship" event are an example of perfect harmony between the Old Testament and the New Testament because both were written by inspired men of God. Notice, however, that when the object of "worship" is visibly present such as the idol Baal, the worshiper has the option of actually "kissing" the object, "kissing toward" the object or throwing a "kiss toward" the object. Apparently, the worshipers kneeled and literally kissed Baal in harmony with the "proskuneo pattern" just as the woman who "loved much" kneeled and literally kissed the feet of Jesus (Luke 7:38).

However, the worshiper "must" always "kiss toward" (*proskuneo*) or throw a "kiss toward" God because God is "a spirit." Therefore, those who worship (*proskuneo*: kiss toward) him must worship (*proskuneo*: kiss toward) him "in spirit . . ." (John 4:20-24). Why? As "spirit," God is present "in spirit" and not "in body." A spirit does not have a physical body and, therefore, God is not visibly present.

(1) I Kings 19:18	(2) Romans 11:4
Yet I reserved 7,000 in Israel—all whose **knees have not bowed** down to Baal and all whose mouths have not **kissed** him.	And what was God's answer to Him? "I have reserved for myself 7,000 men who have **not bowed the knee** to Baal."

"The sum of thy word is truth . . ." (Ps. 119:160 NASV)

THE PROSKUNEO PATTERN OF WORSHIP

REFERENCE	FIRST ACT	SECOND ACT
(1) I Kings 19:18	knees have not bowed	and mouths have not kissed (Baal)
(2) Romans 11:4	not bowed the knee (*gonupeteo*)	
The Sum or Combination of all:	knees have not bowed	and mouths have not kissed (Baal)

Conclusion: In quoting from the Old Testament, the apostle Paul records the *first act only* in the two-act "*proskuneo* pattern" of worship. Why did Paul omit the second part referring to "mouths that have not **kissed** him?" The apostle Paul knew that when either of these two acts are used alone in Scripture, the other act is understood to be present also by necessary inference or in a figure of speech called a synecdoche, whereby a part can be mentioned for the whole. Therefore, the act of "**kissing**" is understood to be present in Paul's account by necessary inference, and the two accounts are in perfect harmony.

Parallel Account # 8
(Heb. 11:21; Gen. 47:31b)

Jacob Kneeled And Worshiped (*Proskuneo*) God

All agree that the Old Testament was written in Hebrew. These two parallel accounts of Jacob's "worship" in the Old Testament document that the Hebrews preferred using the *first act only* in the "*proskuneo* pattern" of worship when referring to the two-act event. They usually used the Hebrew word *shachah* which literally means to "bow down." They apparently knew that the second act of worship (*proskuneo*: kiss toward) was there by necessary inference.

When the Old Testament was translated into Greek in 270 AD (the Septuagint), the Greeks used the word *proskuneo* to replace the Hebrew word *shachah,* knowing that the first act of bowing the knees or kneeling was there by necessary inference. Since the New Testament was written in Greek, their preference of using the *second act only* in the event to stand for the whole was apparently brought forward by the New Testament writers. Therefore, these two parallel accounts of Jacob supplement each other and are in perfect harmony with the "*proskuneo* pattern" of worship as can be seen in the chart that follows the parallel accounts.

Old Testament (Hebrew)	New Testament (Greek)
(1) Genesis 47:31b	(2) Hebrew 11:21
And Israel (Jacob) **bowed himself** (*shachah*) upon the bed's head*.	By faith Jacob when he was dying, blessed both the sons of Joseph and **worshiped** (*proskuneo*: **kissed toward**), leaning upon the top of his staff.

*Scholars say that the writer of Hebrews was quoting from the Greek translation of the OT (The Septuagint) which uses the phrase "top of his staff" rather than the "bed's head."

"The sum of thy word is truth . . ." (Ps. 119:160 NASV)

THE PROSKUNEO PATTERN OF WORSHIP

REFERENCE	FIRST ACT	SECOND ACT
(1) Genesis 47:31b	bowed himself (*shachah*) (kneeled)	
(2) Hebrew 11:21		worshiped (*proskuneo*: kissed toward)
The Sum or Combination of all:	kneeled (and)	worshiped (*proskuneo*: kissed toward)

Conclusion: The sum of God's word documents that the New Testament harmonizes with the Old Testament. Although written in two different languages, these two divinely inspired parallel accounts of the same worship event supplement each other perfectly. Also, the combined accounts document that Jacob bowed himself or kneeled and worshiped (*proskuneo*: kissed toward") God in perfect harmony with the two-act "*proskuneo* pattern" of worship. This finding also means that the pattern has remained the same from Genesis to Revelation. Amazingly, Isaiah 45:22–23 says God has sworn by Himself that He will never change the pattern: "Look unto me, and be ye saved, all the ends of the earth: for I am God, and there is none else. I have sworn by myself, the word is gone out of my mouth in righteousness, and shall not return, that unto me **every knee shall bow.**" The angel in Revelation supplies the second act in the pattern by saying, "worship (proskuneo: kiss toward) God." (Rev. 19:10b; 22:9—the last time that "worship" is mentioned in the Bible).

Parallel Account #9
(Heb. 1:6; Rev. 7:10, 11, 17a)

All the Angels Kneel and Worship (Proskuneo) Jesus and God

Hebrews 1:6	Revelation 7:10, 11, 17a
And again, when he bringeth in the first begotten into the world, he saith, And let all the angels of God **worship** (*proskuneo*: **kiss toward**) him.	10 And cried with a loud voice, saying, Salvation to our God which sitteth upon the throne, and unto the Lamb. 11 And all the angels stood round about the throne, and the elders and the four beasts, and **fell** (*pipto*) **before** the throne on their faces, and **worshiped** (*proskuneo*: **kissed toward**) God. V.17a: For the Lamb . . . in the midst of the throne . . .

"The sum of thy word is truth . . ." (Ps. 119:160 NASV)

THE PROSKUNEO PATTERN OF WORSHIP

REFERENCE	FIRST ACT	SECOND ACT
Heb. 1:6		worshiped (*proskuneo*: kissed toward)
Rev. 7:11-17a	fell...on their faces (kneeled)	worshiped (*proskuneo*: kissed toward)
The Sum or Combination of all:	kneeled (and)	worshiped (*proskuneo*: kissed toward)

Conclusion: The sum of God's word documents that the *second act only,* which is worship (proskuneo: kiss toward), can be mentioned to stand for the whole "*proskuneo* pattern" of worship as it does in Hebrews 1:6. That means the first act in the pattern, which is "bowing the knees," is understood to be present in Hebrews 1:6 by means of a synecdoche whereby a part can be mentioned for the whole. Therefore, these two parallel accounts of "worship" by the angels are in perfect harmony because God's word always harmonizes with itself when we use the words that God used.

Parallel Account # 10

(Ps. 2:12; Luke 7:40b, 45, 47a; Phil. 2:10)

God Says Kneel And Kiss My Son Or Perish

(1) Jesus the Messiah

Psalms 2:12

The King James Version says, "**Kiss** the Son, lest he be angry, and ye perish from the way, when his wrath is kindled but a little. Blessed are all they that put their trust in him."

The Living Bible says, "**Fall down** before his son and **kiss his feet** before his anger is roused and you perish. I am warning you—his wrath will soon begin. But oh, the joys of those who put their trust in him!"

Jackie Stearsman points out that Psalm 2:12 is, "a declaration of the divine purpose to maintain the king's authority and a warning to the world that it **must bow** to him or perish."[10]

(2) Woman Who Kneeled and kissed Jesus loved much
Luke 7:40b, 45, 47a

Simon, I have somewhat to say unto thee. Thou gavest me no **kiss**: but this woman since the time I came in hath not ceased to **kiss** my feet. Her sins, which are many, are forgiven; for she loves much: but to whom little is forgiven, the same loveth little.

(3) Kneel in the Name of Jesus
Philippians 2:10, 11

Note: That at* the name of Jesus **every knee should bow**, of things in heaven, earth, and things under the earth; And that every tongue should confess that Jesus Christ is Lord, to the glory of God the Father: (at* translates literally "in" from the Greek word *en*). "An honest confession is like a **kiss** on the lips" (Proverbs 24:26).

"The sum of thy word is truth . . ." (Ps. 119:160 NASV)

THE PROSKUNEO PATTERN OF WORSHIP

REFERENCE	FIRST ACT	SECOND ACT
(1) Psalm 2:12		Kiss
(2) Luke 7:40b,45,47a		Kiss
(3) Philippians 2:10	Every knee should bow	
The Sum or Combination of All:	Every knee should bow (and)	Every mouth should Kiss (toward) Jesus [worship]

Conclusion: The apostle Paul referred to the two-act "proskuneo pattern" by using the first act while Luke and the writer of Psalms used the second act. God has made it clear in the OT and the NT that "In the name of Jesus every knee should bow" and everyone should worship by "kissing toward" him and "every tongue should confess that Jesus is Lord to the glory of

10. Stearsman, Jackie M. "God's king is the Messiah, the Messiah is His son." *Focusing Psalm 2, Preparing Souls to Serve the Lord* Vol. XIX, No. 4, November 1998, 1.

God the father." If we refuse we shall "perish" (Ps. 2:12). (We can no longer **kiss** Jesus like the woman did in Simon's house, because He has ascended into heaven to be at the right hand of God—in a physical body. Therefore, we have to **kiss toward** Him. On earth, He is present with us the same as the Father is present—"in spirit."

Summary Overall: One important point confirmed by examining these parallel accounts is that the inspired writers often used the single word "worship" (*proskuneo*) when referring to the whole two-act "proskuneo pattern" of worship. Comparing these 10 parallel accounts clearly documents that the two-act "proskuneo pattern" is always referred to in one of three ways: sometimes by the first act, sometimes by the second act, and sometimes by both acts. Also, harmonizing these parallel accounts demonstrates that the inspired writers supplement each other by using acts that are always in harmony with the two-act "proskuneo pattern" of worship. God's Word always harmonizes with itself when we use the words that God used. Therefore, the best interpreter of Scripture is Scripture. By definition and by examining scripture, *proskuneo* is the second act or gesture in the "proskuneo pattern" and is always done while bowing the knees. Understanding these facts is absolutely essential to our understanding the meaning of the "worship" word *proskuneo*, and its usage in the New Testament.

NEXT: The Sequential Accounts document the "proskuneo pattern"—Testimony of Scripture—Part II

The Sequential Accounts will compare what was *said* about worship (proskuneo: kiss toward) with the actual worship acts that were *done* or performed. As already shown, the two-act "proskuneo pattern" of worship is present explicitly in the NT a total of 13 times. By harmonizing the Sequential Accounts and the Parallel Accounts, the two acts can be shown to be together an additional 20 or more times making a total of over 30 times. The introductory paragraph will explain in more detail.

The Testimony of Scripture

Part II

*The Sequential Accounts Document the "*Proskuneo *Pattern" of Worship*

Comparing in Sequence—What Was **Said** *with What Was* **Done**

THE SEQUENTIAL ACCOUNTS ARE *proskuneo* worship events that occur in sequence and should answer the following question: Does what was **said** about worship (*proskuneo*) harmonize with what was **done**? Studying these accounts gives an opportunity to compare exactly what was said about a specific *proskuneo* worship event with the worship acts that were actually done or performed. On close examination, these sequential accounts show that the wise men, Jesus, and the angel in Revelation all used the word "worship" (*proskuneo*) in referring to the two-act "*proskuneo* pattern" of worship that always begins with bowing the knees. It will also become obvious when comparing these events that God's word harmonizes with itself. The first sequential account to be harmonized is that of the wise men. They were the first people who came to worship (*proskuneo*) Jesus. In telling what the wise men *said*, Matthew uses the second act in the *proskuneo* worship pattern, which literally means to "kiss toward." In telling what the wise men *did*, Matthew uses both acts in the "*proskuneo* pattern" of worship as can be seen in the verses on the next page.

Sequential Example #1
Comparing in Sequence—What Was **Said** *with What Was* **Done**

The Wise Men Kneeled and Worshiped (*Proskuneo*) Jesus

(Wise Men Still Do)

The wise men *said* in Matthew 2:2 that they wanted to find the Christ child so that they could "worship (*proskuneo*)" Him. When they found the Christ child, *they did* "worship (*proskuneo*)" Him," but they first **bowed the knees** (Matt. 2:11).

What the wise men **said**	What the wise men **did**
(1) Matthew 2:2	(2) Matthew 2:11
Saying, Where is he that is born king of the Jews? For we have seen his star in the East, and are come to **worship** (*proskuneo*: **kiss toward**) him.	And when they were come into the house, they saw the young child with Mary his mother and **fell** (*pipto*) **down**, and **worshiped** (*proskuneo*: **kissed toward**) him: and when they had opened their treasures, they presented unto him gifts; gold, and frankincense, and myrrh.

"The sum of thy word is truth . . ." (Ps. 119:160 NASV)

THE PROSKUNEO PATTERN OF WORSHIP

REFERENCE	FIRST ACT	SECOND ACT
Matthew 2:2 "We have come to"		worship (proskuneo: kiss toward) him
Matthew 2:11 "they saw the young child with Mary . . . and"	fell down and	worshiped (proskuneo: kissed toward) him
The Sum or Combination of all:	fell down and	worshiped (proskuneo: kissed toward) him

Conclusion: The sum of God's word documents that the wise men did exactly what they said they were going to do because the act of "bowing the knees" and the act of "kissing toward" are the two physical acts or parts that make up the whole "proskuneo pattern" of worship. Therefore, the act of "bowing the knees" or "kneeling" is understood to be present in Matthew 2:2 along with the worship act of "kissing toward" (proskuneo) by a figure of speech called a synecdoche, whereby a part is mentioned for the whole. Therefore, what was *said* harmonizes with what was *done.* In summary, the wise men used the single Greek word *proskuneo* translated as the English word "worship" in referring to the two-act "proskuneo pattern" of worship that they performed when they came into the house where Jesus was. Also, note that after the wise men **kneeled** and kissed toward (*proskuneo*) Jesus, they rose to "serve" (*latreuo*) Him by giving gifts.

~

Sequential Example #2
Comparing in sequence—what Satan wanted **done** *and what Jesus* **said** *in refusal*

Jesus Refused to Kneel and Worship (*Proskuneo*) Satan

According to Matthew's account, Satan requested both physical acts in the "proskuneo pattern" of worship when he said, "If you will **fall down and worship** (*proskuneo*: kiss toward) me." Note that in Jesus' refusal, He only mentioned the second physical act in the "*proskuneo* pattern" of worship when he said, "It is written that thou shalt **worship** (*proskuneo*: kiss toward) the Lord thy God . . ." Jesus knew that Satan knew that the act of "**bowing the knees**" was understood to be present in His reply because He knew that the act of worship (*proskuneo*: kiss toward) is always done while **bowing the knees.**

Satan's **proposal**	Jesus' **refusal**
(1) Matthew 4:9	(2) Matthew 4:10
And saith unto him, all these things will I give to thee, if thou wilt **fall down** and **worship** (*proskuneo*: kiss toward) me.	Then saith Jesus unto him, Get thee hence, Satan: for it is written, Thou shalt **worship** (*proskuneo*: kiss toward) the Lord thy God, and Him only shalt thou serve (*latreuo*).

"The sum of thy word is truth . . ." (Ps. 119:160 NASV)

THE PROSKUNEO PATTERN OF WORSHIP

REFERENCE	FIRST ACT	SECOND ACT
(1) Matthew 4:9 Satan: The proposal:	Fall down and	worship (proskuneo: kiss toward) me
(2) Matthew 4:10 Jesus: The refusal:		worship (proskuneo: kiss toward) God
The Sum Or Combination of all:	Fall down and	worship (proskuneo: kiss toward)

Conclusion: The sum of God's word documents that the act of kneeling is present in the reply of Jesus. Why? This is because the act of "bowing the knees" and the act of "kissing toward" are the two physical acts or parts that make up the whole "proskuneo pattern" of worship. Therefore, the act of "bowing the knees" or "kneeling" is understood to be present in Jesus' reply along with the worship act of "kissing toward" (proskuneo) by a figure of speech called a synecdoche, whereby a part is mentioned for the whole. Also, if the act of kneeling is not understood to be present in the reply of Jesus, then Jesus changed the subject. Note that Jesus used the single Greek word *proskuneo* translated as the English word "worship" in referring to the whole two-act "proskuneo pattern" of worship that Satan wanted Him to perform.

That brings us to a second question: Why didn't Jesus just do these two physical acts in pretense and obtain all the kingdoms of the world? It is because Jesus cannot lie. If Jesus had kneeled down before Satan, it would have been an act of total surrender and submission to Satan's will and authority. If he had "kissed toward" *(proskuneo*) Satan, it would have been an act of unconditional love and adoration. Jesus knew that these two physical acts are gestures of total commitment to serve (*latreuo*) the one that the worshiper is kneeling and kissing toward. Therefore, Jesus would have become Satan's devoted servant and slave. That is why Jesus replied, "It is written that thou shalt **worship** (*proskuneo*: kiss toward) the Lord thy God and Him only shalt thou serve (*latreuo*)."

~

Sequential Example #3
Comparing in sequence—what was **done** *by John with what was* **said** *by the angel*

The Apostle John Kneeled to Worship (*Proskuneo*) the Angel

In John's description of what was *done* when he worshiped (*proskuneo*) the angel, he referred to both physical acts that are essential in the whole "proskuneo pattern" of worship. However, when the angel refused the gestures and instructed John to worship (*proskuneo:* kiss toward) God, the first act in the pattern was omitted. Why? This is because the angel knew that John understood that the act of *proskuneo* is always done while "bowing the knees" and that the two physical acts are inseparable in the "*proskuneo* pattern" of worship.

What John **did**	What the angel **said**
Revelation 19:10a	Revelation 19:10b
(1) And I **fell** (*pipto*) **at his feet** to **worship** (*proskuneo*: **kiss toward**) him.	(2) And he said unto me, See thou do it not: I am thy fellow servant, and of thy brethren that have the testimony of Jesus: **worship** (*proskuneo*: **kiss toward**) God.

"The sum of thy word is truth . . ." (Ps. 119:160 NASV)

THE PROSKUNEO PATTERN OF WORSHIP

REFERENCE	FIRST ACT	SECOND ACT
(1) Revelation 19:10a What John did:	fell at his feet (kneeled)	to worship (proskuneo: kiss toward) . . . the angel
(2) Revelation 19:10b What the angel said:		worship (proskuneo: kiss toward) God
The Sum or Combination of all:	kneeled	to worship (proskuneo: kiss toward)

Conclusion: The sum of God's word documents that the act of kneeling or "falling down" is understood to be present in the reply of the angel along with the act of "kissing toward" (*proskuneo*). Why? The whole of anything is the sum of its parts. The two parts or acts that make up the whole "*proskuneo* pattern" of worship are "bowing the knees" and "kissing toward" the object of worship. Therefore, the act of "bowing the knees" is understood to be present in a figure of speech called a synecdoche, whereby a part can be mentioned for the whole. If the act of kneeling is not understood to be present in the angel's reply, then the angel changed the subject. Note that the angel used the single Greek word *proskuneo* translated as the English word "worship" in referring to the two-act "*proskuneo* pattern" of worship that John was performing.

~

Sequential Example #4
Comparing what was **done** *by John with what was* **said** *by the angel*

Again, the Apostle John Kneeled to Worship (*Proskuneo*) the Angel

Again, in John's description of what happened, he referred to both physical acts that are essential in the "*proskuneo* pattern" of worship. When the angel again instructed John to "worship (*proskuneo*) God," the angel knew that John knew that the act of *proskuneo* is always done while bowing the knees and that the two physical acts are inseparable in the "*proskuneo* pattern" of worship.

What John **did**	What the angel **said**
Revelation 22:8	Revelation 22:9
(1) And I John saw these things, and heard them, and when I had heard and seen I **fell** (*pipto*) **down** to **worship** (*proskuneo*: **kiss toward**) before the feet of the angel which showed me these things.	(2) Then saith he unto me, See thou do it not: for I am thy fellow servant, and of thy brethren the prophets, and of them which keep the sayings of this book: **worship** (*proskuneo*: **kiss toward**) God.

"The sum of thy word is truth . . ." (Ps. 119:160 NASV)

THE PROSKUNEO PATTERN OF WORSHIP

REFERENCE	FIRST ACT	SECOND ACT
Revelation 22:8 What John did:	fell down to (kneeled)	worship (proskuneo: kiss toward) (the angel)
Revelation 22:9 What the angel said:		worship (proskuneo: kiss toward) God
The sum or Combination of all:	Kneeled to	worship (proskuneo: kiss toward)

Conclusion: The whole of anything is the sum of its parts. Therefore, the sum of God's word documents that the act of kneeling or "falling down" is understood to be present in the reply of the angel. Why? The act is understood to be present in a figure of speech called a synecdoche, whereby a part can be mentioned for the whole. If the act of kneeling is not understood to be present in the angel's reply, then the angel changed the subject. Notice again that the angel used the single Greek word *proskuneo* translated as the English word "worship" in referring to the two-act event that John was performing.

Summary:All four examples use the single Greek word *proskuneo* translated as the English word "worship" in referring to the two-act "*proskuneo* pattern" of worship. That is the main fact that is illustrated by the four sequential examples that compare what was *said* with what was *done*. Thus, the meaning of the word worship *(proskuneo)* did not change in the First Century during the writing of the New Testament. The words contain the same meaning now as they did before. If the words changed in meaning, they were changed by men and not by God. We must speak the oracles of God (1 Pet 4:11). When someone uses the English word "worship," would it not be helpful to know the meaning of the Greek "worship" word they are using?

Next: The "Testimony of the Apostles" document the two-act "proskuneo pattern."

The Testimony of Scripture

Part III

*The Testimony of the Apostles Document the "*Proskuneo *Pattern"*

WHY USE THE KJV? Church doctrine was apparently taken from the KJV during the Restoration movement and the later part of the Reformation. The apostles taught and practiced the two-act "*proskuneo* pattern" of worship. Paul, Peter and John wrote 20 of the 27 books of the NT. The following scriptures contain what these three apostles taught and practiced regarding worship that is done while **bowing the knees**. Also included in this section is the testimony of James, who is the writer of the Book of James who was also the brother of Jesus. The *Book of Christian Martyrs of the World* says James kneeled in prayer so often that his knees became hardened like the knees of a camel. James was known as "Old camel knees."

Apostolic Example #1

The Apostle Paul Practiced What He Preached When He Kneeled and Worshiped (Proskuneo) Jesus and God the Father

In the nine Biblical accounts below, the first four tell us what the apostle Paul taught about kneeling to worship (proskuneo: kiss toward) God and Jesus, whereas the last five events tell us what he practiced.

What the Apostle Paul Taught

In Event #1 Paul quotes from I Kings 19:18 to remind us that we should not kneel and kiss idols.

(1a) 7K Refused to Kneel and Kiss Baal	(1b) Parallel Account for Romans 11:4
Romans 11:4 (I Kings 19:18)	I Kings 19:18
And what was God's answer to Him? I have reserved for myself 7,000 men who have not **bowed the knee** (gonupeteo) to Baal.	Yet I reserved 7,000 in Israel—all whose **knees have not bowed** (*kara*) to Baal and all whose **mouths have not kissed** (*nashaq*) him.

When Paul quoted from I Kings 19:18 in event 1a, why did he omit the second act in the "*proskuneo* pattern" of worship which is "mouths have not kissed?" Paul knew that the second act in the pattern was understood to be present by necessary inference or implication because the two acts are inseparable in the two-act event. Also, in I Kings 19:18 the Greek translation of the OT (The Septuagint) used the Greek word *proskuneo* which means "to kiss" or "kiss toward" to replace the Hebrew word for "kiss" (*nashaq*).

In Event 2a, the apostle Paul reminds us of God's oath in Isaiah 45:23, and Paul says, "We shall all stand before the judgment seat" and "give account" regarding God's oath: "Every knee shall bow"!

(2a) We Shall Stand and Give Account	(2b) Parallel account to Romans 14:10–12
Romans 14:10(b)–12 (Isaiah 45:23)	Isaiah 45:22, 23
(10)Then we shall all stand before the judgment seat of Christ (11)For it is written, As I live, saith the Lord, **every knee shall bow** to me, and every tongue shall confess to God. (12)So then every one of us shall give account of himself to God.	(22)Look unto me, and be ye saved, all the ends of the earth: for I am God, and there is none else. (23)I have sworn by myself, the word is gone out of my mouth in righteousness, and shall not return, Thatunto me **every knee shall bow.***

<u>*WOW!!!</u> Isaiah 45:23: God has sworn by Himself that He will never change the pattern: "Every **knee shall bow**"! The only change in the NT is that it now includes His Son, Jesus. See event (4a).

Events 3, 7, and 8 tell us that there was **kneeling** in the assembly during the First Century. For example, in Event 3 the apostle Paul reminds the Corinthians that when we teach as we should, the presence of God will be felt so strongly that even the outsiders will be converted and **fall to their knees** declaring that "God is truly in your midst" (I Corinthians 14:25). The late Furman Kearley says, "What the outsider would do is what the others were doing in the Corinthian assembly."[1]

In event #4a, note that the Bible says clearly that we should **bow our knees** to Jesus, literally.

(3) Kneeling in God's Presence	(4a) Kneel in the Name of Jesus
I Corinthians 14:25	Philippians 2:9, 10a, 11 (Psalms 2:12)
(25)And thus are the secrets of his heart made manifest; and so **falling down** on his face he will **worship** (*proskuneo*: kiss toward) God, and report that God is in you of a truth.	(9)Wherefore God also hath highly exalted him, and given him a name which is above every name: (10a)that at* the name of Jesus **every knee should bow**, (11)and that every tongue should confess that Jesus Christ is Lord to the glory of God the Father. (*at is Literally "in" from Greek word *en*)

(4b) Parallel account for Philippians 2:10
Psalm 2:12—Kiss the Son
Kiss the Son, lest he be angry, and ye perish from the way, when his wrath is kindled but a little. Blessed are all they that put their trust in him.

What the Apostle Paul Practiced

In Events 5-9, Paul shows us by example what is pleasing to God. These five separate Biblical accounts verify that the apostle Paul **kneeled** and **worshiped** (proskuneo: kissed toward) God and Jesus on at least five different occasions. Notice in Event 8 that the apostle Paul went up to Jerusalem to "**worship**" (*proskuneo*: **kiss** toward), which is an act that

1. Kearley, Furman. "Is All of Life worship?" Freed Hardeman University Lectures, 1994, Audiocassette.

is always done while **bowing the knees**. Therefore, the use of the word *proskuneo* that is translated as "**worship**" in this verse does not refer to every act that was done in the corporate assembly, but it verifies the fact that **kneeling to worship** (proskuneo: **kiss** toward) God were gestures that were performed by him in the assembly. Also, the word *proskuneo* that is translated as "worship" in this verse is not used in scripture with any of the "five acts of worship."

(5) On His Knees At Conversion	(6) On His Knees with Ephesian Elders
Acts 22:6b–8a (Acts 9:4; 26:14)	Acts 20:36
(6b) Suddenly there shone from heaven a great light round about me. (7)And I **fell** (*pipto*) to the ground, and heard a voice saying unto me, Saul, Saul, why persecutest thou me? (8a)And I answered 'Who art thou, Lord?'	(36)And when he had thus spoken, he **kneeled** (*gonupeteo*) down, and prayed with them all.

(7) On His Knees with Church at Tyre	(8) On His Knees in Church at Jerusalem
Acts 21:5(b)	Acts 24:11
(5b)And they all brought us on our way, with wives and children, till we were out of the city: and we **kneeled** (*gonupeteo*) down on the shore, and prayed.	(11)Because that thou mayest understand, that there are yet but twelve days since I went up to Jerusalem for to **worship**: (*proskuneo*: kiss toward).

(9) On His Knees in Prison at Rome
Ephesians 3:14
(14)For this cause I **bow my knees** unto the Father of our Lord Jesus Christ.

What Paul Taught

Events 1 to 4—A Summary of What Paul Practiced: Events 5 to 9

"The sum of thy word is truth . . ." (Ps. 119:160 NASV)

THE PROSKUNEO PATTERN OF WORSHIP

REFERENCE	FIRST ACT	SECOND ACT
(1) Romans 11:4 (I Kings 19:18)	Not bowed the knee (*gonupeteo*)	
(2) Romans 14:11 (Isaiah 45:23)	Every knee shall bow (*gonupeteo*)	
(3) I Corinthians 14:25	Will fall (*pipto*) on his face and (kneel)	worship (proskuneo: kiss toward)
(4) Philippians 2:10 (Psalms 2:12)	Every knee should bow (*gonupeteo*)	
(5) Acts 22:6b-8a (Acts 9:4; 26:14)	Fell (*pipto*) unto the ground (kneeled)	
(6) Acts 20:36	Kneeled (*gonupeteo)*	
(7) Acts 21:5a	Kneeled (*gonupeteo)*	
(8) Acts 24:11		worship (proskuneo: kiss toward)
(9) Ephesians 3:14	Bow my knees (*gonupeteo)* (kneel)	
The Sum or Combination of all:	Kneel and	worship (proskuneo: kiss toward)

Conclusion: Paul's example should be a pattern for us. He kneeled publicly and privately. The apostle said, "Be ye imitators of me" (1 Cor. 4:16); and "Be imitators of me, as I am of Christ" (1 Cor. 11:1); and "Be ye imitators together of me . . . ye have us for an example" (Phil. 3:17). Paul said, "Those things, which ye have learned, and received, and heard, and seen in me, do: and the God of peace shall be with you" (Phil. 4:9).

Notice that Paul referred to the two-act "proskuneo pattern" of worship in the three Biblical ways that other New Testament writers used. For example, in six of the accounts above, Paul used the first act in the pattern, which is "**bowing the knees,**" and in two of the accounts he used the second act in the two-act event, which is worship (proskuneo: **kiss toward**). However, in one account he uses both acts that make up the whole two-act "proskuneo pattern" of worship (1 Cor 14:25).

Philippians 2:10 (Event #4) through verse 16, has some very interesting divine instructions. Some have been taught that Paul is talking about everyone **bowing their knees** on the Day of Judgment. However, John says, "I saw the dead, small and great, *stand* before God; and the books were opened (Rev 20:12). Also, Romans 14:10–12 says that "*we shall all stand*" before the judgment seat and *"shall give account*" regarding "**every knee shall bow**." See Event #2 under "What Paul taught." Some say they do it figuratively. Did Christ go to the cross literally or figuratively (Phil 2:8)? Did God highly exalt Jesus literally or figuratively (Phil 2:9)? Beginning with verse five, Paul focuses on some crucial facts about Jesus, and how Christians should respond to those facts. He continues in context through verse 16 telling "what" should be done, "who" should do it, "why" it should be done, and "how" our attitude should be when we obey, "**every knee should bow.**"

What should we do? Verse 10 says, "at the name of Jesus **every knee should bow**, confessing Jesus as Lord."

Who should bow their knees to Jesus? Verse 11 says, "Those in heaven, and those on earth, and those under the earth" (NKJV). That surely means that no one is excluded, unless, of course, there is physical impairment.

Why bow our knees to Jesus?

1. Because v.6 says, Jesus is now "equal with God." That is what is new in the NT re: "bowing the knees."
2. Because v.9 says, "God has highly exalted Him and given Him a name which is above every name."
3. Because v.11 says, it is "to the glory of God the Father."

4. Because v.12 says that the command, "**every knee should bow**" must be "obeyed", and relates to "salvation." Obviously, verse 12 is often taken out of context and treated as an entirely separate topic, as if Paul suddenly changed the subject from Verse 11. Notice that verse 12 begins with "wherefore" or in some versions, "therefore." It is a term of conclusion meaning "consequently"; or "hence", or "for this reason." Therefore, verse 12 is there to emphasize that our salvation depends on obeying Verses 10 and 11. Verse 12 says, "Wherefore, my beloved, as ye have always obeyed, not as in my presence only, but now much more in my absence, work out your own salvation with fear and trembling" (KJV). The Greek word translated "work out" is *katergazomai,* which means "to carry out a task until it is finished."[2] Therefore, as long as we are physically able, we should **bow our knees** in the name of Jesus, confessing Jesus as Lord "to the glory of God the Father" (Phil 2:10, 11) until, "we shall all stand before the judgment seat of Christ. For it is written, As I live, saith the Lord, **every knee shall bow to me**... So then every one of us shall give account of himself to God" (Rom. 14:10–12; Isiah 45:22–23).

5. Because v. 13 says, it is doing God's "will", and "for His good pleasure."

Next, do it "without complaining and disputing."

How should our attitude be regarding "every knee should bow?"
"Do all things without complaining and disputing, that you may become blameless and harmless, children of God without fault in the midst of a crooked and perverse generation, among whom you shine as lights in the world. So that I may rejoice in the day of Christ" (The New King James Version Verses 14–16—Thomas Nelson Publishers, Nashville, TN). Does "day of Christ" mean judgment day?

Question: Is our confusion about "what the Bible says," or is it about, "Am I going to do it?"

2. Zodhiates, Spiros. and Warren Baker. *The Complete Word Study Old Testament,* AMG International, INC. D/B/A Iowa Falls, IA: 1994, 849.

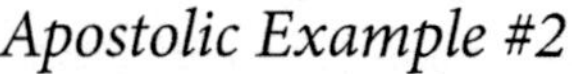

Apostolic Example #2

The Apostle Peter Practiced What He Taught When He Kneeled and Worshiped (Proskuneo) Jesus and God the Father

What the Apostle Peter Taught: 1 Peter 5:6

The KJV says, "**Humble** yourselves, therefore under the mighty hand of God, that he may exalt you in due time."

The Jerusalem Bible says, "**Bow down**, then, before the power of God now, and he will raise you up on the appointed day."

The Greek word translated as "**humble**" in the KJV and "**bow down**" in the Jerusalem Bible Is *tapeinoomai*, and literally means "**to make self low.**"[3]

Mike Warner, an outstanding preacher and Bible scholar asks, "How do we come to God? 'God opposes the proud but gives grace to the humble' (1 Pet 5:5). We come to God **on our knees**, or not at all."[4]

Peter performed both acts in the "*proskuneo* pattern." Events 1, 3, and 6 tell us Peter **bowed the knees** or "**kneeled**" and events 3, 4, and 5 tell us Peter **worshiped** (*proskuneo*: kissed toward).

3. Young, Robert. *Young's Analytical Concordance to the Bible*. Wm. B. Eerdmans Pub. Co. Grand Rapids, MI 1970, 502.

4. Warner, Mike. "Words of Life." *Tyler Morning Telegraph* Sec. 2, September 2, 1994.

What the apostle Peter practiced:

(1) On His Knees after Fish Fill Two Boats	(2) On His Knees after Jesus Walks on Water	(3) On His Knees on Mt. of Transfiguration
Luke 5:8 (Kneeling in confession)	Matthew 14:33 (12 apostles)	Matthew 17:6 (Peter, James & John)
(8)When Simon Peter saw it, he **fell** (*pipto*) **down** at Jesus' knees, saying, "Depart from me; for I am a sinful man,O Lord."	(33)Then they that were in the ship came and **wor-shiped** (*proskuneo*: kissed toward) him, saying, of a truth Thou are the son of God.	(6)And when the disciples heard it, they **fell** (*pipto*) on their face, and were sore afraid.

(4) On His Knees during The Great Commission	(5) On His Knees At the Ascension	(6) On His Knees At Tabitha's House
Matthew 28:17 (11 apostles)	Luke 24:52 (11 apostles)	Acts 9:40 (Kneeling in prayer)
(17) And when they saw him, they **worshiped** (*proskuneo*: kissed toward) him: but some doubted.	(52) And they **worshiped** (*proskuneo*: kissed toward) him, and returned to Jerusalem with great joy.	(40) But Peter put them all out and **kneeled** (*gonu-peteo*) **down**, and prayed.

<u>Event #1</u>: Ronald White said, "When Simon Peter saw this (both boats filled with fish) he **fell at Jesus' knees** and said, 'Go away from me Lord. I am a sinful man'... The reverence we see there by recognizing that he was in the presence of God is the reverence we ought to feel when we **worship**."[5]

5. White, Ronald K. "Attitudes for Worship." Freed Hardeman University Lectures, Henderson, TN, 1994 Audiocassette.

What the apostle Peter practiced—A Summary

"The sum of thy word is truth . . ." (Ps 119:160 NASV)

THE PROSKUNEO PATTERN OF WORSHIP

REFERENCE	FIRST ACT	SECOND ACT
(1) Luke 5:8	fell (*pipto*)* down (kneeled)	
(2) Matthew 14:33		worshiped (proskuneo: kissed toward)
(3) Matthew 17:6	fell (*pipto*)* on their faces (kneeled)	
(4) Matthew 28:17		worshiped (proskuneo: kissed toward)
(5) Luke 24:52		worshiped (proskuneo: kissed toward)
(6) Acts 9:40	kneeled (*gonupeteo*)*	
The Sum or Combination of all:	Kneeled (and)	worshiped (proskuneo: kissed toward)

Conclusion: As our example, Peter humbled himself and kneeled to worship (proskuneo: kiss`toward) Jesus and God the Father in harmony with the "proskuneo pattern" of worship.

~

Apostolic Example #3

The Apostle John Practiced What He Taught When He Kneeled and Worshiped (Proskuneo) Jesus and God the Father

What the Apostle John Taught: Part I

(1) Kneeling and Casting Their Crowns

Revelation 4:10, 11

(10)The four and twenty elders **fall down** before him that sat on the throne and **worship** (*proskuneo*: kiss toward) him that liveth for ever and ever, and cast their crowns before the throne, saying, (11)Thou are worthy, O Lord, to receive glory and honor and power: for thou hast created all things, and for thy pleasure they are and were created.

(2) Kneeling Before the Lamb

Revelation 5:8

(8)And when he had taken the book, the four beasts and four and twenty elders **fell down** before the Lamb, having everyone of them harps, and golden vials full of odours, which are the prayers of the saints.

(3)Kneeling before Jesus

Revelation 5:14(b)

(14b)And the four and twenty elders **fell down** and **worshipped** (*proskuneo*: kissed toward) him that liveth for ever and ever.

(4) All the Angels Kneel

Revelation 7:11 (Hebrews 1:6)

(11)And all the angels stood round about the throne, and about the elders and the four beasts and **fell before** the throne on their faces and **worshipped** (*proskuneo*: kissed toward) God, (12)Saying, Amen: Blessing, and glory, and wisdom, and thanksgiving, and honor, and power, and might, be unto our God for ever and ever. Amen.

(5) Kneeling to Give Thanks and Praise
Revelation 11:16
(16)And the four and twenty elders, which sat before God on their seats, **fell** upon their faces, and **worshipped** (*proskuneo*: kissed toward) God, and (17)Saying, We give thee thanks, O Lord God Almighty, which art, and wast, and art to come; because thou hast taken
to thee the great power, and hast reigned.

(6) "The Eternal Gospel":
Fear God . . . give glory to Him . . . **kneel** and **worship** (proskuneo: kiss toward) Him
Revelation 14: 6,7 (Isa. 45:23, Rom. 14:11, Matt. 4:10)
(6)And I saw another angel fly in the midst of heaven, having the everlasting gospel to preach unto them that dwell on the earth and to every nation and kindred, and tongue, and people, (7)Saying with a loud voice, fear God, and give glory to him; for the hour of his judgment is come: and **worship** (*proskuneo*: kiss toward) him that made heaven, and earth, and the sea, and the fountains of waters.

(7) All Nations Shall Kneel and Worship (*proskuneo*: kiss toward) the Lord
Revelation 15:4 (Isa. 66:23)
(4)Who shall not fear thee, O Lord, and glorify thy name? For thou only art holy: for all nations shall come and **worship** (*proskuneo*: kiss toward) before thee; for thy judgments are made manifest.

(8) Kneel and Say "Amen; Alleluiah"
Revelation 19:4
(4)And the four and twenty and elders and the four beasts **fell down and worshipped** (*proskuneo*: kissed toward) God that sat on the throne, saying, Amen; Alleluiah.

9) The Angel Tells John and Us to Kneel and
Worship (proskuneo: kiss toward) God.
Revelation 19:10b
(10a)And I **fell** at his feet to **worship** (*proskuneo*: kiss toward) him. (10b) And he said unto me, see thou do it not: I am thy fellowservant, and of

thy brethren that have the testimony of Jesus: **worship** (*proskuneo*: kiss toward) God: for the testimony of Jesus is the spirit of prophesy.

(10) Those Who Have Not Kneeled and Worshiped (proskuneo: kissed toward) the Beast
Revelation 20:4
(4)And I saw thrones, and they say upon them and judgment was given unto them: and I saw the souls of men that were beheaded for the witness of Jesus, and for the word of God, and which had not **worshiped** (*proskuneo*: kissed toward) the beast, neither his image, neither had received his mark upon their foreheads, or in their hands; and they lived and reigned with Christ a thousand years.

(11) Again, the Angel of the Lord Tells John and Us to Kneel and Worship (proskuneo: kiss toward) God.
Revelation 22:9
(8)And I John saw those things and heard them. And when I had heard and seen, I **fell down** to **worship** (*proskuneo*: kiss toward) before the feet of the angel which shewed me these things. (9)Then saith he unto me, see thou do it not: for I am they fellow servant, and of thy brethren the prophets,and of them which keep the sayings of this book: **worship** (proskuneo: kiss toward) God.

What the Apostle John Taught: Part I—A Summary

"The sum of thy word is truth . . ." (Ps. 119:160 NASV)

THE PROSKUNEO PATTERN OF WORSHIP

REFERENCE	FIRST ACT	SECOND ACT
(1) Revelation 4:10,11	Fall (*pipto*) down and (kneel)	worshiped (proskuneo: kissed toward)
(2) Revelation 5:8	Fell (*pipto*) down and (kneeled)	
(3) Revelation 5:14(b)	Fell (*pipto*) down and (kneeled)	worshiped (proskuneo: kissed toward)

(4) Revelation 7:11	Fell (*pipto*) down and (kneel)	worshiped (proskuneo: kissed toward)
(5) Revelation 11:16	Fell (*pipto*) down upon their faces and (kneeled)	worshiped (proskuneo: kissed toward)
(6) Revelation 14:6,7		worship (proskuneo: kiss toward)
(7) Revelation 15:4		worship (proskuneo: kiss
(8) Revelation 19:4		worshiped (proskuneo: kissed toward)
(10) Revelation 19:10b		worshiped (proskuneo: kissed toward)
(11) Revelation 20:4		worshiped (proskuneo: kissed toward)
The Sum or Combination of all:	Kneeled (and)	worshiped (proskuneo: kissed toward)

<u>Summary</u>: In the events above the apostle John taught both by precept and by example that we should **kneel and worship** (proskuneo: kiss toward) Jesus and God the Father.

<u>Question</u>: What posture was John in when the angel said, "Do it not: for I am thy fellow servant, and of thy brethren the prophets, and of them which keep the sayings of this book: **worship** (proskuneo: kiss toward) God." Someone said, The word of God is the "final supreme court of appeal." Therefore, should we **bow our knees** literally or figuratively? The apostle John says at the beginning of Revelation, "Blessed is he who reads and those who hear the words of this prophecy, and keep those things which are written it; for the time is near" (Rev. 1:3 NKJV).

What the Apostle John Taught: Part II

The following nine events tell us about those people who **worship** (*proskuneo*: kiss toward) Satan and his demons rather than Jesus and God the Father.

(1) Those of Satan Will Kneel and **Worship** (*proskuneo*: kiss toward) God at the feet of the Philadelphia Congregation—Revelation 3:9
(9) Behold, I will make them of the synagogue of Satan, which say they are Jews, and are not, but do lie; behold, I will make them to come and **worship** (*proskuneo*: kiss toward) **before thy feet,** and to know that I have loved thee.

(2) Those Who Did Not Repent—Revelation 9:20
(20)And the rest of the men which were not killed by these plagues yet repented not of the works of their hands, that they should not **worship** (*proskuneo*: kiss toward) devils, and idols of and silver, and brass, and stone, and of wood: which neither can see, nor hear, nor walk:

(3) Those of "The World" Kneeled and Worshiped (*proskuneo*: kissed toward) the Dragon—Revelation 13:4(a)
(4a)And they **worshiped** (*proskuneo*: kissed toward) the dragon which gave power unto the beast:

(4) Those of "The World" Also Kneeled and Worshiped (*proskuneo:* kissed toward) the Beast—Revelation 13:4(b)
(4b)and they **worshiped** (*proskuneo*: kissed toward) the beast saying, who is like unto the beast? Who is able to make war with him?

(5) All Those Whose Names Are Not Written in the Book of Life Kneel and Worship (*proskuneo*: kiss toward) the Beast—Revelation 13:8
(8)And all that dwell upon the earth shall **worship** (*proskuneo*: kiss toward) him, whose names are not written in the book of life of the lamb slain from the foundation of the world.

The Earth Dwellers Kneel and Worship (*proskuneo*: kiss toward) the First Beast—Revelation 13
(12)And he exerciseth all the power of the first beast before him, and causeth the earth and them that dwell therein to **worship** (*proskuneo*: kiss toward) the first beast, whose deadly wound was healed.

(7) Those Who Receive the Mark of the Beast Kneel and Worship (*proskuneo*: kiss toward) him—Revelation 14:9, 10(a)

(9)And the third angel followed them, saying with a loud voice, If any man **worship** (*proskuneo*: kiss toward) the beast and his image, and receive his mark in his forehead, or in his hand,
(10a)The same shall drink of the wine of the wrath of God.

(8) Those Who Have the Mark of the Beast Kneeled and Worshiped (*proskuneo*: kissed toward) him—Revelation 16:2
(2)And the first went and poured out his vial upon the earth; and there fell a noisome and grievous sore upon the men which had the mark of the beast, and upon them which **worshiped** (*proskuneo*: kissed toward) his image.

(9) Those Who Received the Mark of the Beast Kneeled and Worshiped (*proskuneo*: kissed toward) his Image—Revelation 19:20
(20)And the beast was taken, and with him the false prophet that wrought miracles before him, with which he deceived them that had received the mark of the beast and them that **worshiped** (*proskuneo*: kissed toward) his image. These both were cast alive into a lake of fire burning with brimstone.

What the Apostle John Practiced

(1) On His Knees After Jesus Walked on Water	(2) On His Knees After Jesus Transfigured	(3) On His Knees During The Great Commission
Matthew 14:33 (12 apostles)	Matthew 17:6 (Peter, James & John)	Matthew 28:17 (11 apostles)
(33)Then they that were in the ship came and **worshiped** (*proskuneo*: kissed toward) him, saying, Of a truth thou art the son of God.	(6)And when the disciples heard it, they **fell** (*pipto*) on their face, and were sore afraid.	(17)And when they saw him, they **worshiped** (*proskuneo*: kissed toward) him: but some doubted.

(4) On His Knees At the Ascension	(5) On His Knees On the Lord's Day	(6) On His Knees When the Angel Refused the worship gestures
Luke 24:52 (11 apostles)	Revelation 1:17 (At the feet of Jesus)	Revelation 19:10(a)
(52)And they **worshiped** (*proskuneo*: kissed toward) him and returned to Jerusalem with great joy:	(17)And when I saw him, I **fell** (*pipto*) **at his feet** as dead. And he laid his right hand upon me, saying unto me, Fear not; I am the first and the last:	(10) I **fell** (*pipto*) **at his feet** to **worship** (*proskuneo*: kiss) toward) him. And he said unto See thou do it not: I am thy fellow servant, and of thy brethren that have the

(7) On His Knees
When the Angel Again Refused Worship (proskuneo: kiss toward)—Revelation 22:8, 9
(8)And I John saw these things, and heard them, and when I had heard and seen I **fell** (pipto) **down** to **worship** (proskuneo: kiss toward) before the feet of the angel which showed me these things. (9)Then saith he unto me, see thou do it not: for I am thy fellow servant, and of thy brethren the prophets, and of them which keep the sayings of this book: **worship** (proskuneo: kiss toward) God.

What the Apostle John Practiced—A Summary

"The sum of thy word is truth . . ." (Ps. 119:160 NASV)

THE PROSKUNEO PATTERN OF WORSHIP

REFERENCE	FIRST ACT	SECOND ACT
(1) Matthew 14:33		worshiped (proskuneo: kissed toward)
(2) Matthew 17:6	Fell (pipto) on their faces (kneeled)	
(3) Matthew 28:17		worshiped (proskuneo: kissed toward)

(4) Luke 24:52		worshiped (proskuneo: kissed toward)
(5) Revelation 1:17	Fell (pipto) at his feet (kneeled)	
(6) Revelation 19:10(a) Revelation 19:10(b) (the angel said)	Fell (pipto) at his feet to (kneeled)	worship (proskuneo: kissed toward) worship (proskuneo: kissed toward) God
(7) Revelation 22:8 Revelation 22:9 (the angel said)	Fell (pipto) down (kneeled)	to [worship] (proskuneo) kiss toward worship (proskuneo: kissed toward) God
The Sum or Combination of all:	Kneeled (and)	worshiped (proskuneo: kissed toward)

Summary: John **kneeled and worshiped** (*proskuneo*: kissed toward) Jesus and God the Father in harmony with the two-act "*proskuneo* pattern" of worship. He **kneeled** before the angel twice but the angel said, "**Worship** (*proskuneo*: kiss toward) God!" The angel knew that the act of **bowing the knees** was understood to be present in the reply by necessary inference. If the act of **bowing the knees** was not understood to be present in the reply, then the angel changed the subject. Also, the angel said the command to **worship** (*proskuneo*) is "the testimony of Jesus" (V. 19:10 KJV).

In context, this instruction from the angel of the Lord to "**worship** (proskuneo: kiss toward) God" while **bowing the knees** appears to be a command to be obeyed literally rather than figuratively. Remember that the apostle John, at the beginning of Revelation, says, "Blessed is he who reads and those who hear the words of this prophecy, and keep those things which are written it; for the time is near" (Rev. 1:3 NKJV).

#4 A Non-Apostolic Example

James, the brother of Jesus, practiced what he preached when he kneeled before the Lord

(The Brother of Jesus Who Wrote the Book of James)

What James, the Brother of Jesus, Taught: James 4:10

The KJV says, "Humble* yourselves in the sight of the Lord, and He shall lift you up."

The NLT (New Living Translation) says, "When you bow down before the Lord and admit your dependence on him, he will lift you up and give you honor."

*Note: The Greek word translated "**humble**" in the KJV and "**bow down**" in the NLT literally means "**to make self low.**" Some believe that the word translated "**humble**" or "**bow down**" in James 4:10 is related to **kneeling** in humility that is also required in proskuneo, which is also spelled proskyneo in some references. For example, Brian Kenyon, in his article "Confusing the Subject of Worship", refers to James 4:10 when illustrating that proskyneo "requires humility" on the part of the worshiper when performing the two-act pattern of worship. "First, proskyneo reveals that **worship** involves humility on the part of the worshiper (Jas. 4:10). To **prostrate oneself** before another and to **kiss** another's feet requires humility (Matt. 2:11; 28:9)."

Ronald White referred to James 4:10 and summarized it well when he said, "At some point, our worship must **bring us low** before we can be lifted up."

What James practiced:

Fox's Book of Christian Martyrs says, "Of James, the brother of the Lord, we read the following: James, being considered a just and perfect man, governed the Church with the apostles . . . He would enter into the temple

... **fall on his knees**, and ask remission for the people, doing this so often that his knees lost their sense of feeling and became hardened like the knees of a camel. Because of his holy life James was called "The Just" and "the safeguard of the people."

John Scott is a highly regarded preacher who communicated it well by saying, "James, the author had a nickname, and his nickname was 'Old Camel Knees'. That was a compliment to James because James, the brother of the Master, was known as such a man of prayer that he had literally developed calluses on his knees, and he was called 'Old Camel Knees' because his life was devoted to prayer ... He was a towering man of faith."

Summary of all: The Testimony of Scripture documents that the apostles taught and practiced the two-act "proskuneo pattern" of worship. Their example should be a "pattern" for us. The writer of Hebrews said to "imitate those who through faith and patience inherit the promises" (Heb. 6:12). The apostle Paul wrote, "Be ye imitators together of me: ye have us for an example" (Phil. 3:17). He **kneeled** publicly and privately. The apostle said, "Be ye imitators of me" (1 Cor. 4:16); and "Be imitators of me, as I am of Christ" (1 Cor. 11:1). Finally, "Those things, which ye have learned, and received, and heard, and seen in me, do: and the God of peace shall be with you" (Phil. 4:9).

Next: The "Testimony of Jesus" documents the "proskuneo pattern"—Testimony of Scripture: Part IV

The Testimony of Scripture

Part IV

The Testimony of Jesus Documents the "Proskuneo *Pattern*"

JESUS TAUGHT AND PRACTICED KNEELING AS OUR EXAMPLE

Jesus Practiced What He Preached When He **Kneeled** *Before God.*

What Jesus taught

AGAIN, THE KJV IS used because Church doctrine was apparently taken from the KJV during the later part of the Reformation as well as during the Restoration movement. According to Matthew, Jesus referred to the two-act "*proskuneo* pattern" of worship in all three of the standard Scriptural ways that the other inspired writers used throughout the New Testament. For example, in event #1, Jesus used an expression that indicates that the worshipper **bowed the knees,** which is the first act in the pattern. In event #2, He used the second act in the pattern, which is **worship** (*proskuneo*: **kiss toward**), and in event #3, Jesus used both acts when referring to the two-act "*proskuneo* pattern" of worship.

(1) "Wicked" Servant Does Not Forgive Fellow Servant
Matthew 18:29, 30
(29)And his fellow servant **fell down** at his feet and besought him, saying, Have patience with me and I will pay thee all. And he would not: but went and cast him into prison, till he should pay the debt.

(2) Jesus Refused to Kneel and Serve Satan	(3) The Lord Forgives the "wicked" Servant
Matthew 4:10(b) (Luke 4:8)	Matthew 18:26
Then saith Jesus unto him, Get thee hence, Satan: For it is written, Thou shalt **worship** (*proskuneo*: kiss toward) the Lord thy God, and him only shalt thou serve (*latreuo*).	(26)The servant therefore **fell down**, and **worshipped** (*proskuneo*: **kissed toward**) him, saying, Lord have patience with me, and I will pay thee all.

In events four through eight, Jesus discussed "true worshipers" with the Samaritan woman at the well. Notice that He used the second act in the two-act "*proskuneo* pattern" of **worship** each time, knowing that the act is always done while **bowing the knees.**

(4) God is Present Everywhere "In Spirit"
John 4:21
(21)Jesus saith unto her, Woman, believe me, the hour cometh, when ye shall neither in this mountain, nor yet at Jerusalem, **worship** (*proskuneo*:**kiss toward**) the Father.

5) Woman Doesn't Know "What" She's Worshiping	(6) Woman Doesn't Know God is her "Father"
John 4:22	John 4:23
22) Ye **worship** (*proskuneo*: **kiss toward**) ye know not what: We know what we **worship** (*proskuneo*: kiss toward): for salvation is of the Jews.	(23) But the hour cometh, and now is, when the **true worshippers** (*proskunetes*: those who **kiss toward**) shall **worship** (*proskuneo*: **kiss toward**) the Father in spirit and in truth: for the Father seeketh such to worship (*proskuneo*: **kiss toward**) him.

(7) Woman Doesn't Know God is a "Spirit" and "Must" be worshiped "in Spirit" & "in truth"	(8) Jesus said to the congregation at Philadelphia
John 4:24	Revelation 3:9
(24) God is a Spirit: and they that **worship** (*proskuneo*: kiss toward) Him must **worship** (*proskuneo*: kiss toward) Him in spirit and in truth.	(9) Behold, I will make them of the synagogue of Satan, which say they are Jews, and are not but do lie; behold, I will make them to come and **worship** (*proskuneo*: **kiss toward**) before thy feet, and to know that I have loved thee.

What Jesus practiced at Gethsemane:

(9) Jesus Kneeled and Touched His Forehead to the Ground	(10) Jesus Kneeled on the Ground
Matthew 26:39	Mark 14:35
(39) And he went a little farther, and **fell** on his face, and prayed, saying, O my Father, if it be possible, let this cup pass from me: nevertheless not as I will, but as thou wilt.	(35) And he went forward a little, and **fell** on the ground, and prayed that, if it were possible, the hour might pass from him.

(11) Jesus Kneeled and Prayed
"Thy will be done"

Luke 22:41

(41)And He was withdrawn from them about a stone's cast, and **kneeled** down and prayed.

In 1992, Ken Neller discussed John 4:21–24 at the Harding University Lectures. He said, "This word *proskuneo*, this word for **bowing one's self** or **prostrating one's self**, is the word Jesus uses in a very important passage on **worship** found in John 4. Just for emphasis sake, I want to read this passage to you substituting, instead of our word worship, the literal phrase **prostrating one's self**, and you can kind of get an idea of what **worship** is all about . . ."[1]

Jesus declared, Believe me woman, a time is coming when you will **prostrate yourself** before the Father, neither on this mountain or yet at Jerusalem. You Samaritans **prostrate yourselves** before what you do not know. We **prostrate ourselves** before him whom we do know . . . Yet, a time is coming and is now come, when the **true prostraters** will **prostrate themselves** before the Father in spirit and in truth.

For they are the kind of people whom God seeks to **prostrate themselves** before him. God is spirit and those who **prostrate themselves** before him must do so in spirit and in truth. (John 4:21–24)

The 2001 Analytical-Literal Translation of the NT (ALT) translates John 4:21-24 on page 186 as follows:

> Jesus says to her, "An hour is coming when neither in this mountain nor in Jerusalem will you **prostrate yourselves** in worship before the Father. You **prostrate yourselves** in worship before what you do not know; we **prostrate ourselves** in worship before what we know … But an hour is coming and now is when the true worshipers will **prostrate themselves** in worship before the Father in spirit and truth, for indeed the Father is seeking such to be **prostrating themselves** in worship before Him. God [is] Spirit [or, [is] as to His essence Spirit], and it is necessary [for] the ones **prostrating**

1. Ken Neller, "*Revelation and Christian Worship.*" Harding University Lectures, Searcy, AR., 1992, Audiocassette.

themselves in worship before Him to be **prostrating** in worship in spirit and truth."

What Jesus Taught: Events 1 to 8
What Jesus Practiced: Events 9 to 11

"The sum of God's word is truth." (Psalm 119:160 NASV)

THE PROSKUNEO PATTERN OF WORSHIP

REFERENCE	FIRST ACT	SECOND ACT
(1) Matthew 18:29,30	fell (*pipto*) down (kneeled)	
(2) Matthew 4:10(b) (Luke 4:8)		worship (proskuneo: kiss toward) the Lord thy God
(3) Matthew 18:26	fell (*pipto*) down and (kneeled)	worshiped (proskuneo: kissed toward)
(4) John 4:21		worship (proskuneo: kiss toward)
(5) John 4:22		worship (proskuneo: kiss toward)
(6) John 4:23		worship (proskuneo: kiss toward)
(7) John 4:24		worship (proskuneo: kiss toward)
(8) Revelation 3:9		worship (proskuneo: kiss toward)
(9) Matthew 26:39	fell (*pipto*) on his face (kneeled)	
(10) Mark 14:35	fell (*pipto*) on the ground (kneeled)	
(11) Luke 22:41	kneeled (*gonupeteo*)	
The Sum or Combination of all:	**kneeled** and	**worshiped** (proskuneo: **kissed toward**)

The testimony of Jesus documents that the two-act "*proskuneo* pattern" of worship was practiced in the first century. All Christians agree that we should follow Him and imitate Him. His way is "The Way."

Most dictionaries say the term **"prostrate"** means to **kneel** and touch the forehead to the ground. In the New Testament, the word *proskuneo* that is translated **"worship"** in the KJV, which means to "do reverence or homage to someone" by **"kneeling or prostrating** oneself before him."[2] Since both previous examples use a form of the term **"prostrate"** in translating John 4:21-24, the following modification of John 4:21-24 is presented using a form of the term **"kneel."** The text follows the KJV, but the format is similar to the 2001 Analytical-Literal Translation of the NT except the word **"kneel"** is used instead of the word **"prostrate"**:

> Jesus saith unto her, Woman believe me, the hour cometh, when ye shall neither in this mountain, nor yet at Jerusalem, **kneel** in worship before the father. Ye **kneel** in worship before ye know not what: we know what we **kneel** in worship before ... But the hour cometh, and now is, when the **true kneelers** shall **kneel** in **worship** before the father in spirit and in truth: for the father seeketh such to **kneel** in worship before him. God is a spirit: and they that **kneel** in worship before him must **kneel** in worship before him in spirit and in truth.

Next: A summary of the Explicit, Parallel, & Sequential Accounts of the "proskuneo pattern" in the New Testament.

2. Zodhiates, Spiros. and Warren Baker. *The Complete Word Study Old Testament*, AMG International, INC. D/B/A Iowa Falls, IA: 1994, 1234.

The Testimony of Scripture

Part V

A Summary of the Explicit Accounts, Parallel Accounts, and Sequential Accounts of the "Proskuneo *Pattern*"

The "Proskuneo Pattern" is Documented 35 times in the NT here —Later 99 times

THE FOLLOWING TABLE CONTAINS Bible references of the thirty-five (35) accounts of the "*proskuneo* pattern" in the New Testament. In addition, there are three (3) accounts of the pattern that were brought forward from the OT by the NT writers that harmonize perfectly with the events in the NT, making a total of thirty-eight (38) accounts. Among the 38 accounts, there are twenty (20) parallel accounts, four (4) sequential accounts, and fourteen (14) explicit accounts of the two-act "*proskuneo* pattern." The OT also refers to the two-act "*proskuneo* pattern" of worship in three ways: by the first act (Gen 47:31–Event 29), by the second act (Ps 2:12—Event 25), and by both acts (1 Kings 19:18—Event 21). God's word always harmonizes with itself when we use the words that God used. These accounts harmonize and combine perfectly to document that the two-act "*proskuneo* pattern" is obviously present in each of these 38 worship events.

“The sum of thy word is truth . . .” (Ps 119:160 NASV)

THE PROSKUNEO PATTERN OF WORSHIP

WORSHIPER(S)	REFERENCE	FIRST ACT	SECOND ACT	OBJECT
Wise men Sequential: —*what was said* uses 2nd act only —*What was done* is explicit 2-act pattern:	1)Matthew 2:2 2) Matthew 2:11	Fell down and	Worship (*proskuneo*) Worshiped (*proskuneo*)	Jesus
Jesus (Satan's proposal) —Explicit 2-act pattern: —Luke's parallel account uses 2nd act only: —Jesus' refusal uses 2nd act only in 2-act pattern:	3)Matthew 4:9 4)Luke 4:7 5)Matthew 4:10 6)Luke 4:8	If Fall down and	Worship (*proskuneo*) me Worship (*proskuneo*) me Worship (*proskuneo*) Worship (*proskuneo*)	Satan (Jesus refused) God God
A Leper —The 3 parallel accounts supplement & combine to form the 2-act “proskuneo pattern”	7) Matthew 8:2 8) Mark 1:40 9) Luke 5:12	Kneeling Fell on his face	Worshiped (*proskuneo*)	Jesus
Jairus —The 3 parallel accounts supplement each other to form the 2-act “proskuneo pattern”	10)Matthew 9:18 11)Mark 5:22 12)Luke 8:41	Fell at his feet Fell down at his feet	Worshiped (*proskuneo*)	Jesus

WORSHIPER(S)	REFERENCE	FIRST ACT	SECOND ACT	OBJECT
Woman of Canaan —The 2 parallel accounts supplement & combine to form the 2-act pattern:	13)Matthew15:25 14)Mark 7:25	 Fell at his feet	Worshiped (*proskuneo*)	Jesus
Wicked servant —Explicit 2-act pattern:	15)Matthew 18:26	Fell down and	Worshiped (*proskuneo*)	A king
Roman soldiers —Explicit 2-act pattern: —Matthew uses the 1st act only to stand for the whole 2-act "pattern":	16)Mark15:19 17)Matthew 27:29	Bowing their knees Bowed the knee	Worshiped (*proskuneo*)	Jesus
Legion —The 2 parallel accounts supplement each other to form the 2-act pattern:	18)Mark 5:26 19)Luke 8:28	 Fell down at his feet	Worshiped (*Proskuneo*)	Jesus
Cornelius —Explicit 2-act pattern:	20)Acts 10:25	Fell at his feet and	Worshiped (*proskuneo*)	Peter
SEVEN THOUSAND —Paul Uses 1st act only: —Parallel account is the explicit 2-act pattern recorded in OT, literally:	21) Romans 11:4 22) 1 Kings19:18	Not bowed the knee Knees have not bowed	Mouths have not kissed	Baal

WORSHIPER(S)	REFERENCE	FIRST ACT	SECOND ACT	OBJECT
The Outsider —Explicit 2-act pattern:	23)1 Corinthians 14:25	Fall on his face and	Worship (*proskuneo*)	God
Every knee —The 3 parallel accounts supplement each other	24)Philipians 2:10	Every knee should bow		
to form the 2-act "proskuneo pattern"	25)Luke 7:38		Kissed his feet	Jesus
in the NT & OT, literally:	26)Psalm 2:12		Kiss my Son	
All the angels —Writer of Heb. uses 2nd act in the 2-act pattern:	27) Hebrews 1:6		Worship (*proskuneo*)	Jesus
—Explicit 2-act "proskuneo pattern"	28) Revelation 7:11–17	Fell before the throne	Worshiped (*proskuneo*)	The lamb (& God)
Jacob —The 2 parallel accounts supplement & combine	29) Hebrews 11:21		Worshiped (*proskuneo*)	God
to form 2-act pattern:	30) Genesis 47:31	Bowed himself		
24 Elders —Explicit 2-act "proskuneo pattern":	31) Revelation 4:10	Fall down and	Worship (*proskuneo*)	God

WORSHIPER(S)	REFERENCE	FIRST ACT	SECOND ACT	OBJECT
24 Elders —Explicit 2-act "proskuneo pattern":	32) Revelation 5:14	Fell down and	Worshiped (*proskuneo*)	"Him that liveth forever"
24 Elders —Explicit 2-act "proskuneo pattern":	33) Revelation 11:16	Fell upon their faces	Worshiped (*proskuneo*)	God
Elders and creatures —Explicit 2-act "proskuneo pattern":	34) Revelation 19:4	Fell down	Worshiped (*proskuneo*)	God
John–Sequential: —Explicit 2-act pattern: —The angel's reply uses 2nd act for the "pattern":	35) Revelation 19:10a 36) Revelation 19:10b	Fell down to	Worship (*proskuneo*) Worship (*proskuneo*)	The angel God
John (again)–Sequential: —Explicit 2-act pattern: —The angel's reply uses 2nd act for the "pattern":	37) Revelation 22:8 38) Revelation 22:9	Fell down to	Worship (*proskuneo*) Worship (*proskuneo*)	The angel God

Conclusion: The two-act "*proskuneo* pattern" is documented 35 times in the NT, and referred to in the three classic ways in OT. The Worship Chart will document the "*proskuneo* pattern" a total of 99 times.

NEXT: Introducing the Worship Chart—A Documentary of 99 Accounts of the "Proskuneo Pattern" in the NT

5

The Worship Chart

Part I

Introduction to the Worship Chart

A Documentary of 99 Accounts of the "proskuneo pattern"

"On EARTH as it is in HEAVEN" A Study Guide to be used with Prayer and an Open Bible

BEFORE PRESENTING THE WORSHIP chart that contains 99 Worship Events presented in chart format, an introduction seems appropriate. These 99 worship events were discovered in the New Testament during my exploration of "*The Wonderful World of Worship on* ***Bended knee.***" Each worship event is presented in a format that compares the content of each event with the criteria set forth by Jesus for true worshipers: "The true worshipers (*proskunetes*) shall worship (*proskuneo*) the Father in spirit and in truth: for the Father seeketh such to worship (*proskuneo*) him. God is a Spirit: and they that worship (*proskuneo*) him must worship (*proskuneo*) him in spirit and in truth" (John 4:23, 24 KJV).

THE WORSHIP CHART HEADINGS

The six headings for the various columns in the Worship Chart, from left to right, are as follows: (a) Bible Reference(s) of Worship Events; (b) Worshipers or Kneelers; (c) Worship Acts Performed; (d) Object of Worship; (e) Presence: In Spirit or In Body; and (f) Genuineness: In Truth or In Pretense. These six headings will be explained in detail and in sequence.

I. Bible Reference(s) of Worship Events—refers to the Bible verse(s) that tell about each specific act or gesture in the two-act "proskuneo pattern" of worship.

II. Worshipers or Kneelers—refers to the worshipers or kneelers who performed the acts of worship. The first worshipers or kneelers listed in the chart are the wise men who came to kneel before the baby Jesus as recorded in Matthew, chapter two. The 99th and last worshiper or kneeler listed is the apostle John, whose worship was rejected by the angel of the Lord as recorded in the last chapter of the Bible, Revelation 22.

III. Worship Acts Performed—refers to acts in the two-act "proskuneo pattern" of worship performed by the worshipers.

IV. Object of Worship—refers to the object of worship, and is always someone who is divine or thought to be divine[1]

V. Presence: In Spirit or In Body—indicates whether the object of worship mentioned in the verse was present "in spirit" or "in body." The various interpretations of "in spirit" (*pneuma*) that were encountered during this study are as follows: "with sincerity," "with the right attitude," "with a reverent spirit," "with enthusiasm," "in a spiritual manner," "in communion with the Divine world," "in the right way," "with emotion," "through the Holy Spirit," and "through Jesus." Should we do all of the above? Yes. However, with so many different opinions about the scriptural meaning of the phrase "in spirit," what criteria was used to determine the words and phrases to use as headings in the chart format? For the most part, Scripture, Bible scholars, and Lexicons were used. Hugo McCord is a Bible scholar who said, "The true test of any translated word is to interchange it

1. Greeven, Heinrich. *Theological Dictionary of NT* Eerdmans, William. B., Pubishing Co. Grand Rapids, MI 1968, 73.

with the original word wherever used."[2] Using McCord's criteria, which of the above definitions or interpretations of "in spirit" can be interchanged with the original words?

In an attempt to use the exact English equivalents of the words that Jesus used, the words in John 4:23–24 were re-examined and, after much research, were left intact. Notice in John 4:23–24 that the phrase "a spirit" occurs once, the phrase "in spirit" occurs twice, and the word "spirit" occurs three times. Jesus said, "The true worshipers shall worship the Father in spirit and in truth: for the Father seeketh such to worship him. God is a Spirit: and they that worship him must worship him in spirit and in truth" (John 4:23–24 KJV).

Staying in context with Scripture, what is the meaning of the word "spirit", the phrase "a spirit," and the phrase "in spirit?" Jack Reese is a highly regarded Bible scholar and teacher who concluded, "An excellent way of determining the meaning of a word is by examining that with which the term is contrasted."[3] With this concept in mind, therefore, the Scriptures were searched for the contrast of "a spirit" and "in spirit." Also, the Greek dictionary was consulted for the meaning of the Greek word "spirit."[4]

A. How does the Greek dictionary define the word "spirit" in John 4:23-24?

The Greek dictionary says the word *spirit* is translated from the Greek word *pneuma,* meaning "breath" or "spirit." In John 4:24, "God is spirit", refers to His "incorporeality."[5] "Incorporeality" is a word that is defined by The American Heritage Dictionary as "lacking material form or substance, spiritual."[6] The Greek antonym or opposite of "spirit" is *soma,* which means "body", or a material substance that is visible.[7]

2. McCord, Hugo. *Spiritual Sword.* Published by The Getwell Church of Christ, Memphis, TN January 1994, 8.

3. Reese, Jack. *A Comparative Study of the Servant Words in the New Testament.* Abilene: ACU Press, 1978, 10.

4. Ibid: Zodhiates, Spiros. and Warren Baker. *The Complete Word Study Old Testament,* AMG International, INC. D/B/A Iowa Falls, IA: 1994, 1992.

5. 1180–82.

6. *American Heritage Dictionary.* Houghton Mifflin Co. 1 Beacon St., Boston Massachusetts, 667.

7. Ibid: Zodhiates, Spiros. and Warren Baker. *The Complete Word Study Old Testament,* AMG International, INC. D/B/A Iowa Falls, IA: 1994, 1185.

B. How does Scripture contrast "a spirit?"

In the context of *presence*, Jesus contrasted "a spirit" with "flesh and bones" referring to His own physical body (Luke 24:37–39). Luke tells us that when Jesus appeared to His disciples after His resurrection, they were frightened because they thought they had seen "a spirit" (Luke 24:36). Jesus ended their confusion by way of contrast when He explained that, "a spirit hath not flesh and bones, as you see me have" (Luke 24:39 KJV). In context, Jesus was literally present on earth in a physical body or "flesh and bones," and He was, therefore, visible. In contrast, God the Father is literally present "in spirit," and He is invisible. As spirit, He is real, and He is literally present in heaven and on earth, anywhere and everywhere "in spirit." That is why Jesus explained to the Samaritan woman that the place of worship is no longer an issue (John 4:21).

C. How does Scripture contrast "in spirit?"

In the context of *presence*, the Apostle Paul used the phrase "in spirit" in contrast with the phrase "in body." Paul told the Corinthian church, "For I verily, as absent in body, but present in spirit" (1 Corinthians 5:3 KJV). Also, in the context of *presence*, Paul tells the Colossian church, "though I am absent in body, nevertheless I am with you in spirit" (Col. 2:5 NAS). It is interesting that the Apostle Paul contrasted the exact phrase, "in spirit" with the exact phrase "in body" referring to the nature of his *presence*. Since the best interpreter of Scripture is Scripture, the exact phrases that Paul used in the context of presence were placed in the worship chart heading as, "Presence: In Spirit or In Body." Although Paul may have been speaking figuratively regarding his own presence "in spirit," we know that God is present "in spirit", literally.

C. R. Nichol is in agreement. He says, "During the personal ministry of Christ, he was with them physically. When Christians assemble to eat the Lord's supper, the Lord himself is there also, and eats with them in the "new" way as he is present, not in physical presence, but in a "new" way—in Spirit . . ."[8]

Commenting on John 4:24, Everett Ferguson says, "In view of the context, to worship in spirit here means worship that is not tied to a place;

8. Nichol, C. R. *The Lord's Supper, Prayers*. Clifton: Nichol Pub. Co., 1957, 18–19.

it is what takes place in the spiritual realm. Such passages express a contrast with the flesh and things pertaining to the flesh . . ."[9]

The *Exegetical Dictionary* says that, "Worship 'in spirit and truth' . . . is not a matter of the 'inwardness' of worship. "Spirit' is the opposite of 'flesh.'"[10]

D. Had the woman at the well been worshiping (*proskuneo*) God "in spirit?"

It is said that context determines the real meaning of a word. In the context of her conversation with Jesus, had the woman been worshiping (*proskuneo*) God "in spirit?" The question is actually three questions rolled into one as follows: First, had she actually been worshiping (*proskuneo*), which means doing the right acts? Second, had she been worshiping (*proskuneo*) God, the correct object? And third, had she been worshiping (*proskuneo*) God "in spirit?" Early in the conversation, Jesus answered all three of these questions in just six words: "Ye worship (*proskuneo*) ye know not what" (John 4:22 KJV). The first two words in the sentence imply that she definitely had been worshiping (*proskuneo*), which means doing the right acts—or at least that she had been going through the motions. However, the last four words, "Ye know not what," indicate that she did not really know God as the object of worship, or at least she was unsure of God's presence. Therefore, she had not been worshiping God "in spirit" because her spirit had not been having an encounter with God. She did not realize that God is "a spirit" and that He is literally present "in spirit." That is why Jesus explained to her, "God is a spirit: and they that worship (*proskuneo*) him must worship (*proskuneo*) him in spirit . . . "(John 4:24). As spirit, God is present "in spirit," and it is not possible to worship God "in body" or in "flesh and bones." Consequently, since "God is a spirit," He "must" be worshiped "in spirit."

E. Conclusions

There are three main reasons that the heading, "**Presence: In Spirit or in Body,**" is in harmony with Scripture. First, the Greek word, *pneuma*, which means breath or "spirit" is identical in both of the verses quoted.

9. Ferguson, Everett. *The Church of Christ*. Grand Rapids: William B. Eerdmans Publishing Co., 1996, 213.

10. *Exegetical Dictionary of the New Testament*, Vol. 3, Horst Balz and Gerhard Schneider eds. Grand Rapids: William. B. Eerdman's Publishing Co., 1990, 174.

Second, in the context of "presence," the Bible contrasts "a spirit" with "flesh and bones" (Luke 24:37–39). Third, in the context of "presence," the Bible contrasts the phrase "in spirit" with the phrase "in body" on two occasions (1 Cor. 5:3; Col. 2:5). Therefore, the heading chosen is in harmony with Scripture. Also, these contrasts found in Scripture that compare being present "in spirit" with being present "in body" should help us grasp the Biblical fact that "God is a spirit." As spirit, therefore, He is omnipresent, which means He is present anywhere and everywhere "in spirit," literally (John 4:23–24). Consequently, since God is not present "in body" or in "flesh and bones," He *must* be worshiped "in spirit." Although God is not visible (because He is a spirit), "He that comes to God must believe that He is, and that He is a rewarder of those who diligently seek Him" (Heb. 11:6 NKJV).

Frank Pack understands the concept of God's *presence*. He has expressed it succinctly as follows: "As spirit, God is not confined to one sacred spot."[11]

In regard to the *presence of God* in the worship assembly, there is much concern among many who call themselves Christians, that people are not experiencing *the presence of God* when they assemble. When I asked a Greek Orthodox minister why members of some protestant churches do not **kneel**, here is how he responded: "They do not **kneel** because they do not experience the *presence of God*."

George Barna revealed in his book, *Experience God in Worship* that, "Among adults who regularly attend church services, one-half admit that they haven't experienced *God's presence* at any time during the past year."[12]

Edwin White who wrote the book entitled *Sense of Presence* says, "My belief is that hunger and thirst for God is lost to the Churches of Christ in this generation. The awareness of God is lost to the Churches of Christ in this generation."[13]

Why is it that some individuals do not experience the *presence of God*? Like the woman at the well, many of us do not know or do not grasp

11. Pack, Frank. The *Living Word Commentary of The Gospel According To John.* Everett Ferguson ed. Sweet Publishing Co., P.O. Box 55127 Hurst, TX 76054, 1975, 76.

12. Barna, George. et all. *Experience God in Worship*. Loveland: Group Pub. Inc., 2000 14–15

13. White, Edwin. "*A Sense of Presence #1.*" IBC Lectureship, Florence, AL, 1994, Audiocassette.

the Biblical fact that "God is a spirit" and that He is literally present "in spirit" even though He is not visible. Could part of the problem be that many of us have been taught that "in spirit" means something other than "in spirit?" Therefore, we may miss the awe and reverence that is felt in the *presence of God* because we are not focused on the fact that God is *present* "in spirit."

VI. Genuineness: In Truth or In Pretense—indicates whether the "proskuneo pattern" was performed by the various worshipers "in truth" or "in pretense." What does "in truth" mean? The various interpretations of "in truth" that have been encountered during this study are as follows: "according to truth," "doing the right things," "with the right guide," "according to God's word," "doing the right acts," "with reason," "scripturally," "in reality," and "in genuineness." Surely, we should do all the above. However, with so many different opinions as to the meanings of "in truth," what criteria were utilized to determine the words and phrases to use as headings in the chart format? For the most part, Scripture, Bible scholars, and Lexicons (or Greek dictionaries) were employed. Also, in an attempt to use the English equivalents of the words that Jesus used, the Greek dictionaries were consulted for the meaning of the word "truth," and then the Scriptures were searched for contrast of the phrase "in truth." Finally, the phrase "in truth" that Jesus used was left intact and the contrasting phrase "in pretense" was placed as found in scripture. Further explanations are provided in the following list:

A. How does the Greek dictionary define the word "truth" in John 4:23–24? From the Greek word *aletheia,* meaning "truth, verity, reality;" also, "love of truth, both in words and conduct . . . veracity." In "John 4:23–24, with a sincere mind, with sincerity of heart, not merely with external rites;" Antonym: a "falsehood, lie."[14] Scripture says, "I am the truth" (John 14:6); "The spirit is truth" (1 John 5:6), and "Thy word is truth" (John 17:17). The word "true" as in "true worshiper" (John 4:23) is *alethinos* and means "true or genuine."[15]

B. How does Scripture contrast the phrase "in truth?"

14. Ibid: Zodhiates, Spiros. and Warren Baker. *The Complete Word Study Old Testament,* AMG International, INC. D/B/A Iowa Falls, IA: 1994, 120–21.

15. Ibid, 122.

In the context of genuineness, God's word contrasts the phrase, "in truth" with "in pretense."

a. In the context of genuine preaching, the apostle Paul wrote to the Philippian church, "Whether in pretense, or in truth, Christ is preached;" (Phil. 1:18).

b. In the context of genuine prayer, Jesus also used the word, "pretense." He said, "Woe unto you scribes and Pharisees, hypocrites! for ye, for a pretense make long prayer" (Matt. 23:14).

c. In the context of genuine love, the apostle John contrasts loving "in word and in tongue" with loving "in deed and in truth." John said, "Let us not love in word, neither in tongue; but in deed and in truth" (1 John 3:18).

d. The Old Testament also uses the phrase "in truth" in the context of genuine prayer: "The Lord is nigh unto all them that call upon him, to all that call upon him in truth" (Psalm 145:18).

C. Had the woman at the well been worshiping (proskuneo) God "in truth?"

In the context of her conversation with Jesus, the woman had been worshiping (*proskuneo*) God "in pretense" and not "in truth." Jesus said to her: "For thou hast had five husbands; and he whom thou now hast is not thy husband" (John 4:18). Jesus knew that she had been worshiping (*proskuneo*) by doing the right acts, but she had just been going through the motions. Worship **on bended knee** is designed to change the worthless sinner into a faithful servant of the living God. She had been arising from her knees to continue the same promiscuous lifestyle. She had not fully surrendered her will to Him, and her spirit was not being transformed. Therefore, she had been worshiping (*proskuneo*) "in pretense" and not "in truth." Jesus said to her, "The true worshipers (*proskunetes*) shall worship (*proskuneo*) the Father in spirit and in truth: for the Father seeketh such to worship (*proskuneo*) him. Again, "The Lord is nigh unto all them that call upon him, to all that call upon him in truth" (Psalm 145:18). Someone has said, "God still heals broken hearts, but He has to have all the pieces."

D. Conclusions

According to the contrast of "in truth" as revealed in God's word, the heading, "**Genuineness: In Truth or In Pretense**" is in harmony with Scripture. What do some of the Bible scholars say the phrase "in truth" means? Everett Ferguson, a highly regarded professor and author, also speaks of genuineness in contrast to pretense when discussing "in truth" as recorded in John 4:23–24. He says, "'In truth' refers to 'reality', as opposed to what is false or what is not permanent (John 3:21; 4:23; 8:44; 18:37; I John 1:6; 2:21) or to 'sincerity' or 'genuineness' in contrast to pretense or mere words (I John 3:18), 'in reality' is possible here too; (2 John 1; 3 John 1; cf I Phil. 1:18). The adjective 'true' in John 4:23 suggests the 'real' or 'genuine' worshipers. 'Truth' in John is related to Jesus (John 1:14; 14:6), the Spirit (John 14:17; I John 5:6), and the word of God (John 17:17)."[16]

Jimmy Jividen, in his book, *More Than a Feeling*, explains that, "Worshiping 'in truth' involves the right acts and the right forms, but the focus of the passage probably goes further, involving the truthfulness, sincerity, and *genuineness* of the inner person in worship—the spiritual integrity of an honest heart."[17]

Frank Pack, in *The Living Word Commentary* says, "True or genuine worshipers are not concerned with the outward place but offer worship to God in spirit and truth, a spiritual worship that conforms to his divine nature. It is according to the truth as it is revealed in Jesus Christ, but truth also carries the meaning of *genuineness*."[18]

Richard C. Leonard also uses the term "genuine" when referring to John 4:23. He says, "Although Jesus had spoken of genuine worship of the Father as worship 'in spirit and in truth' (En pneumai kai aletheia, John 4:23), this did not mean that Christian worship was so spiritual that it was invisible . . . Within the assembly of believers, acts of worship were visible acts. The word translated 'worship' (*proskuneo*), as noted above, means to **kneel**, **bow**, or **prostrate one's self**, and such actions must accompany the vocal expressions of praise and supplication. Paul, for one, expressed his faith in prayer, 'I **kneel** before the Father' (Eph. 3:14) . . . Paul, commending

16. Ferguson, Everett. *The Church of Christ*. Grand Rapids: William B. Eerdmans Publishing Co., 1996, 213.

17. Jividen, Jimmy. *More Than a Feeling—Worship That Pleases God*. Nashville: The Gospel Advocate Company, 1999, 26.

18. Pack, Frank. The *Living Word Commentary of The Gospel According To John*, Everett Ferguson ed. Sweet Publishing Co. Memphis, TN 1975, 76.

to the Philippians Christ's attitude of humility, declares that his obedience even to death on the cross led to His exultation; God 'gave Him the name that is above every name, that at the name of Jesus **every knee should bow** . . . and every tongue confess that Jesus Christ is Lord, to the glory of God the Father' (Phil. 2:9–11)."[19]

Next: The Worship Chart—A Documentary of 99 accounts of the "proskuneo pattern." The format of the Worship Chart was designed to facilitate comparison of each event with the criteria set forth by Jesus for true worshipers in John 4:23–24. All 99 worship events in the NT that contained one or both acts that make up the "proskuneo pattern" qualified for entry into the chart. For example, thirty-five (35) of the worship events entered came from verses of scripture that referred to the pattern by the first act, which is some form of **"bowing the knees."** Forty-seven (47) of the entries came from verses that referred to the pattern by the second act which is *proskuneo* translated as "worship," and indicates that the worshiper "kissed" or "kissed toward" or "threw a kiss toward" the object of worship. The act in each event that is there by necessary inference is placed in parentheses. However, thirteen (13) of the entries came from verses where both acts in the two-act "*proskuneo* pattern" are explicitly present. The other four (4) entries came from verses that contain the literal English word "kiss," making a total of 99 events.

An example where the English word "kiss" is present literally is Luke 7:38, which tells of the woman in Simon's house who "ceased not to kiss" Jesus' feet after wetting them with her tears and drying them with her hair. In context, it appears that the woman performed both acts in the "*proskuneo* pattern" of worship because the act of kissing His feet implies that she also **bowed the knees.**

When the Greek word *proskuneo* is translated literally into any other language, including English, we have the very Word of God. For example, the parallel accounts of the same *proskuneo* worship events by different writers can only be harmonized by using the literal translation of *proskuneo*. By doing so, God's Word always harmonizes with itself. "Literally" means using the English equivalents of the words that God used when He spoke through the inspired writers. It is speaking "the oracles of God"

19. Leonard, Richard C. "New Testament Vocabulary of Worship." *The Biblical foundations of Christian Worship*. Robert E. Webber ed., Nashville: Start Song Publishing Group, 1993, 19–23.

(1 Pet. 4:11). You will recall the example in 1 Kings 19:18 where God said to Elijah, "Yet, I have left me seven thousand in Israel, all the **knees which have not bowed** unto Baal, and every mouth which hath not **kissed** him" (1 Kgs. 19:18 KJV). When the Greeks translated that verse into the Greek language (the Septuagint), they used the word *proskuneo* in place of the Hebrew word for "kissed." Why were the other 12 Greek terms translated as "worship" in the NT excluded? Because, in contrast to *proskuneo*, those 12 Greek terms can all be done in a posture that does not require **bowing the knees**. Also, each of those terms will be discussed in detail following the presentation of the worship chart.

This study obviously focuses on "worship" translated from the Greek word *proskuneo* and the two-act "*proskuneo* pattern." In the worship chart, the act in the "*proskuneo* pattern" that is there by necessary inference is placed in parentheses. One question that should be addressed at the beginning is as follows: When placing the first act in parenthesis that is there by necessary inference, why use a form of the word "kneel" instead of the terms "fell *(pipto)* down," "fell *(pipto)* on his face," "fell *(pipto)* at his feet," etc.?

For review, the word for "kneel" in the New Testament is *gonupeteo*, derived from *gonu*, knee, and *pipto*, to fall. *Gonupeteo* means to "fall on the knees" or "kneel" before another in submission, reverence, homage, and adoration.[20]

In the New Testament, "fell (*pipto*) on his face" and kneeling (*gonupeteo*) are used interchangeably by the Holy Spirit in the parallel accounts of the leper. For example, Luke 5:12 says the leper "fell (*pipto*) on his face" whereas Mark 1:40 says the leper came "kneeling" (*gonupeteo*). Also, the newer translations use the term "kneel" or an equivalent expression at least one or more times in translating the Greek word *proskuneo*. For uniformity and consistency, therefore, the term "kneel" was selected for use in the Worship Chart in an effort to lessen confusion and to better communicate the worship gesture to our present culture.

For comparison purposes, the worship chart displays three different translations of the specific worship acts performed. Under the heading, "Worship Acts Performed," the KJV is listed first, the NIV is listed second, and the LTG—which stands for the literal translation of the Greek word *proskuneo*—is placed third in each of the 99 worship events. The KJV

20. Zodhiates, Spiros. and Warren Baker. *The Complete Word Study Old Testament*, AMG International, INC. D/B/A Iowa Falls, IA: 1994, 380.

and the NIV translations are the two most popular selling versions of the Bible. Further explanations are placed appropriately throughout the Worship Chart.

Next: The Worship Chart—A Documentary of 99 accounts of the "proskuneo pattern."

The Worship Chart

Part II

A Documentary of 99 Accounts of the "proskuneo pattern"

(EVENTS CONTAINING THE FIRST act, or second act, or both acts of the "proskuneo puzzle" qualified for entry into the "Worship Chart.") "The true worshipers (*proskunetes*) shall worship (*proskuneo*) The Father in Spirit and in Truth" (John 4:23). The Analytical Literal Translation uses "**prostrate**" instead of "worship." The chart format is designed to summarize the criteria for "true worshipers" in John 4:23–24. In the NT, *proskuneo* means "to kiss" or "kiss toward", or throw a "kiss toward" someone in worship, or adoration, while **kneeling or prostrating** oneself.[1]

1. Zodhiates, Spiros. and Warren Baker. *The Complete Word Study Old Testament*, AMG International, INC. D/B/A Iowa Falls, IA: 1994, 1233–34.

The Worship Chart—Part II

BIBLE REFERENCE OF Worship Events	WORSHIPER(S) KNEELER(S)	WORSHIP ACTS PERFORMED "EVERY KNEE SHALL BOW" Isaiah 45:23 "We shall all stand before the judgment seat . . . For it is written . . . every knee shall bow to Me . . . Each of us shall give account." (Rom 14:10b-12a)	OBJECT OF WORSHIP	PRESENCE "IN SPIRIT" OR IN BODY	GENUINENESS "IN TRUTH" OR IN PRETENSE
1) Matt. 2:2	Wise men	KJV: "Are come to **worship** (*proskuneo*) him" NIV: "Have come to **worship** (*proskuneo*) him" LTG*: "Have come to (kneel and) **worship** (*proskuneo*: **kiss toward** Him)"	Jesus	In Body	In Truth (intent to serve)
2) Matt. 2:8	King Herod	KJV: "I may come and **worship** (*proskuneo*) him" NIV: "I may go and **worship** (*proskuneo*) him" LTG: "I may go to (kneel and) **worship** (*proskuneo*: **kiss toward**) Him)"	Jesus	In Body	In Pretense (no intent to serve)
3) Matt. 2:11	Wise men (*did* what they *said* in Matt. 2:2)	KJV: "**Fell down** and **worshiped** (*proskuneo*) him" NIV: "**Bowed down** and **worshiped** (*proskuneo*) him" LTG: "**Kneeled** and **worshiped** (*proskuneo*: **kissed toward**) Him"	Jesus	In Body	In Truth (arose to serve: gave gifts)
4) Matt. 4:9 (Luke 4:7)	Jesus ("tempted")	KJV: "If you will **fall down** and **worship** (*proskuneo*) me" NIV: "If you will **bow down** and **worship** (*proskuneo*) me" LTG: "If you will **kneel** and **worship** (*proskuneo*: **kiss toward**) me"	Satan ("temptor")	In Body?	Jesus refused to kneel & kiss toward Satan

Isaiah 45:23: "I have sworn by Myself, the word has gone forth from My mouth in righteousness and will not turn back, that to Me every knee will bow, every tongue will swear allegiance" (NASV). Paul quoted from this verse in Rom. 14:10–12 and added, "we shall all stand" and "give account."

*LTG-refers to the literal translation of the Greek word proskuneo. Also, the act that is present by "necessary inference" in the two-act "proskuneo pattern" is placed in parenthesis.

BIBLE REFERENCE OF Worship Events	**WORSHIPER(S) KNEELER(S)**	**WORSHIP ACTS PERFORMED "EVERY KNEE SHALL BOW" Isaiah 45:23 "We shall all stand before the judgment seat . . . For it is written . . . every knee shall bow to Me . . . Each of us shall give account" (Rom 14:10b–12a)**	**OBJECT OF WORSHIP**	**PRESENCE "IN SPIRIT" OR IN BODY**	**GENUINENESS "IN TRUTH" OR IN PRETENSE**
5) Matt. 4:10 (Luke 4:8) (Isa. 45:23) (Rom. 14:11) (Rev. 14:7) (Rev. 22:9)	"You shall" ("It is written")	KJV: "Worship (proskuneo) the Lord your God" NIV: "Worship (proskuneo) the Lord your God" LTG*: "(Kneel and) worship (proskuneo: kiss toward) the Lord your God."	"The Lord Your God"	In Spirit	In Truth ["and serve (latreuo) Him only"]
6) Matt. 8:2 (Mark 1:40) (Luke 5:12)	A leper	KJV: "Worshiped (proskuneo) him" NIV: "Knelt (proskuneo) before him" LTG: "(Kneeled and) worshiped (proskuneo: kissed toward) Him"	Jesus	In Body	In Truth (leprosy healed)
7) Matt. 9:18 (Mark 5:22) (Luke 8:41)	Jairus (a ruler)	KJV: "Worshiped (proskuneo) him" NIV: "Knelt (proskuneo) before him" LTG: "(Kneeled and) worshiped (proskuneo: kissed toward) Him"	Jesus	In Body	In Truth (daughter healed)
8) Matt. 14:33 (Jesus walks on water)	The 12 Apostles	KJV: "Worshiped (proskuneo) him" NIV: "Worshiped (proskuneo) him" LTG: "(Kneeled and) worshiped (proskuneo: kissed toward) Him"	Jesus	In Body	In Truth (arose to serve)

*Again, LTG refers to the literal translation of the Greek word proskuneo, and the act that is present by necessary inference in the two-act "proskuneo pattern" is placed in parenthesis.

The Worship Chart—Part II

BIBLE REFERENCE OF Worship Events	WORSHIPER(S) KNEELER(S)	WORSHIP ACTS PERFORMED "EVERY KNEE SHALL BOW" Isaiah 45:23 "We shall all stand before the judgment seat . . . For it is written . . . every knee shall bow to Me . . . Each of us shall give account" (Rom 14:10b–12a)	OBJECT OF WORSHIP	<u>PRESENCE</u> "IN SPIRIT" OR IN BODY	<u>GENUINENESS</u> "IN TRUTH" OR IN PRETENSE
9) Matt. 15:25 (Mark 7:25)*	Woman of Canaan (See Event #26 for commentary	KJV: "Worshiped (proskuneo) him" NIV: "Knelt (proskuneo) before him" LTG: "(Kneeled and) worshiped (proskuneo: kissed toward) Him"	Jesus	In Body	In Truth ("great is thy faith")
10) Matt. 17:6 (Jesus transfigured)	Apostles (3) (Peter, James & John)	KJV: "Fell on their faces" NIV: "Fell face down to the ground" LTG: "Kneeled, (worshiped/kissed toward) and touched forehead to the ground"	Jesus	In Body	In Truth (arose to serve)
11) Matt. 17:14	Man with a lunatic son	KJV: "Kneeling down to him" NIV: "Knelt before him" LTG: "Kneeled (and worshiped/kissed toward) Him"	Jesus	In Body	In Truth (son healed)
12) Matt. 18:26	"Wicked Servant" (false worshiper)	KJV: "Fell down and worshiped (proskuneo) him" NIV: "Fell on his knees (proskuneo) before him" LTG: "Kneeled and worshiped (proskuneo/kissed toward) Him"	"A King"	In Body	In Pretense! (Arose & had no mercy)
13) Matt. 18:29	"Fellow Servant"	KJV: "Fell down at his feet" NIV: "Fell to his knees" LTG: "Kneeled (and worshiped/kissed toward) His feet"	"Wicked Servant"	In Body	In Truth (begged for mercy)

*<u>Event #9</u> (Matt. 15:25) See Event #26 on page 122 for Mark's parallel account of the woman of Canaan and a fascinating commentary by Mary Martini. Note: The Holy Spirit has also authorized the use of the term **kneeling** as an option to **prostration**. For example, in the parallel accounts of the leper, (Mark 1:40), the leper came "kneeling."

BIBLE REFERENCE OF Worship Events	WORSHIPER(S) KNEELER(S)	WORSHIP ACTS PERFORMED "EVERY KNEE SHALL BOW" Isaiah 45:23 "We shall all stand before the judgment seat . . . For it is written . . . every knee shall bow to Me . . . Each of us shall give account" (Rom 14:10b–12a)	OBJECT OF WORSHIP	PRESENCE "IN SPIRIT" OR IN BODY	GENUINENESS "IN TRUTH" OR IN PRETENSE
14) Matt. 20:20	Mother of James & John	KJV: "**Worshiping** (proskuneo) him" NIV: "**Kneeling down** (proskuneo)" LTG: "(Kneeling and) **worshiping** (proskuneo: kissing toward) Him"	Jesus	In Body	In Truth? (selfish motive?)
15) Matt. 26:39 (Mark 14:35) (Luke 22:41)	Jesus (Gethsemane)	KJV: "**Fell** on his face" NIV: "**Fell** with his face to the ground" LTG: "**Kneeled**, (and worshiped/kissed toward) and touched forehead to the ground"	"My Father"	In Spirit	In Truth (surrendered His will)
16) Matt. 26:49 (Mark 14:45) (Luke 22:47)	Judas (false worshiper)*	KJV: "said, Hail, Master; and **kissed** him" NIV: "said, 'Greetings, Rabbi!' And **kissed** him" LTG: "said, Hail Master; and (kneeled and) **kissed** (kataphileo) Him" [worshiped]	Jesus	In Body	In Pretense! (betrayal kiss)
17) Matt. 27:29 (Mark 15:19) (Crown of thorns)	Roman Soldiers (false worshipers)	KJV: "**Bowed the knee** before him" NIV: "**Knelt** in front of him" LTG: "**Kneeled** (and worshiped/kissed toward) Him"	Jesus	In Body	In Pretense! (mocked Him)

*Event #16: It is not possible to know for sure that Judas bowed the knees when he kissed Jesus. If he did not, then he is the only person in the New Testament who kissed Jesus while standing up. However, he was one of the 12 apostles who bowed their knees after Jesus walked on water (Matt. 14:33). Notice the words "in pretense" in the last column under "In Truth or In Pretense." Jesus said, "Judas, betrayest thou the Son of man with a kiss?" (Luke 22:47–48). Those who kneeled and worshiped (proskuneo) Jesus "in truth" rose to serve Him and became His followers.

BIBLE REFERENCE OF Worship Events	WORSHIPER(S) KNEELER(S)	WORSHIP ACTS PERFORMED "EVERY KNEE SHALL BOW" Isaiah 45:23 "We shall all stand before the judgment seat . . . For it is written . . . every knee shall bow to Me . . . Each of us shall give account" (Rom 14:10b–12a)	OBJECT OF WORSHIP	PRESENCE "IN SPIRIT" OR IN BODY	GENUINENESS "IN TRUTH" OR IN PRETENSE
18) Matt. 28:4	Roman Guards	KJV: *"Became as dead men" NIV: *"Became like dead men" LTG: * "Kneeled (and worshiped/kissed toward) and became like dead men"[2]*	The Angel	In Body	In Fear?
19) Matt. 28:9 (Jesus resurrected)	Mary Magdalene and the other Mary**	KJV: "Held him by the feet and worshiped (proskuneo) him" NIV: "Clasped his feet and worshiped (proskuneo) him" LTG: "(Kneeled and) held His feet and worshiped (proskuneo: kissed) Him"	Jesus	In Body	In Truth (arose & told apostles)
20) Matt. 28:17 (At the Great Commission)	The 11 Apostles***	KJV: "Worshiped (proskuneo) him" NIV: "Worshiped (proskuneo) him" LTG: "(Kneeled and) worshiped (proskuneo: kissed toward) Him"	Jesus	In Body	In Truth (they arose to serve)
21) Mark 1:40 (Matt. 8:2) (Luke 5:12)	A Leper	KJV: "Kneeling down to him" NIV: "On his knees" LTG: "Kneeling (and worshiping/kissing toward) Him"	Jesus	In Body	In Truth (leprosy healed)

*Event #18 is listed here as a worship event by necessary inference. Also, the late J. W. Davidson who was a minister of the Gospel listed this event as an example of "**prostration**" in the New Testament.

Event #19: Mary Magdalene and the other Mary were apparently the first to **kneel and **kiss** Jesus' nail-scarred feet. I have heard others say, (including my Aunt, Jewell Scott), that the first thing they intend to do when they get to heaven is "**kneel** before Jesus and **kiss** His nail-scarred feet." Regarding posture and necessary inference: To hold Jesus by the feet, wouldn't the two Marys also have to **bow their knees**?

***Event #20 The 11 apostles (Judas is no longer with them) **kneeled** & worshiped Jesus "in truth." They arose to put the great commission into action.

2. Strong, James. *Strong's Exhaustive Concordance of the Bible*. Thomas Nelson Pub. Cambridge, Ontario 1990, 4352.

BIBLE REFERENCE OF Worship Events	WORSHIPER(S) KNEELER(S)	WORSHIP ACTS PERFORMED "EVERY KNEE SHALL BOW" Isaiah 45:23 "We shall all stand before the judgment seat . . . For it is written . . . every knee shall bow to Me . . . Each of us shall give account" (Rom 14:10b–12a)	OBJECT OF WORSHIP	PRESENCE "IN SPIRIT" OR IN BODY	GENUINENESS "IN TRUTH" OR IN PRETENSE
22) Mark 3:11	"Evil Spirits"	KJV: "Fell down before him" NIV: "Fell down before him" LTG: "Kneeled (and worshiped/kissed toward) Him"	Jesus	In Body	In Pretense! (no intent to serve)
23) Mark 5:6 (Luke 8:28)	Legion (possessed with an evil spirit)	KJV: "Worshiped (proskuneo) him: NIV: "Fell on his knees (proskuneo) in front of him" LTG: "(Kneeled and) worshiped (proskuneo: kissed toward) Him"	Jesus	In Body	In Truth (was healed & arose to tell others)
24) Mark 5:22 (Matt. 9:18) (Luke 8:41)	Jairus (a ruler)	KJV: "Fell at his feet" NIV: "Fell at his feet" LTG: "Kneeled (and worshiped/kissed toward) Him"	Jesus	In Body	In Truth (daughter arose)
25) Mark 5:33 (Luke 8:47)	Woman with bleeding	KJV: "Fell down before Him" NIV: "Fell at his feet" LTG: "Kneeled (and worshiped/kissed toward) Him"	Jesus	In Body	In Truth ("told Him all")
26) Mark 7:25* (Matt. 15:25)	Woman of Canaan	KJV: "Fell at his feet" NIV: "Fell at his feet" LTG: "Kneeled (and worshiped/kissed toward) Him"	Jesus	In Body	In Truth (she kept asking)

*Event #26 (Mark 7:25): This is the parallel account for Matthew 15:25 (Event #9) that says she "worshiped (proskuneo: kissed toward) Him." Apparently, the woman's kisses to Jesus' hand reminded him of an affectionate puppy. Mary Martini has captured this scene beautifully in her essay entitled Women in the book of Mark. Interestingly, and appropriately, she wrote the following: "She sought Him out and fell at His feet ... She came and worshiped Him saying: 'Lord, help me!' (Matt. 15:25). The word 'worship' as used here is interesting. Apparently, she prostrated herself in front of Him ... notice the irony of the literal meaning of the word worship: 'to kiss like a dog licking his master's hand' The next exchange of words is among the most fascinating in the Bible. Jesus said, 'Let the children be filled first, for it is not good to take the children's bread and throw it to the little dogs.' (v. 27) ... With quick wit and reason she replied: 'Yes, Lord, yet even the little dogs under the table eat from the children's crumbs' (v. 28)."[4]

3. Martini, Mary. "Women in the Book of Mark." *The Restorer* July/August 1999, 20.

BIBLE REFERENCE OF Worship Events	WORSHIPER(S) KNEELER(S)	WORSHIP ACTS PERFORMED "EVERY KNEE SHALL BOW" Isaiah 45:23 "We shall all stand before the judgment seat . . . For it is written . . . every knee shall bow to Me . . . Each of us shall give account" (Rom 14:10b–12a)	OBJECT OF WORSHIP	PRESENCE "IN SPIRIT" OR IN BODY	GENUINENESS "IN TRUTH" OR IN PRETENSE
27) Mark 10:17	Rich young ruler* (false worshiper)	KJV: "Kneeled to him" NIV: "Fell on his knees before him" LTG: "Kneeled (and worshiped/kissed toward) Him"	Jesus	In Body	In Pretense! (arose and served not)
28) Mark 14:35 (Matt. 26:39) (Luke 22:41)	Jesus (Gethsemane)	KJV: "Fell on the ground" NIV: "Fell to the ground" LTG: "Kneeled (and worshiped/kissed toward) Him"	"Abba, Father"	In Spirit	In Truth (surrendered His will)
29) Mark 14:45 (Matt. 26:49) (Luke 22:47)	Judas (false worshiper)	KJV: "saith ... Master; and kissed him" NIV: "said, 'Rabbi!' and kissed him" LTG: "said, 'Master' and (kneeled and) kissed (kataphileo) Him" [worshiped]	Jesus	In Body	In Pretense! (Betrayal kiss)
30) Mark 15:19 (Matt. 27:29) (crown of thorns)	Roman soldiers** (false worshipers)	KJV: "Bowing their knees worshiped (proskuneo) him" NIV: "Falling on their knees, they worshiped (proskuneo) him" LTG: "Kneeling, they worshiped (proskuneo: kissed toward) Him"	Jesus	In Body	In Pretense! (in mockery; not in truth)

*Event # 27: The rich young ruler was told to go and sell what he had and give it to the poor, but instead, he went away sorrowful because he had great possessions. He kneeled "in pretense" and not "in truth" because he did not obey Jesus as a faithful servant and did not rise to follow Him.

**Event #30: The Roman soldiers bowed their knees and worshiped (proskuneo: kissed toward) Jesus "in pretense" and not "in truth" because everyone knows they did it in mockery with no intent to serve and become His follower.

BIBLE REFERENCE OF Worship Events	WORSHIPER(S) KNEELER(S)	WORSHIP ACTS PERFORMED "EVERY KNEE SHALL BOW" Isaiah 45:23 "We shall all stand before the judgment seat . . . For it is written . . . every knee shall bow to Me . . . Each of us shall give account" (Rom 14:10b–12a)	OBJECT OF WORSHIP	PRESENCE "IN SPIRIT" OR IN BODY	GENUINENESS "IN TRUTH" OR IN PRETENSE
31) Luke 4:7* (Matt. 4:9)	Jesus "Tempted"	KJV: "If you will worship (proskuneo) me" NIV: "If you will worship (proskuneo) me" LTG: "If you will (kneel and) worship (proskuneo: kiss toward) me"	Satan "Temptor"	In Spirit?	Refused to kneel and serve Satan
32) Luke 4:8 (Matt. 4:10) (Isa. 45:23) (Rev. 22:9)	"You shall"	KJV: "Worship (proskuneo) the Lord thy God" NIV: "Worship (proskuneo) the Lord thy God" LTG: "(Kneel and) worship (proskuneo: kiss toward) the Lord thy God"	"The Lord your God"	In Spirit	In Truth ["and serve, (latreuo) Him only"]
33) Luke 5:8 (fishermen)	Peter (Simon becomes Peter the apostle)	KJV: "Fell down at Jesus' knees" NIV: "Fell at Jesus' knees" LTG: "Kneeled (and worshiped/kissed toward) at Jesus' knees"	Jesus	In Body	In Truth (became a fisher of men)
34) Luke 5:12 (Matt. 8:2) (Mark 1:40)	A Leper	KJV: "Fell on his face" NIV: "Fell with his face to the ground" LTG: "Kneeled (and worshiped/kissed toward) and touched forehead to the ground"	Jesus	In Body	In Truth (leprosy healed)

*Event #31: (Luke 4:7) In Matthew's parallel account (Luke 4:9), Satan said, "All these things will I give to thee, if thou wilt fall down and worship (proskuneo: kiss toward) me." Why didn't Jesus do these two acts "in pretense" and the joke would have been on Satan? Jesus refused because He cannot lie. Jesus knew that He would have to become Satan's humble servant and rise to follow him because He would have done the acts "in truth" and not "in pretense."

BIBLE REFERENCE OF Worship Events	WORSHIPER(S) KNEELER(S)	WORSHIP ACTS PERFORMED "EVERY KNEE SHALL BOW" Isaiah 45:23 "We shall all stand before the judgment seat . . . For it is written . . . every knee shall bow to Me . . . Each of us shall give account" (Rom 14:10b–12a)	OBJECT OF WORSHIP	PRESENCE "IN SPIRIT" OR IN BODY	GENUINENESS "IN TRUTH" OR IN PRETENSE
35) Luke 7:38*† (Psalm 2:12)	A sinful woman	KJV: "Kissed (kataphileo) his feet" NIV: "Kissed (kataphileo) his feet" LTG: "(Kneeled and) kissed (kataphileo) His feet" [worshiped]	Jesus	In Body	In Truth ("she loved much" v. 47)
36) Luke 8:28 (Mark 5:6)	Legion (possessed with an evil spirit)	KJV: "Fell down at his feet" NIV: "Fell at his feet" LTG: "Kneeled (and worshiped/kissed toward) Him"	Jesus	In Body	In Truth (arose to tell others)
37) Luke 8:41 (Matt. 9:18) (Mark 5:22)	Jairus (a ruler)	KJV: "Fell down at his feet" NIV: "Fell at his feet" LTG: "Kneeled (and worshiped/kissed toward) Him"	Jesus	In Body	In Truth (daughter arose)
38) Luke 8:47 (Mark 5:33)	Woman with bleeding	KJV: "Falling down before him" NIV: "Fell at his feet" LTG: "Kneeled (and worshiped/kissed toward) Him"	Jesus	In Body	In Truth (your faith has healed you)

*Event #35: (Luke 7:38) David Thomas captures the essence of the event and also issues a challenge. He says, "In Luke 7:36-50 there is a beautiful example of a woman who worshiped Jesus in a manner consistent with both the Hebrew and Greek meaning of the word 'worship'. Describe her act of worship." He then adds, "Worship also requires open, public expression. Concealed love is to be questioned." The woman "ceased not to kiss" Jesus' feet. In context, it appears that the woman performed both acts in the "proskuneo pattern" of worship, because to **kiss** His feet she must have also **bowed the knees**.[4]

†John Scott reminds us that, "God loves a broken heart, a wet eye, and a **bent knee**."[5]

4. David Thomas, worship@accucomm.net. Accessed 2000.
5. Scott, John. Saturn Road Church of Christ, Garland, Texas, 1997, Audiocassette.

BIBLE REFERENCE OF Worship Events	WORSHIPER(S) KNEELER(S)	**WORSHIP ACTS PERFORMED "EVERY KNEE SHALL BOW" Isaiah 45:23 "We shall all stand before the judgment seat . . . For it is written . . . every knee shall bow to Me . . . Each of us shall give account" (Rom 14:10b–12a)**	OBJECT OF WORSHIP	PRESENCE "IN SPIRIT" OR IN BODY	GENUINENESS "IN TRUTH" OR IN PRETENSE
39) Luke 17:16	A leper (1 of 10)	KJV: "Fell down on his face at his feet" NIV: "Threw himself at Jesus' feet" LTG: "Kneeled (and worshiped/kissed toward) at His feet"	Jesus	In Body	In Truth (thanked Jesus)
40) Luke 22:41 (Matt. 26:39) (Mark 14:35)	Jesus (Gethsemane)*†	KJV: "Kneeled down and prayed" NIV: "Knelt down and prayed" LTG: "Kneeled (and worshiped/kissed toward) and prayed"	"Father"	In Spirit	In Truth (surrendered His will)
41) Luke 22:47 (Matt. 26:49) (Mark 14:45)	Judas (false worshiper)	KJV: "Drew near unto Jesus and kissed him" NIV: "Approached Jesus to kiss him" LTG: "Drew near unto Jesus, (kneeled) and kissed (kataphileo) Him" [worshiped]	Jesus	In Body	In Pretense! (betrayal kiss)
42) Luke 24:5	"the Women"	KJV: "Bowed down their faces to the earth" NIV: "Bowed down with their faces to the ground" LTG: "Kneeled (and worshiped/kissed toward) and touched their foreheads to the ground"	Angels at tomb	In Body	In Truth (they arose to tell)

*Event #40: (Luke 22:41): Speaking from the Garden of Gethsemane on Easter morning Darlene Matthews said, "When Jesus went to **bow down** at that rock, He went determined not to get up until His will was surrendered . . . There was a battle that went on at this place. It was a battle between the Father's will and Jesus' will . . . There is no other way for you to live for God except for you to give your will. You will have to have a Gethsemane in your life. You must get down **on your knees** and forever give your will to the Father. You must make up your mind . . . Jesus did not need to pray for Himself at the cross. He prayed at Gethsemane."[6]

†Ella Wheeler Wilcox wrote a poem entitled, "The Purpose in Gethsemane." It says, "All those who journey, soon or late, must pass within the garden's gate; **Must kneel** alone in darkness there and battle with some fierce despair, 'Not my will but Thine.'"[7]

6. Matthews, Darlene. "Live broadcast from the Garden of Gethsemane." KLTV Channel 7, Tyler, Texas, on Easter, 1987, Videocassette.
7. Wilcox, Ella Wheeler. "The Purpose in Gethsemane." *Tapestries of Life*. Nashville: Holman Bible Publishers, 1974, 217.

BIBLE REFERENCE OF Worship Events	WORSHIPER(S) KNEELER(S)	WORSHIP ACTS PERFORMED "EVERY KNEE SHALL BOW" Isaiah 45:23 "We shall all stand before the judgment seat . . . For it is written . . . every knee shall bow to Me . . . Each of us shall give account" (Rom 14:10b–12a)	OBJECT OF WORSHIP	PRESENCE "IN SPIRIT" OR IN BODY	GENUINENESS "IN TRUTH" OR IN PRETENSE
43) Luke 24:52 (the ascension of Jesus)	The 11 Apostles	KJV: "Worshiped (proskuneo) him" NIV: "Worshiped (proskuneo) him" LTG: "(Kneeled and) worshiped (proskuneo: kissed toward) Him"	Jesus	In Body	In Truth (they arose to serve)
44) John 4:20(a) (Mt. Garizim)	"Our fathers" (Samaritans)	KJV: "Worshiped (proskuneo) in this mountain" NIV: "Worshiped (proskuneo) on this mountain" LTG: "(Kneeled and) worshiped (proskuneo: kissed toward) on this mountain"	God	In Spirit?	In Truth?
45) John 4:20(b)	"You" (Jesus & Jews)	KJV: "Say...ought to worship (proskuneo)...in Jerusalem" NIV: "Claim must worship (proskuneo)...in Jerusalem" LTG: "Say must (kneel and) worship (proskuneo: kiss toward) in Jerusalem"	God	In Spirit?	In Truth?
46) John 4:21	"Woman" (at the well)	KJV: "Ye shall worship (proskuneo) the Father neither in this mountain nor yet in Jerusalem" NIV: "You will worship (proskuneo) the Father neither on this mountain nor in Jerusalem" LTG: "You will (kneel and) worship (proskuneo: kiss toward) the Father neither on this mountain nor in Jerusalem"	"the Father"	In Spirit	In Truth

BIBLE REFERENCE OF Worship Events	WORSHIPER(S) KNEELER(S)	WORSHIP ACTS PERFORMED "EVERY KNEE SHALL BOW" Isaiah 45:23 "We shall all stand before the judgment seat . . . For it is written . . . every knee shall bow to Me . . . Each of us shall give account" (Rom 14:10b–12a)	OBJECT OF WORSHIP	PRESENCE "IN SPIRIT" OR IN BODY	GENUINENESS "IN TRUTH" OR IN PRETENSE
47) John 4:22(a)	"You" (Woman at the well)	KJV: "Worship (proskuneo) ye know not what" NIV: "Worship (proskuneo) what you do not know" LTG: "(Kneel and) worship (proskuneo: kiss toward) you know not what"	God	"know not what"	In Pretense! (the woman: was arising to same sinful lifestyle)
48) John 4:22(b)	"We" (Jesus & Jews)	KJV: "Worship (proskuneo) ... we know what" NIV: "Worship (proskuneo) ... what we do know" LTG: "(Kneel and) worship (proskuneo: kiss toward) we know what"	"the Father"	In Spirit	In Truth
49) John 4:23(a)*	The true worshipers (proskunetes)	KJV: "Shall worship (proskuneo) the Father in spirit and in truth" NIV: "Will worship (proskuneo) the Father in spirit and in truth" LTG: "Shall (kneel and) worship (proskuneo: kiss toward) the Father in spirit and in truth"	God, "the Father"	"In Spirit"	In Truth

*Event #49–51: James Pullin says, "John 4:23–24 declares that we must worship God in spirit and in truth. In doing so, we must reverence His glory, **fall prostrate** before Him, expose all our faults and errors to Him and repent of them . . . God loves and cares for us all as unique individuals."[8]

8. Pullin, James. "The Spiritual Preparation for Leading Worship." *Worship Leader* June–July, 1992, 12.

The Worship Chart—Part II

BIBLE REFERENCE OF Worship Events	WORSHIPER(S) KNEELER(S)	WORSHIP ACTS PERFORMED "EVERY KNEE SHALL BOW" Isaiah 45:23 "We shall all stand before the judgment seat . . . For it is written . . . every knee shall bow to Me . . . Each of us shall give account" (Rom 14:10b–12a)	OBJECT OF WORSHIP	PRESENCE "IN SPIRIT" OR IN BODY	GENUINENESS "IN TRUTH" OR IN PRETENSE
50) John 4:23(b)	True worshipers (proskunetes)	KJV: "The Father seeketh such to worship (proskuneo) him: NIV: "They are the kind of worshipers (proskuneo) the Father seeks" LTG: "The Father seeks such to (kneel and) worship (proskuneo: kiss toward) Him"	God, "the Father"	In Spirit	In Truth
51) John 4:24 "God is a Spirit"	They that worship (proskuneo: kiss toward) Him	KJV: "Must worship (proskuneo) him in spirit and in truth" NIV: "Must worship (proskuneo) in Spirit and in truth" LTG: "Must (kneel and) worship (proskuneo: kiss toward) Him in spirit and in truth"	God is "the Father" & "God is a spirit"	"In Spirit" (God is present "in Spirit")	"In Truth" (& not in pretense)
52) John 9:38	Blind man	KJV: "Worshiped (proskuneo) him" NIV: "Worshiped (proskuneo) him" LTG: "(Kneeled and) worshiped (proskuneo: kissed toward) Him"	Jesus	In Body	In Truth ("Lord I believe")
53) John 11:32	Mary (sister of Lazarus)	KJV: "Fell down at his feet" NIV: "Fell down at his feet" LTG: "Kneeled (and worshiped/kissed toward) His feet"	Jesus	In Body	In Truth ("You are the Christ")
54) John 12:20	Certain Greeks	KJV: "Came up to worship (proskuneo)" NIV: "Went up to worship (proskuneo)" LTG: "Went up to (kneel and) worship (proskuneo: kiss toward)"	God	In Spirit	In Truth ("Sir, we would see Jesus")

BIBLE REFERENCE OF Worship Events	WORSHIPER(S) KNEELER(S)	WORSHIP ACTS PERFORMED "EVERY KNEE SHALL BOW" Isaiah 45:23 "We shall all stand before the judgment seat . . . For it is written . . . every knee shall bow to Me . . . Each of us shall give account" (Rom 14:10b–12a)	OBJECT OF WORSHIP	PRESENCE "IN SPIRIT" OR IN BODY	GENUINENESS "IN TRUTH" OR IN PRETENSE
55) Acts 7:43	Israelites	KJV: "Worship (proskuneo)" NIV: "Worship (proskuneo)" LTG: "(Kneel and) worship (proskuneo: kiss toward)"	Idols	In Body (figures of idols)	In Truth (believed in & served the idols)
56) Acts 7:60 (the stoning of Steven)	Steven	KJV: "Kneeled down" NIV: "Fell on his knees" LTG: "Kneeled (and worshiped/kissed toward)"	"God" "Jesus"	In Spirit:God In Body: Jesus	In Truth (worshiped while dying)
57) Acts 8:27*	Ethiopian Eunuch	KJV: "Had come ... to worship (proskuneo)" NIV: "Had gone ... to worship (proskuneo)" LTG: "Had been ... to (kneel and) worship (proskuneo: kiss toward)"	God	In Spirit	In Truth ("reading Isaiah")
58) Acts 9:4 (Acts 22:7) (Acts 26:14)	Saul (Paul)	KJV: "Fell to the earth" NIV: "Fell to the ground" LTG: "Kneeled (and worshiped/kissed toward)"	Jesus	In Spirit (saw a light from heaven)	In Truth (arose to serve)

*Event #57: (Acts 8:27) Earl Edwards says, "The eunuch had come to Jerusalem to proskuneo, 'worship'. He was to **bow down** to God and **worship**, a given act of worship that he was to do…"[9]

9. Edwards, Earl. "Focus on God's Plan for Worship." Lectureship at Hartsville Pike Church of Christ, Gallitin, TN, 1995, Audiocassette.

The Worship Chart—Part II

BIBLE REFERENCE OF Worship Events	WORSHIPER(S) KNEELER(S)	WORSHIP ACTS PERFORMED "EVERY KNEE SHALL BOW" Isaiah 45:23 "We shall all stand before the judgment seat . . . For it is written . . . every knee shall bow to Me . . . Each of us shall give account" (Rom 14:10b–12a)	OBJECT OF WORSHIP	<u>PRESENCE</u> "IN SPIRIT" OR IN BODY	<u>GENUINENESS</u> "IN TRUTH" OR IN PRETENSE
59) Acts 9:40 (Tabitha raised)	Peter (an apostle)	KJV: "Kneeled down and prayed" NIV: "Got down on his knees and prayed" LTG: "Kneeled (and worshiped/kissed toward) and prayed"	God	In Spirit	In Truth (Tabitha arose)
60) Acts 10:25	Cornelius (a Gentile)	KJV: "Fell at his feet and worshiped (proskuneo) him" NIV: "Fell at his feet in reverence (proskuneo)" LTG: "Kneeled and worshiped (proskuneo: kissed toward) Him"	Peter	In Body	In Error! (wrong object)
61) Acts 16:29	Phillipian Jailer	KJV: "Fell down before Paul and Silas" NIV: "Fell trembling before Paul and Silas" LTG: "Kneeled (and worshiped/kissed toward) Paul and Silas"	Paul & Silas	In Body	In Error! (wrong object)
62) Acts 20:36	Paul (with the Ephesian elders)	KJV: "Kneeled down and prayed with them all" NIV: "Knelt with all of them and prayed" LTG: "Kneeled (and worshiped/kissed toward) and prayed with them all"	God	In Spirit	In Truth (Paul arose to serve)
63) Acts 21:5	Paul (an apostle) (with church at Tyre)	KJV: "We kneeled down on the shore, and prayed" NIV: "There on the beach we knelt to pray" LTG: "We kneeled (and worshiped/kissed toward) on the shore and prayed"	God	In Spirit	In Truth (Paul arose to serve)
64) Acts 22:7 (Acts 9:4) (Acts 26:14)	Paul (an apostle)	KJV: "Fell unto the ground" NIV: "Fell to the ground" LTG: "Kneeled on the ground (and worshiped/kissed toward)"	Jesus	In Spirit (saw a light from heaven)	In Truth ("What shall I do, Lord")

BIBLE REFERENCE OF Worship Events	**WORSHIPER(S) KNEELER(S)**	**WORSHIP ACTS PERFORMED "EVERY KNEE SHALL BOW" Isaiah 45:23 "We shall all stand before the judgment seat . . . For it is written . . . every knee shall bow to Me . . . Each of us shall give account" (Rom 14:10b–12a)**	**OBJECT OF WORSHIP**	**PRESENCE "IN SPIRIT" OR IN BODY**	**GENUINENESS "IN TRUTH" OR IN PRETENSE**
65) Acts 24:11*	Paul (an apostle) (with church at Jerusalem)	KJV: "Went up to Jerusalem for to worship (proskuneo)" NIV: "Went to Jerusalem to worship (proskuneo)" LTG: "Went to Jerusalem to (kneel and) worship (proskuneo: kiss toward)"	God	In Spirit	In Truth (arose to serve)
66) Acts 26:14 (Acts 22:7) (Acts 9:4)	Paul (an apostle, and all with him)	KJV: "Fallen to the earth" NIV: "Fell to the ground" LTG: "Kneeled on the ground (and worshiped/kissed toward)"	Jesus "I am Jesus"	In Spirit (saw a light from heaven)	In Truth (arose & did as told)
67) Rom. 11:4 (I Kgs. 19:18)	"Seven thousand"	KJV: "Have not bowed the knee to Baal" NIV: "Have not bowed the knee to Baal" LTG: "Have not bowed the knee to Baal [and whose mouths have not kissed (proskuneo) him]" [worshiped]	Baal (Idol)	In Body	The 7K Refused (to kneel & kiss Baal)
68) Rom. 14:11** (Isa. 45:23) (Matt. 4:10) (Rev. 14:7)	"Every knee"	KJV: "Every knee shall bow to me" NIV: "Before me every knee shall bow" LTG: "Every knee shall bow (and every mouth shall worship/ kiss toward) me"	God	In Spirit ("must" John 4:24)	In Truth ("must" John 4:24)

*Event #65: (Acts 24:11) After Earl Edwards did a good job explaining that proskuneo means 'to **fall down** before, to kiss toward, to do obedience to', he then used the eunuch and the apostle Paul as examples to illustrate. He said, "The eunuch had come to Jerusalem to proskuneo, worship. He was to **bow down** to God and **worship** in the temple--an outward expression, a given act of worship . . . Now let's come to another example of Paul in Acts 24:11. Paul went up to Jerusalem to worship, proskuneo." do. . ."[10]

**Event #68 is Quoted from I Kings 19:18.

10. Edwards, Earl. "Focus on God's Plan for Worship." Lectureship at Hartsville Pike Church of Christ, Gallitin, TN, 1995, Audiocassette.

BIBLE REFERENCE OF Worship Events	**WORSHIPER(S) KNEELER(S)**	**WORSHIP ACTS PERFORMED "EVERY KNEE SHALL BOW" Isaiah 45:23 "We shall all stand before the judgment seat . . . For it is written . . . every knee shall bow to Me . . . Each of us shall give account" (Rom 14:10b–12a)**	**OBJECT OF WORSHIP**	**PRESENCE "IN SPIRIT" OR IN BODY**	**GENUINENESS "IN TRUTH" OR IN PRETENSE**
69) I Cor. 14:25* (assembly at Corinth)	The "Outsider"	KJV: "Will fall on his face and worship (proskuneo) God" NIV: "Will fall down and worship (proskuneo) God" LTG: "Will kneel and worship (proskuneo: kiss toward) God"	God	In Spirit	In Truth ("God is really among you")
70) Eph. 3:14**	Paul (an apostle)	KJV: "I bow my knees to the Father" NIV: "I kneel before the Father" LTG: "I kneel (and worship/kiss toward) the Father"	"The Father" (God)	In Spirit	In Truth (in His service)
71) Phil. 2:10*** (Ps. 2:12) (Jesus equal with God)	"Every knee"	KJV: "At the name of Jesus every knee should bow" NIV: "At the name of Jesus every knee should bow" LTG: "In the name of Jesus every knee should bow (and every mouth should worship/kiss toward Him)"	Jesus	In Spirit	In Truth

*Event #69: (1Cor. 14:25) "Even an unbeliever, when he enters the assembly, should be able to understand what is taking place, so that he will **fall down and worship**, exclaiming, 'God is really among you' (v. 25)."[11]

Event #70: (Eph. 3:14) Adam Clark writes, "Quoting from Ephesians 3:14 the author says, '*I bow my knees to the Father.***' The apostle prays to God the Father; and **bows his knees**. . . What can a man think of himself, who, in his addresses to God, either sits on his seat or stands in the presence of his Maker and Judge of all men?"[12]

***Event #71: (Phil. 2:10): Alexander Campbell says, "I know how reluctant men are to submit to God's government; and yet they must all **bow** to it at last. 'To Jesus **every knee shall bow** and to him every tongue confess.' But they object to **bowing** now and invent excuses."[13]

11. Frame, John M. *Worship in Spirit and Truth*. Phillipsburg: Presbyterian and Reformed Publishing Company, 1996, 8.
12. Clark, Adam. *Clark's Commentary*, Vol. VI Romans/Revelation, New York: Abingdon Press, Jan. 9 1832 446.
13. Campbell, Alexander. *The Christian System*. Nashville: The Gospel Advocate Co., 1964, 209.

BIBLE REFERENCE OF Worship Events	WORSHIPER(S) KNEELER(S)	WORSHIP ACTS PERFORMED "EVERY KNEE SHALL BOW" Isaiah 45:23 "We shall all stand before the judgment seat . . . For it is written . . . every knee shall bow to Me . . . Each of us shall give account" (Rom 14:10b–12a)	OBJECT OF WORSHIP	PRESENCE "IN SPIRIT" OR IN BODY	GENUINENESS "IN TRUTH" OR IN PRETENSE
72) Heb. 1:6 (Rev. 7:11)	"All the Angels"	KJV: "Worship (proskuneo) him" NIV: "Worship (proskuneo) Him" LTG: "(Kneel and) worship (proskuneo: kiss toward) Him"	Jesus ("The Lamb")	In Body (serve Him day & night)	In Truth
73) Heb. 11:21 (Gen. 47:31)	Jacob	KJV: "Worshiped (proskuneo) leaning on the top of his staff" NIV: "Worshiped (proskuneo) as he leaned on the top of his staff" LTG: "(Kneeled and) worshiped (proskuneo: kissed toward) as he leaned on the top of his staff"	God	In Spirit	In Truth ("when he was dying")
74) Rev. 1:17*	John (an apostle)	KJV: "Fell at his feet" NIV: "Fell at his feet" LTG: "Kneeled (and worshiped/kissed toward) at His feet"	Jesus	In Body	In Truth ("on the Lord's day")
75) Rev. 3:9	Those of Satan	KJV: "To ... worship (proskuneo) before thy feet" NIV: "Will ... fall down (proskuneo) at your feet" LTG: "Will ... (Kneel and) worship (proskuneo: kiss toward) at your feet"	Congre-gation at Phila-delphia	In Body	In Truth?

*Event #74: (Rev. 1:17) "In Revelation when the Apostle John saw the Lord, he **fell at His feet** . . . When confronted with deity that's what people did."[16]

14. Lockhart, Jay. "You Have Life . . . Now Grow!" Sermon at West Erwin Church of Christ, Tyler, TX, July 16, 1995, Audiocassette.

BIBLE REFERENCE OF Worship Events	WORSHIPER(S) KNEELER(S)	WORSHIP ACTS PERFORMED "EVERY KNEE SHALL BOW" Isaiah 45:23 "We shall all stand before the judgment seat . . . For it is written . . . every knee shall bow to Me . . . Each of us shall give account" (Rom 14:10b–12a)	OBJECT OF WORSHIP	PRESENCE "IN SPIRIT" OR IN BODY	GENUINENESS "IN TRUTH" OR IN PRETENSE
76) Rev. 4:10*	24 Elders	KJV: "Fall down ... and worship (proskuneo)" NIV: "Fall down ... and worship (proskuneo)" LTG: "Kneel ... and worship (proskuneo: kiss toward)"	"Lord God Almighty"	In Spirit	In Truth ("cast their crowns")
77) Rev. 5:8*	Elders & Creatures	KJV: "Fell down before the Lamb" NIV: "Fell down before the Lamb" LTG: "Kneeled and worshiped (proskuneo: kissed toward) the Lamb"	"The Lamb" (Jesus)	In Body	In Truth ("Thou art worthy")
78) Rev. 5:14	24 Elders	KJV: "Fell down and worshiped (proskuneo)" NIV: "Fell down and worshiped (proskuneo)" LTG: "Kneeled and worshiped (proskuneo: kissed toward)"	"The Lamb" (Jesus)	In Body	In Truth ("worthy is the Lamb" v. 12)
79) Rev. 7:11, 17 (Heb. 1:6)	"All the Angels"	KJV: "Fell before the throne on their faces and worshiped (proskuneo) God" NIV: "Fell down on their faces before the throne and worshiped (proskuneo) God:" LTG: "Kneeled before the throne and worshiped (proskuneo: kissed toward) God"—v.17: and "Lamb" in the midst of the throne	"God" v.11 (& "Lamb" in the midst of the throne v. 17)	In Spirit	In Truth ("our God forever" v. 12)

*<u>Event #76 & 77</u>: <u>Joseph Carroll</u>: "Here is true worship, and the order is significant. The first thing in Rev. 4, verse 10 is that they **fall down** . . . That is first, and that is always first. The **falling down** speaks of submission . . . John reveals the essentials of worship. The first is **falling down**, the submission is the casting of the crown . . . Notice the order in Rev. 5, V#8. First, they **fall down**."[15]

15. Carroll, Joseph S. *How to Worship Jesus Christ*. Chicago: Moody Press, 1984, 36–37.

BIBLE REFERENCE OF Worship Events	WORSHIPER(S) KNEELER(S)	WORSHIP ACTS PERFORMED "EVERY KNEE SHALL BOW" Isaiah 45:23 "We shall all stand before the judgment seat . . . For it is written . . . every knee shall bow to Me . . . Each of us shall give account" (Rom 14:10b–12a)	OBJECT OF WORSHIP	PRESENCE "IN SPIRIT" OR IN BODY	GENUINENESS "IN TRUTH" OR IN PRETENSE
80) Rev. 9:20	Those who did not repent	KJV: "Worship (proskuneo)" NIV: "Worshiping (proskuneo)" LTG: "(Kneel and) worship (proskuneo: kiss toward)"	Idols, Demons	In Body? (works of their hands)	In Truth (served idols & demons)
81) Rev. 11:1	Those counted ("measured")	KJV: "Worship (proskuneo)" NIV: "Worshipers (proskuneo)" LTG: "(Kneel and) worship (proskuneo: kiss toward)"	God	In Spirit	In Truth (in God's temple)
82) Rev. 11:16*	24 Elders	KJV: "Fell upon their faces and worshiped (proskuneo) God" NIV: "Fell down on their faces and worshiped (proskuneo) God" LTG: "Kneeled and worshiped (proskuneo: kissed toward) God"	God	In Spirit	In Truth ("Thanks, O Lord God Almighty")
83)Rev. 13:4(a)	"The World"	KJV: "Worshiped (proskuneo)" NIV: "Worshiped (proskuneo)" LTG: "(Kneeled and) and worshiped (proskuneo: kissed toward)"	"The Dragon"	In Body?	In Truth (served Satan)

*Event #82: (Rev. 11:6) "Too many of us stow away **humble prostration**, found in Revelation to the distant future, never realizing that this is also a picture of the emerging Church of Jesus Christ! Jesus taught His disciples to pray to the Father, 'Thy will be done on earth as it is in Heaven.' By actions, we pray, 'Father, Thy will will have to wait till we finally get to Heaven!'"[16]

16. Garlington, Joseph L. *Worship: The Pattern of Things in Heaven*. Shippensburg: Destiny Image Publishers, Inc., 1998, 156.

BIBLE REFERENCE OF Worship Events	WORSHIPER(S) KNEELER(S)	WORSHIP ACTS PERFORMED "EVERY KNEE SHALL BOW" Isaiah 45:23 "We shall all stand before the judgment seat . . . For it is written . . . every knee shall bow to Me . . . Each of us shall give account" (Rom 14:10b–12a)	OBJECT OF WORSHIP	PRESENCE "IN SPIRIT" OR IN BODY	GENUINENESS "IN TRUTH" OR IN PRETENSE
84)Rev. 13:4(b)	"The World"	KJV: "Worshiped (proskuneo)" NIV: "Worshiped (proskuneo)" LTG: "(Kneeled and) and worshiped (proskuneo: kissed toward)"	"The Beast"	In Body?	In Truth (served Satan)
85) Rev. 13:8	All not in Book of Life	KJV: "Worshiped (proskuneo)" NIV: "Worshiped (proskuneo)" LTG: "(Kneeled and) and worshiped (proskuneo: kissed toward)"	"The Beast"	In Body	In Truth (served Satan)
86) Rev. 13:12	Earth Dwellers	KJV: "Worshiped (proskuneo)" NIV: "Worshiped (proskuneo)" LTG: "(Kneeled and) and worshiped (proskuneo: kissed toward)"	"The first Beast"	In Body	In Truth (served Satan)
87) Rev. 13:15	All who refused	KJV: "To worship (proskuneo) the image...be killed" NIV: "To worship (proskuneo) the image to be killed" LTG: "To (kneel and) worship (proskuneo: kiss toward) the image to be killed"	Image of the Beast	In Body (his image)	In Truth (served Satan)

BIBLE REFERENCE OF Worship Events	**WORSHIPER(S) KNEELER(S)**	**WORSHIP ACTS PERFORMED "EVERY KNEE SHALL BOW" Isaiah 45:23 "We shall all stand before the judgment seat . . . For it is written . . . every knee shall bow to Me . . . Each of us shall give account" (Rom 14:10b–12a)**	**OBJECT OF WORSHIP**	**PRESENCE "IN SPIRIT" OR IN BODY**	**GENUINENESS "IN TRUTH" OR IN PRETENSE**
88) Rev. 14:7* (Isa. 45:23) (Rom. 14:11–12) (Luke 4:8) (Rev. 19:10b) (Rev. 22:9)	"Every nation" (warned by Angel with "everlasting gospel")	KJV: "Fear God, and give glory to him; for the hour of his judgment is come: and worship (proskuneo) him.". NIV: "Fear God and give him glory ... the hour of his judgment is come. Worship (proskuneo) him" . . . LTG: "Fear God ... give Him glory ... judgment is come.(Kneel and) worship (proskuneo: kiss toward) Him."	God	In Spirit (God is present "in spirit")	In Truth
89) Rev. 14:9	Those who receive mark of the Beast	KJV: "Worship (proskuneo)" NIV: "Worship (proskuneo)" LTG: "(Kneel and) worship (proskuneo: kiss toward)"	"The Beast"	In Body (his image)	In Truth (served Satan)
90) Rev. 14:11	Beast Worshipers	KJV: "Worship (proskuneo)" NIV: "Worship (proskuneo)" LTG: "(Kneel and) worship (proskuneo: kiss toward)"	"The Beast & his image"	In Body (his image)	In Truth (served Satan)
91) Rev. 15:4 (Isa. 66:23)	"All Nations"	KJV: "Shall come and worship (proskuneo)" NIV: "Will come and worship (proskuneo)" LTG: "Will come and (kneel and) worship (proskuneo: kiss toward)"	God	In Spirit (God is present "in spirit")	In Truth ("must" John 4:24)

*Event #88: (Rev. 14:7)" The Analytical Literal Translation says, "Fear God and give glory to Him, because the hour of His judgment came, and **prostrate yourselves in worship** before the One having made heaven and the earth and the sea and springs of waters. The Contemporay Englishing Version says, "**Worship** and honor God! The time has come for him to judge everyone. **Kneel down** before the one who created heaven and earth, the oceans, and every stream."

The Worship Chart—Part II

BIBLE REFERENCE OF Worship Events	WORSHIPER(S) KNEELER(S)	WORSHIP ACTS PERFORMED "EVERY KNEE SHALL BOW" Isaiah 45:23 "We shall all stand before the judgment seat . . . For it is written . . . every knee shall bow to Me . . . Each of us shall give account" (Rom 14:10b–12a)	OBJECT OF WORSHIP	PRESENCE "IN SPIRIT" OR IN BODY	GENUINENESS "IN TRUTH" OR IN PRETENSE
92) Rev. 16:2	Those with the mark of the Beast	KJV: "Worshiped (proskuneo) his image" NIV: "Worshiped (proskuneo) his image" LTG: "(Kneeled and) worshiped (proskuneo: kissed toward) his image"	The Beast (his image)	In Body? (his image)	In Truth (served Satan)
93) Rev. 19:4	Elders & Creatures	KJV: "Fell down and worshiped (proskuneo)" NIV: "Fell down and worshiped (proskuneo)" LTG: "Kneeled and worshiped (proskuneo: kissed toward)"	God	In Spirit	In Truth (said "Amen! Allelujah!)
94) Rev. .9:10a	John (an apostle)	KJV: "Fell at his feet to worship (proskuneo) him" NIV: "Fell at his feet to worship (proskuneo) him" LTG: "Kneeled at his feet to worship (proskuneo: kiss toward)"	"The Angel"	In Body	In Error! (wrong object)
95) Rev. 19:10b (Rom. 14:11) (Rev. 14:7)	John (an apostle) was told by the angel:	KJV: "Worship (proskuneo) God:" NIV: "Worship (proskuneo) God!" LTG: "(Kneel and) worship (proskuneo: kiss toward)" God"	"God"	In Spirit (God is present "in spirit")	In Truth ("must" John 4:24)
96) Rev. 19:20	Beast Worshipers	KJV: "Worship (proskuneo)" NIV: "Worship (proskuneo)" LTG: "(Kneel and) worship (proskuneo: kiss toward)"	"The Beast"	In Body? (his image)	In Truth (served Satan)
97) Rev. 20:4	Witnesses of Jesus (and the word of God)	KJV: "Had not worshiped (proskuneo)" NIV: "Had not worshiped (proskuneo)" LTG: "Had not (kneeled and) worshiped (proskuneo: kissed toward)"	"The Beast"	In Body? (his image)	Refused (to kneel and kiss toward the beast)

BIBLE REFERENCE OF Worship Events	**WORSHIPER(S) KNEELER(S)**	**WORSHIP ACTS PERFORMED "EVERY KNEE SHALL BOW" Isaiah 45:23 "We shall all stand before the judgment seat . . . For it is written . . . every knee shall bow to Me . . . Each of us shall give account" (Rom 14:10b–12a)**	**OBJECT OF WORSHIP**	**PRESENCE "IN SPIRIT" OR IN BODY**	**GENUINENESS "IN TRUTH" OR IN PRETENSE**
98) Rev. 22:8	John (an apostle)	KJV: "Fell down to worship (proskuneo) before the feet of the angel" NIV: "Fell down to worship (proskuneo) at the feet of the angel" LTG: "Kneeled to worship (proskuneo: kiss toward) at the feet of the angel"	"The Angel"	In Body	In Error! (wrong object)
99) Rev. 22:9 (Isa. 45:23) (Rom. 14:11) (Rev. 14:7)	John (an apostle) was told by the angel:	KJV: "Worship (proskuneo) God!" NIV: "Worship (proskuneo) God!" LTG: "(Kneel and) worship (proskuneo: kiss toward) God!"	"God"	In Spirit (God is present "in spirit")	In Truth ("must" John 4:24)

Question #1: Are events #95 and #99 commands, literally? In those two commands, the angel supplies the 2nd act in the two-act "proskuneo pattern" that supplements the first act in Isaiah 45:23 and Romans 14:11—"**every knee shall bow**." Also, God has sworn by Himself that He will never change the pattern and it is the final command recorded in the last chapter in the Bible—which is God's Word—the "Final Supreme court of Appeal.

Question #2: Is the confusion about what the Bible says? Or is it about, "Am I going to do it?"

Next: The 13 different "worship" words in the KJV—an overview.

6

The 13 Different "Worship" Words in the KJV

An Overview

When someone uses the English word "worship," what kind of worship do they mean? Are they referring to worship *(doxa)* that occurs when someone shows *humility* by taking the lowest seat at a wedding (Luke 14:10, KJV)? Or is it worship (*therapueo*) that occurs when someone attempts to *cure* God's ailments by giving Him therapy with healing hands (Acts 17:25)? And if someone uses the word worshiper (*neokoros*), are they referring to a person who *sweeps* and guards the temple (Acts 19:35)? Hopefully, this detailed study of the 13 Greek words translated as worship or worshiped in the New Testament will help us all to gain a better insight into the meaning of "worship."

As stated earlier the primary focus of this study is the Greek "worship" word *proskuneo* that is found in John 4, and in the NT, it is always done while **kneeling** or **bowing the knees**. Before examining the other 12 "worship" words in detail, an attempt will be made to clarify some of the misunderstandings that have occurred as a result of translating all the "worship" words as the same. It seems that translating more of the Greek words literally would have prevented some of the divisive issues related to "worship."

1) What is "worship?"—Do all Bible scholars define worship the same?

Beginning in the 1990's, the word "worship" in many churches has been a topic of confusion, controversy, and division. Why is there confusion if 'God is not the author of confusion' (I Cor 14:33)? This is one of the most frequently asked questions when discussing the topic of "Worship." We know that we should search the scriptures for what we believe and practice in religion (Acts 17:11). Other helpful resources include the Lexicons or Greek dictionaries, Bible translations, historical facts, and Bible scholars. Many Bible scholars have already searched these various sources, and the section on Testimony of the Bible Scholars is in the next chapter. However, it seems that we should present some of their testimonies now by first asking some of the challenging questions regarding "worship" and then let the Bible scholars answer. The first question in the series is probably the most controversial, and that question is as follows:

Chuck Fromm, publisher and chief editor of *Worship Leader* has concluded from his vast experience that, "What worship is defies simple definition. Whatever position you choose (or even if you decide to straddle the fence), one thing that is for certain: the word 'worship' means different things to different people."[1]

John Gipson spoke on the topic, "What is worship" at Freed-Hardeman University in 1994. He is an outstanding preacher and communicator who summarized the problem of defining "worship" in the following quote: "Words, words, words! That's what we encounter when we make an effort to define *worship*. To complicate the matter even more, there are a number of different words in the Bible which have all been translated *worship*. Various shades of meaning are found in the original words: 'to bow down, do obeisance, to do, serve, to bow self down, glory, esteem, to be reverential, pious, religious observance, to worship publicly, to kiss (the hand) toward, to venerate, and reckon venerable.' Quite a list, don't you think? With so many nuances it's no wonder that every book I pick up gives a different definition of what worship is."[2]

Brian Kenyon has also expressed the problem well. He says, "Both in and out of the church of Christ, many people do not understand the meaning of New Testament worship. Some misunderstand worship to be a purely internal position, while others suppose it to be a mere ritualistic performance of external activities. These misunderstandings lead to a confusion over the issue of worship, prevent people from acceptably worshiping God, and ultimately result in souls being lost."[3]

1. Fromm, Chuck. "Trying to define what 'It' Is." *Worship Leader* Summer 2001, 6.

2. Gipson, John. "What is worship." *Worship in Spirit and Truth.* Freed Hardeman University Lectures, Henderson, TN 1994, 106.

3. Kenyon, Brian. "True Worship: A Word Study." Florida School of Preaching, Vol. XIX, No. 9, April 1999, 1.

George Barna agrees that, "A majority of adults attending Christian churches have no idea what worship means. Two out of three cannot provide an appropriate definition or description of worship."[4]

Wendal Willis states the fact clearly and concisely: "The confusion is not only about practice and style, which is usually where the debate is conducted, but also I think there is confusion as to the purpose and the meaning of the public worship."[5]

David L. Lipe has observed that, "The theme of worship is an area of concern with which many churches are struggling. For some churches, issues concerning worship threaten the precious unity of the body of Christ in a way not threatened before."[6]

Stafford North, Professor at Oklahoma Christian University, has discerned that, "In the last decade, worship has been a hot topic in all religious bodies. Some changes have been generally accepted; some have been divisive, some have been scriptural; and some have not."[7]

2) Is "all of life" worship?

The late Furman Kearley, former editor of the *Gospel Advocate* and Academic Dean of Magnolia Bible College addressed the question by saying, "Is all of life worship? Well, actually the question boils down to how we're going to define the English word worship in terms of translating the word from the original ... The word "worship" is always changing."[8]

3) Does "worship" in the KJV refer to any of the "five acts of worship?"

During the "Open Forum" on worship at the International Bible College, a man from the audience stepped to the microphone and stated a fact that is not widely known. He said, "The problem that I have in reading the New

4. Barna, George. *Habits of Highly Effective Churches*. Ventura: Regal Books, 1999, 84–85.

5. Willis, Wendell. "Our Present Confusion—Worship." ACU Lectures, Abilene, TX. 1997, Audiocassette.

6. Lipe, David L. *Worship in Spirit and Truth*. Freed Hardeman University Annual Bible Lectureship, Henderson, TN, 1994, V.

7. North, Stafford. "Unlocking Our Hearts to God is Key to Making Our Worship Meaningful." *Christian Chronicle* May 2000, 31.

8. Kearley, Furman. "Open Forum: Is All of Life Worship?" IBC Lectures, Worship Styles in the 90's, Florence, Al, 1994, Audiocassette.

Testament is finding one single example of "worship" referring to singing, prayer, Bible study, giving, or communion."[9]
(The gentleman is correct. The Scriptures are SILENT when it comes to calling any of the "five acts" an act of "worship." However, each of the five acts do "ascribe worth" or "declare the worth of" Deity. Some have listed 22 acts in the Bible that "ascribe worth").

4) Which Greek words in the NT translate as our English word "worship?"

Richard C. Leonard was chosen by Robert Webber to write the "The New Testament Vocabulary of Worship" in Vol. 1 of *The Biblical Foundations of Worship*. He states plainly that, "There is no New Testament term that exactly corresponds to our English word *worship*. The biblical expressions are concrete, whereas the word *worship*, etymologically, conveys the more abstract idea of 'ascribing worth.' A common term in the New Testament . . . is the verb *proskuneo*, which means literally to **'fall to the knee** before,' to **bow down** or **prostrate** oneself."[10]

5) Is the word "worship" defined in the Bible?

Gary Workman, editor of the *The Restorer*, presented an informative Editorial on "What is Worship?" He began by saying, "Ideas about the exact meaning of worship and what might constitute worship are numerous and varied. One reason for this is that the Bible does not explain the term in any stated definition . . . "[11]

6) Why does the KJV translate 13 different Greek words as "worship?"

The reason the KJV translated so many words as "worship" is attributed by some to the broad usage of the term "worship" in British culture at the time the KJV was translated in 1610. For example, the wedding ceremony

9. An anonymous gentleman at the "Open Forum: *Is All of Life Worship*?" International Bible College, Florence, AL, 1994, Audiocassette.

10. Leonard, Richard C. "New Testament Vocabulary of Worship." *The Biblical foundations of Christian Worship*, Robert E. Webber, ed. Nashville: Start Song Publishing Group., 1993, 15, 19–23.

11. Workman, Gary. Editorial: "What is Worship?" *The Restorer*, Feb/Mar. 1993 Vol. 13 No. 2, 2.

from the Anglican Book of Common Prayer that is used by the Church of England includes the following clause on "worship" in the wedding vows: "With this ring I thee wed, with my body I thee worship, and with all my worldly goods I thee endow."[12] The Book of Common Prayer was published in 1662 and the ceremony is still practiced by the Church of England.

Also, the act of **kneeling** and pledging "earthly worship" to the Queen of England is still practiced today. For example, during the coronation of Queen Elizabeth II in 1953 all the Archbishops, Bishops, Dukes, and Earls, paid "homage" to her. They each in turn **kneeled** before her and stated a pledge of "earthly worship." After arising from their knees, they each **kissed** her right hand. For illustration purposes, the following excerpt was taken directly from the written protocol of the coronation ceremony. You will recall that the most common Greek word translated "worship" in the KJV is *proskuneo* which literally means to "kiss" or "kiss toward" or throw a "kiss toward" the object of worship and is always done while **bowing the knees.** Notice in the following protocol, however, that the kiss bestowed to the Queen's right hand is performed AFTER "arising" from the knees.

> ... The Dukes first by themselves, and so of the Marquesses, Earls, Viscounts, and Barons in that order shall ascend the steps of the Throne, and having first removed his coronet, shall **kneel down** before her Majesty, and placing his hands between the Queen's shall pronounce the words of Homage, saying: "I do become your liege man of life and limb, and of earthly worship; and faith and truth will I bear unto you, to live and die, against all manner of folks. So help me God ... And *arising*, he shall touch the Crown upon her Majesty's head ... and then shall he **kiss** the Queen's right hand.[13]

Upon completion of the King James translation of the Bible, the translators wrote two and one half pages of dedicatory remarks to King James. In those remarks, the King was addressed as "Your Highness" five (5) times and as "Your Majesty" a total of nine (9) times.[14]

12. Suter, John Wallace. *The Anglican Book of Common Prayer*, published by Church Publishing, Inc. London, England. 1662 http://www.chicagomarriage.com/Book%20of%20Common%20Prayer%201662%20Wedding%20Ceremon pages 1 through 6.

13. *The Coronation of Queen Elizabeth II 1953*, Accessed on 2002 Online: www.oremas.org/liturgy/coronation.

14. "The Epistle Dedicatory." Preface to the *King James Version—Eight Translation New Testament*, Wheaton: Tyndale House Publishers, Inc., 1974, x–xi.

The phrase "your worship" is often used in British culture as "a title of honor when addressing magistrates, mayors, and certain other dignitaries."[15] The term "Worshipful" is sometimes used as an adjective and "Worshipfulness" is used a noun.

7) Did the KJV translators practice kneeling?

King James and the translators of the KJV were members of the Church of England, which is also known as the Anglican Church and in the US is known as the Episcopal Church. Members of the Church of England practiced **kneeling** at the time the KJV was translated, and all the groups mentioned still practice **kneeling** today. The translators, therefore, rendered the Greek word *proskuneo* as "worship" each time in the KJV, realizing that **bowing the knees** is done in "worship." It is interesting that *proskuneo* is the only Greek word translated as "worship" that is always done while **bowing the knees.** The translators further illustrated the definition of *proskuneo* by their actions: They **kneeled** in worship - literally. You will recall that **Kneeling** is the first act in the "*proskuneo* pattern" of worship.

8) What is the advantage of growing up in a monarchy?

Ron Owens, author of *Return to Worship*, points out the difference between growing up in a monarchy and a democracy. He says, "Those of us who grew up under a monarchy can perhaps relate better to the practice of **bowing and doing homage** than those who live in the United States."[16] Being now an American citizen, he also reminds us that we never refer to our president as "Your Highness" or to our judges as "Your Worship."

Jack Lewis is a former professor who is considered an authority on "worship" words. He brings to our attention the difficulty that can occur when **bowing the knees** is taken figuratively. He says, "One of the most common words in the New Testament for worship is p*roskynein*, and its basic meaning is to **prostrate oneself** in the presence of a superior. In a democracy, we do not **prostrate ourselves** before superiors, and that atti-

15. *The American Heritage Dictionary*. William Morris ed., Houghton Mifflin Co., Boston Mass.1976, 1476.

16. Owens, Ron. *Return to Worship*. Nashville: Broadman & Holman, 1999.

tude carries over into our relationship with God. The idea of **prostration**, even when taken figuratively and emotionally, comes hard for us."[17]

Joseph Garlington, in his book, *Worship, the Pattern of Things in Heaven*, is very much in agreement. He says, "In England, and in other countries which still maintain a monarchy or social system of royalty, the citizens have an innate understanding of words like *worship, king, and kingdom.* Americans, however, suffer a distinct disadvantage in this area. When you talk about the Lordship of Jesus Christ, you're talking about somebody who says, 'Your very existence depends on Me.' So when we offer worship to such an all-powerful being, even the **posture of our body** and the words of our mouths should frame the worth, value, and respect due His name and person."[18]

9) What is the origin of the English word "worship?"

Hal Hougey, author of *The Quest for Understandable Hermeneutics,* points out that the English word "worship" is an Anglo-Saxon word derived from "worth-ship" or "worthiness." It means showing reverence and honor to one who is "worthy." He uses a form of *proskuneo* (*proskunesis*) to illustrate. He says, "When man, the sinful creature, finds himself in the Presence of the King of the Universe . . . the unholy cannot stand in the presence of the Holy . . . The Greek word which best conveys this concept is *proskunesis.* Literally, it means 'to kiss toward.'"

"The idea is that when man comes into the Presence of God, he **falls down** before him, sinful and unworthy, to do obeisance before the Worthy One. The ancient practice was to **fall down** before a conquering king and **kiss** his foot, or the ground on which that foot stood, as a pledge of obedience and loyalty to the conquering master. That is what worship is really all about."[19]

10) "Worship" is an Anglo-Saxon word, but who are they?— And who are the Anglicans?

According to *The World Book Encyclopedia*, Anglo-Saxon is the name given the Germanic tribes that settled in England in the A.D. 400's and

17. Lewis, Jack P. "Time for Worship." *Gospel Advocate* April 1998, 34–35.

18. Garlington, Joseph L. *Worship, the Pattern of Things in Heaven,* Shippensburg: Destiny Image Publishers, Pa. 1997 p18.

19. Hougey, Hal. *The Quest for Understandable Hermeneutics.* Manna Publishing, Santa Cruz, CA 1997, 460–61.

500's. These tribes were the Angles, Saxons and Jutes. The word *England* was taken from the Old English words *Engla* and *land*, meaning *land of the Angles*. 'The Anglo-Saxons left their mark on the English language in its grammar and in thousands of words, including perhaps half the words we use today.

Further, *The Encyclopedia* says that, "Anglicans are Christians who belong to churches that developed from the Church of England. Other major churches in the Anglican Communion include the Anglican Church of Canada and the Episcopal Church in the U.S. The Church of England separated from the Roman Catholic Church during the Reformation of the 1500's. Anglicanism spread as British colonists settled in North and South America, Africa, and Asia. The highest ranking bishop is the Archbishop of Canterbury."[20]

One of the most quoted people on "worship" is William Temple, an Anglican who was also the Archbishop of Canterbury. His famous definition of worship is as follows:

> To worship is to quicken the conscience by the holiness of God, to feed the mind with the truth of God, to purge the imagination with the beauty of God, to open the heart to the love of God, and to devote the will to the purpose of God. In other words, worship is all that we are responding to all that He is."[21]

11) What is the solution to the "worship" confusion and controversy?

First, it appears that there are several Greek words translated as "worship" that could be translated more *literally* to provide a better insight into their real meaning. In fact, there appears to be a trend among the newer Bible versions to translate more of the worship words *literally*. Second, a better understanding of the "worship" words could help eliminate some of our confusion regarding "worship." Third, eliminating confusion regarding worship should lead to a better communication among Christians. And fourth, a better communication should lead to fewer divisions among Christians over "worship."

20. *The World Book Encyclopedia*. Chicago: Field Enterprises Educational Corp., 1971, 441–42.

21. http://en.wikipedia.org/wiki/William_Temple_(archbishop) Accessed 2000: http://www.mpc.org.uk/article_trueworship.htm.

Bryan Kenyon agrees that, "In the King James translation, anyway, there are 13 words that are translated with some form of the word "worship." Now, some of these words have no business being translated that way . . ."[22]

Jimmy Clark also agrees that in the King James Version, "There are a few passages that use the word 'worship' that could be better translated with another term."[23]

Hal Hougey has also expressed concern regarding translation of the worship words. He says, "Regrettably, translators have seriously damaged the whole concept of worship by rendering several different Greek words as 'worship', when that is not what they mean. This has led us to think that 'worship' is a word with many meanings, so broad as to become almost meaningless."[24]

12) What is the first step in understanding the 13 Greek words translated as "worship" or worshiped?

Brian Kenyon has emphasized that, "A first step in understanding true worship is to examine the words the Holy Spirit chose to use in teaching about the subject . . . "[25]

Stafford North reinforces a very important fact: He says, "The Bible teaches that as Christians we should search the Scriptures to determine what we should believe and practice in religion (Acts 17:11). To this end, we are committed concerning what the Bible teaches on the subject of worship."[26]

Gary Workman summarized it well when he said, "After all, the Bible was written in Hebrew, Aramaic and Greek. It is to those *original* words that we must look for the proper meaning and application. We must be-

22. Kenyon, Bryan. *Defining Worship*. Florida School of Preaching Lectureship, 2002, Audiocassette.

23. Clark, Jimmy. "Significant Greek Terms Relating to Worship." *Do You Understand Worship*? Florida School Of Preaching, 27th annual Lectureship, 2002, 64.

24. Hougey, Hal. *The Quest for Understandable Hermeneutics*. Manna Publishing Co., Santa Cruz, CA .1997, 460–61.

25. Kenyon, Brian. "True Worship: A Word Study." *Florida School of Preaching*, Vol. XIX No. 9, April, 1999, 1.

26. North, Stafford. "Unlocking Our Hearts to God is Key to Making Our Worship Meaningful." *Christian Chronicle* May 2000, 31.

gin with Bible words and concepts and then try to find adequate English equivalents."[27]

Jimmy Clark is exactly right when he says, "The inspired word of God is only present where the text is accurately translated."[28]

13) What are the 13 Greek words translated by a form of "worship?"

In the King James Version of the New Testament, there are 13 different Greek words that are translated by a form of "worship"—eight verbs and five nouns. The words are listed here along with their definitions. The three most common Greek words translated as "worship" in order of their frequency are *proskuneo*, *sebomai*, and *latreuo*. Since *proskuneo* has already been discussed, the other two Greek worship words will be discussed last. It appears that the first five Greek words listed are some that could be better translated with a more literal term. Examples of verses that contain those words are also listed. The first word that should be translated with a more *literal* term is *doxa*.

#1 Doxa; meaning honor, praise, applause, or glory.[29] Luke 14:10 is actually an example of Jesus teaching *humility* to his disciples. Jesus tells them plainly that when they are invited to a wedding they should take the lowest seat, and then when the bridegroom comes, he may ask them to go up higher. The KJV reads as follows:

> But when thou art bidden, go and sit down in the lowest room; then when he that bade thee cometh, he may say unto thee, Friend, go up higher; then shalt thou have worship (*doxa*) in the presence of them that sit at meat with thee (Luke 14:10, KJV).

In context, it seems that "honor" would be a better rendering than "glory" since it is talking about man rather than God. Also, the next verse states "for whosoever exalteth himself shall be abased, and he that humbleth himself shall be exalted" (Luke 14:11). Did Jesus say a Greek word that means "worship", or did he say a word that means "honor?" The English

27. Workman, Gary. Editorial: "What is Worship?" *The Restorer* Feb/Mar 1993, Vol. 13, No. 2, 2.

28. Clark, Jimmy. "Significant Greek Terms Relating to Worship." *Do You Understand Worship*? FSOP 27th annual Lectureship, 2002, 63.

29. Ibid: Zodhiates, Spiros. and Warren Baker. *The Complete Word Study Old Testament,* AMG International, INC. D/B/A Iowa Falls, IA: 1994, 478.

word "worship" was probably inserted into the verse by the King James translators because of the culture in which they lived.

Also, when the word "worship" is left in the verse as it is, it contradicts Jesus himself when He said that "worship" is for God only. In Matthew 4:10, Jesus said "It is written that thou shalt worship (*proskuneo*) the Lord, thy God, and Him only shalt thou serve (*latreuo*)." Notice, however, that the word translated "worship" in Matthew 4:10 is *proskuneo* and refers to a specific kind of "worship" that is always done while bowing the knees. *Doxa* or honor, on the other hand, can be bestowed while in any posture. Translating *doxa* as "worship" causes confusion and God is not the author of confusion (1Cor 14:33). The NIV, RSV, TEV, JB, and NASB translate the word honor or honored. The following table shows the trend toward a more literal translation of the Greek word *doxa*. For comparison purposes the KJV is placed first.

TESTIMONY OF THE TRANSLATORS

Worship word	KJV	NIV	RSV	TEV	JB	NKJV	ASV	NASB
Doxa Luke 14:11	worship	honored	honored	honor	honored	glory	glory	honor

It appears that the more literal translations convey a better understanding of the word *doxa*.

#2 *Therapeuo*, meaning "to heal, cure, restore to health."[30] Therefore, Acts 17:25 is another worship passage that could be understood more clearly when translated literally. The apostle Paul speaks to those in Athens concerning God's wellness and wholeness saying, "Neither is worshiped (*therapeuo*) with men's hands, as though he needed anything, seeing he giveth to all life, and breath, and all things" (Acts 17:25).

The Greek word translated as "worshipped" in the KJV is "*therapeuo*." Most of the recent Bible versions render the word "served" or "minister to."[31] The English words, therapy and therapeutic are derived from this word. The lesson to be learned from the passage is that God does not

30. Thayer, Joseph Henry. *Thayer's Greek-Lexicon of the NT*. Zondervan, Publishing House Grand Rapids, MI 1977, 288.

31. Ibid.

need healing or medical therapy from men because He is never sick. He is always in perfect health, seeing that "He giveth to all life, and breath, and all things."

The following table shows the trend toward a more literal translation of the Greek word *therapeuo*. The KJV is placed first for comparison.

TESTIMONY OF THE TRANSLATORS

Worship word	KJV	NIV	RSV	TLB	PME	ESv	ASV	NASB
Therapeuo Acts 17:25	wor-shipped	served	served	minister to	minis-tered to	served	served	served

The more literal TLB and PME communicate a better understanding of the word *therapeuo.*

#3 ***Neokoros***, a noun meaning "temple keeper", is found in the NT only in Acts 19:35.[32]

> And when the town clerk had appeased the people, he said, Ye men of Ephesus, what man is there that knoweth not how the city of the Ephesians is a worshipper (*neokoros*) of the great goddess Diana, and of the image that fell down from Jupiter? (Acts 19:35)

The word is translated as "worshiper" in the KJV, but most other versions translate the word more accurately as "temple keeper" or "guardian of the temple." The word is derived from *Neos*, meaning "temple" and from *Koreo*, meaning "to sweep."[33] It appears that translating the actual words that God used according to their real English meaning helps to eliminate part of the confusion related to the use of the word "worship."

The following table shows the trend toward a more literal translation of the Greek word *neokoros*. The KJV is placed first for comparison.

32. Bauer, Walter. *A Greek-English Lexicon of the NT*. 2d ed. publisher: American Bible Society, 1865 Broadway New York, NY 10023 1979, 723–24. 1979, 537.

33. Madvig, D. H. *Neokoros in the New International Dictionary of New Testament Theology*, ed. Collin Brown, Grand Rapids: Zondervan, 1986, 3:796.

TESTIMONY OF THE TRANSLATORS

Worship word	KJV	NIV	RSV	TEV	TJB	NKJV	ASV	NASB
Neokoros Acts 19:35	wor-shipper	guardian of the temple	temple keeper	keeper of the temple	guardian of the temple	temple guardian	temple keeper	guardian of the temple

The more literal translations definitely help us to understand the true meaning of *neokoros.*

#4 ***Threskia***, a noun that refers to "a religious observance"[34] is translated worshiping in Colossians 2:18.

> Let no man beguile you of your reward in a voluntary humility and worshipping (*threskia*) of angels, intruding into those things which he hath not seen, vainly puffed up by his fleshly mind (Col 2:18).

#5 Ethelothreskia, is a noun related to *threskia* which means "self-made" or "would-be religion."[35] In Collossians 2:23 it is translated as "will-worship" in the KJV.

> Which things have indeed a shew of wisdom in will-worship (*ethelothreskia*), and humility, and neglecting the body: not in any honor to the satisfying of the flesh (Col. 2:23).

The following table shows the trend toward a more literal translation of the word e*thelothreskia.*

TESTIMONY OF THE TRANSLATORS

Worship word	KJV	NIV	NASB	PME	TJB	ESV	NKJV
Ethelo-Threskia Col. 2:23	Will-worship	Self-imposed worship	Self-made religion	Self-imposed efforts at piety	Self-imposed devo-tions	Self-made religion	Self-imposed religion

34. Young, Robert. *Young's Analytical Concordance to the Bible.* Wm. B. Eerdmans Pub. Co. Grand Rapids, MI, 1970, 1075.

35. Bauer, Walter. *A Greek-English Lexicon of the NT.* 2ded. publisher: American Bible Society, 1865 Broadway New York, NY 10023 1979, 723-24.

The more literal translations help us to better comprehend the meaning of *ethelothreskia.* As stated earlier, the three most common Greek words translated by a form of "worship" in the NT in order of their frequency are *proskuneo, sebomai,* and *latreuo.* However, since *proskuneo* (Kiss toward) and *latreuo* (serve or service) are the two topics discussed most often in the context of "true worship," these two words will be presented last. The term *Sebomai* will be presented next.

The following five words are various forms of the Greek word *sebomai* derived from the Greek term *sebo.* The root *seb-* originally meant to step back or keep one's distance, and then later *sebomai* came to mean religious veneration associated with acts of "worship." Interestingly, in the New Testament, *sebomai* is always associated with deity (Matt. 15:9; Mark 7:7; Acts 13:43, 50; 16:14; 17:4, 17; 18:17, 13; 19:27).[36]

The next five terms (6–10) are all derived from the root word *sebo*:

#6 *Sebomai*: a verb meaning "*to revere, to worship.*"[37] This is the word translated as "worship" in the often-quoted passage that has come to be known as an example of "vain worship."

> This people draweth nigh unto me with their mouth, and honoureth me with their lips; but their heart is far from me. But in vain they do worship [*sebomai*] me, teaching for doctrines the commandments of men (Matt. 15:8–9).

#7 *Eusebo*: is a noun form of *sebomai,* which means "worship" (Acts 17:23). This familiar passage has become widely known as an example of "ignorant worship."

> For as I passed by, and beheld your devotions, I found an altar with this inscription, To the Unknown God. Whom therefore ye ignorantly worship (*eusebo*), him declare I unto you (Acts 17:23).

#8 *Theosebes*: is another noun form of *sebomai*, which means "worshiper of God" (John 9:31). The phrase "worshipper of God" in the following passage is translated from the one Greek word, *theosebes.*[38]

36. Ibid, 747.

37. Thayer, Joseph Henry. *Thayer's Greek-Lexicon of the NT*. Zondervan Publishing House, Grand Rapids, MI 1977, 548.

38. Clark, Jimmy. "Significant Greek Terms Relating to Worship." *Do You Understand Worship?* Florida School of Preaching 27th annual Lectureship, 2002, 72.

> Now we know that God heareth not sinners: but if any man be a worshipper (*theosebes*) of God, and doeth his will, him he heareth" (John 9:31).

#9 *Sebazomai*: is a verb form of *sebomai*, which means "worship" (Rom. 1:25). Putting the creature first before the Creator also seems very common is our culture today.

> Who changed the truth of God into a lie, and worshiped [*sebazomai*] and served [*latreuo*] the creature more that the Creator, who is blessed for ever. Amen (Rom. 1:25).

#10 *Sebazma:* is another noun form of *sebomai* and refers to an object of worship. In the following passage, Paul again addresses those who fall away and put themselves first before God.

> Who opposeth and exalteth himself above all that is called God, or that is worshipped [*sebazma*]; so that he as God sitteth in the temple of God, shewing himself that he is God (2 Thess. 2:4).

#11 *Proskuneo* or Proskyneo: is a verb, and is the most common Greek word translated "worship" in the NT, which is a total of 60 times. The entire focus of this study has been and continues to be the "worship" word *proskuneo* as well as the "proskuneo pattern" of worship. Both are discussed in detail elsewhere. For review, the "worship" word *proskuneo* is used eight (8) times in the conversation between Jesus and the woman at the well (John 4:20–24). The Greek word translated "worshippers" in the passage is the noun *proskunetes.*

> Our fathers worshiped (*proskuneo*) in this mountain; and ye say, that in Jerusalem is the place where men ought to worship (*proskuneo*). Jesus saith unto her, Woman, believe me, the hour cometh, when ye shall neither in this mountain, nor yet at Jerusalem, worship (*proskuneo*) the Father. Ye worship (*proskuneo*) ye know not what: we know what we worship (*proskuneo*): for salvation is of the Jews. But the hour cometh, and now is, when the true worshippers (proskunetes) shall worship (proskuneo) the Father in spirit and in truth: for the Father seeketh such to worship (*proskuneo*) him. God is a spirit: and they that worship (*proskuneo*) him must worship (*proskuneo*) him in spirit and in truth (John 4:20–24 KJV).

#12 *Proskunetes:* is the noun form of *proskuneo* and the only occurrence in the KJV is translated "*worshipper*" (John 4:23).

#13 *Latreuo*: is a verb meaning to "serve" in the "carrying out of religious duties."[39] *Latreuo* is the verb form that occurs twenty-one (21) times in the KJV and is translated seventeen (17) times as "serve" and four (4) times as "worship" or "worshipper." The noun form of *latreuo* is *latreia* and is translated as "service" in all its five occurrences. The root meaning of the word is "service rendered for hire; then any service or ministration ... the service of God."[40]

Interestingly, much of the present controversy concerning "worship" centers around the way the noun *latreia* is translated in Romans 12:1. Some Bible versions translate *latreia* in the verse as "worship" rather than "service." Therefore, some Christians believe that "all of life is worship." Many others, however, believe that "all worship is service, but not all service is worship." Some are convinced that "worship and service are synonymous," and it does not matter which word is used. The KJV translates the noun *latreia* in Romans 12:1 as follows:

> I beseech you therefore, brethren, by the mercies of God, that ye present your bodies a living sacrifice, holy, acceptable unto God, which is your reasonable service [*latreia*](Rom. 12:1).

The following table compares how some of the various bible versions translate the noun *latreia* in Romans 12:1. The KJV is placed first for comparison.

TESTIMONY OF THE TRANSLATORS

Worship word	KJV	ASV	RSV	NIV	NKJV	ESV	ALT
Latreia Rom. 12:1	reason-able service	spiritual service	spiritual worship	spiritual worship	reason-able service	spiritual worship	sacred service

Conclusion: The controversy between "worship" and "service" continues.

NEXT: Comparing *proskuneo* and *latreuo*

39. Ibid: Bauer, Walter. *A Greek-English Lexicon of the NT*. 2ded. publisher: American Bible Society, 1865 Broadway New York, NY, 10023. 1979, 467.

40. Ibid: Thayer, Joseph Henry. *Thayer's Greek-Lexicon of the NT*. Zondervan, Publishing House 5300 Patterson Ave. SE, Grand Rapids, MI 49530. 1977, 372.

The following section is designed to compare "worship" (*proskuneo*) and "service" (*latreuo*). Are all of these statements true? One: "All of life is worship." Two: "All worship is service but not all service is worship." Three: Worship and service are synonymous." In an attempt to determine the meaning of the two words and how they are used in Scripture, the Lexicons were consulted, the Scriptures were searched (Acts 17:11), and the findings were placed in a table format. Hopefully, this study will help to lessen some of the confusion and controversy surrounding the two words.

Furman Kearley, the editor of *Gospel Advocate* said, "We would have been better served, had the KJV, or any other translation, never translated *latreuo* as "worship" and always kept it as "serve" or "service." He also stressed that the Greek words *proskuneo* and *latreuo*, "are describing two different categories of activities."[41]

Next: A table format is used to compare the scriptural difference between Worship (*proskuneo*) and Service (*latreuo*).

41. Kearley, Furman. "Open Forum: Is All of Life Worship?" IBC Lectures, Worship Styles in the 90's, Florence, AL,1994, Audiocassette.

Comparing Worship (*Proskuneo*) and Service (*Latreuo*)

Testimony of Scripture and Lexicons

There is an ongoing controversy among many Christians regarding "worship" and "service." Some say that worship includes everything a Christian does, and therefore, "all of life is worship." Others say that "all of worship is service, but not all service is worship." Still, others say that "worship" and "service" are identical.

The most common Greek word translated as "worship" in the NT is *proskuneo*—in all 60 occurrences. The most common word translated as "serve" is *latreuo*—17 times as "serve" but four (4) times as "worship." The noun form of *latreuo* is *latreia* and in the KJV is translated "service" all five (5) times. Is all of worship (*proskuneo*) the same as service (*latreia*) or serve (*latreuo*)? What does the Bible say? In an attempt to determine the meaning of these Greek terms and how they are used in the New Testament, the Lexicons were consulted, the Scriptures were searched (Acts 17:11), and the findings were placed in a table format for comparison. (See pages 161–163).

Testimony of Scripture & Lexicons Greek Words

COMPARING	*PROSKUNEO*	*LATREUO*
The Definition	From *pros*, "to" or "toward" and *kuneo*, to "kiss." Literally "to kiss" or to "kiss toward" or throw a "kiss toward" someone who is divine or thought to be divine.[1]	To "serve" in carrying out religious duties,[2] Or"... *the service of God*."[3] This religious "service" may include false gods (Rom. 1:25) or the true God (Matt. 4:10b; Rev. 22:3). According to some, *latreuo* may mean "worship" in some contexts.
Posture of performance	Done in NT while bowing the knees by kneeling or prostrating oneself before the object of worship.[4] Examples: (Matt. 2:11; 4:9; 18:26)	*Latreuo* must be done in any and all Postures—If it is done "day and night" (Luke 2:37; 2 Tim. 1:3; Rev. 7:13) and "without ceasing" (2 Tim. 1:3; Rom. 1:9).
Duration of action	Does not begin until the knees bend. Ends when the knees extend. Examples: (Acts 10:25; 1 Cor. 14:25; Rev. 5:10; 5:14)	"Without ceasing" (Rom. 1:9; 2 Tim. 1:3) "Day & night" (Luke 2:37; 2 Tim. 1:3; Rev. 7:15).

1. Zodhiates, Spiros. and Warren Baker. *The Complete Word Study Old Testament*, AMG International, INC. D/B/A Iowa Falls, IA: 1994, 1233–34.

2. Bauer, Walter. *A Greek-English Lexicon of the NT*. 2d ed. publisher: American Bible Society 1865 Broadway New York, NY 10023 1979, 1979, 467.

3. Thayer, Joseph Henry. *Thayer's Greek-Lexicon of the NT*. Zondervan Pub. Grand Rapids, MI 1977, 372.

4. Ibid: Zodhiates, Spiros. and Warren Baker. *The Complete Word Study Old Testament*, AMG International, INC. D/B/A Iowa Falls, IA: 1994, 1234.

Comparing Worship (Proskuneo) *and Service* (Latreuo)

COMPARING	*PROSKUNEO*	*LATREUO*
Number of Occurrences NT	Verb: *proskuneo* occurs 60 times in NT. Noun: *proskunetes* occurs one (1) time	Verb: *latreuo* occurs 21 times in NT Noun: *Latreia* occurs five (5) times in NT
Translation in KJV	Verb: *proskuneo*:"worship or worshipped" Noun: *proskunetes*: "worshipper"	Verb: *latreuo*: "serve" 17X, "worship" 4X Noun: *latreia*: "service" five (5) times
Location of Performance	On Earth examples: (Matt 2:11; John 4:24; 1 Cor. 14:25; Acts 24:11) In Heaven examples: (Rev. 4:10; 5:14; 7:11) (See Worship Chart of 99 Events for His will "being done on earth as it is in heaven"	On Earth examples: (Rom. 1:9; Luke 2:37; 2 Tim. 1:3; Heb. 9:14;12:28). In Heaven examples: (Rev. 7:15; 22:3)
The Pattern of Performance	*Proskuneo* is always the second act in the two-act "*proskuneo* pattern" of worship. For example, the wise men "fell down and worshiped (*proskuneo*: kissed toward)" Jesus (Matt. 2:11).	The "*latreuo* pattern" of service to God is "night and day" & "without ceasing" (Luke 2:37; Rom. 1:9; 2 Tim. 1:3; 7:15). Jesus is our "example" (I Pet. 2:21). To serve like Jesus, a Christian is "on call" day and night even when asleep (Mark 4:38–39).
The "Object" of both is "God"	"Thou shalt worship (*proskuneo*) the Lord thy God" (Matt. 4:10a).	". . . and Him only shalt thou serve (*latreuo*)" (Matt. 4:10b).

COMPARING	***PROSKUNEO***	***LATREUO***
Sequence of the two words in NT	Jesus placed "worship" (*proskuneo*) before "serve" (*latreuo*) (Matt. 4:10; Luke 4:8).	Jesus placed "serve" (*latreuo*) after "worship" (*proskuneo*) (Matt. 4:10; Luke 4:8).

The table compares seven differences and two similarities between *proskuneo* and *latreuo*. The two similarities are the "location of performance," which is on earth and in heaven, and "the object" of both words is God. Discussion questions: From findings, what conclusions can be drawn? What is the application?

Next: ***The Testimony of Bible Scholars.*** These informative quotations from the various Bible scholars were selected from a wide variety of sources including religious journals, books on worship, seminars on worship, Sunday sermons, and other helpful resources. Non-Bible scholars include Abraham Lincoln, Sir Isaac Newton, Corrie Ten Boom, and several others. ***The Testimony of Bible Scholars*** is confirmation that we should **kneel,** *Literally.*

7

Literally Kneel? The Testimony of Bible Scholars

THE TOPIC OF **KNEELING** in **worship** always raises a few questions in the minds of many faithful Christians. This presentation on The Testimony of Bible Scholars will attempt to address many of those questions by placing them in a series and then allowing the Bible scholars to answer. From the answers given, we should soon be able to conclude whether or not the Bible authorizes **kneeling** in **worship**—literally. For example, I once asked a Greek Orthodox minister, "Why is it that some Christian groups do not **kneel** in **worship** when they assemble?" Without hesitation, he said, "It is because they do not experience the *presence of God.*" Therefore, our first question in this series will be, "What would we do if we sensed the presence of God?" Also, an occasional Bible scholar quote from Chapter I and elsewhere may be repeated here, depending on the question asked. For ease of recognition the terms used for **bowing the knees** or **kneeling** are bolded.

1. What would we do if we sensed the *presence* of God or Jesus?

Robert Webber quotes David Mims who said, "If Christ came physically, and actually stood in the midst of a people at **worship**, we would begin with a symbol, not words. We would probably **kneel**, maybe even **fall prostrate before** Him. We would be so overwhelmed by God's *presence* that we would be at a loss for words. **Kneeling** or lying **prostrate before** Him would say it all. It's an action worth a thousand words."[1]

1. Webber, Robert. *Worship is a Verb*. Nashville: Star Song Publishing Group, 1992, 91–92.

Jay Lockhart: "I know what we would do if we sensed the *presence* of God because I know what others did who have felt His *presence*. We would **fall down** and we would **worship**. But the fact is—God is in this place."[2]

Bruce Leafblad: "As Lord, He is supreme, the Lord of Lords, and we come into His *presence* **bowing** and **kneeling**—A God before whom we, together with all creation, assume a place of *humble* stature. As creator, God is the solitary source by whom everything was made, and we come before Him as **lowly** creatures."[3]

Lawrence Richards: "When one is afforded a vision of the glory of God, the response is always the same. When Ezekiel beheld God on the throne, he **fell on his face** (Ezekiel 1:28). When John saw the glorified Christ on Patmos, he **fell at His feet** (Revelation 1:17). In true **worship**, one sees the contrast between the glory of God and his own unworthiness."[4]

Charles Hodge: "You come to **worship** to see God and **to fall before** God and praise God and the glory is, you become like the God you **worship**."[5]

Roland Bowen asks, "What would you do if Jesus appeared right here before us at this very moment? How would you react? Have we forgotten that when we assemble together we are actually in His *presence*? I want us to see how some people reacted when they came into Jesus' *presence*. Acts chapter 9, verse 1, Saul: Suddenly a light from heaven flashed around him. He **fell to the ground** and heard a voice say unto him, 'Saul, Saul, why do you persecute me?' And what did he do when he came into Jesus' *presence*? He **fell to the ground.** Acts 26 tells us that not only he but everybody with him **fell to the ground.** He **fell to the ground** in *humility* and **worship**."[6]

2. Lockhart, Jay. "The God We Worship"—West Erwin Church of Christ, Tyler, TX, October 2, 1994, Audiocassette.

3. Leafblad, Bruce H. "Recovering the Priority of God"—*Worship Leader,* April-May 1992.

4. Richards, Lawrence O. *Zondervan Expository Dictionary of Bible Words.* Grand Rapids: Zondervan Publishing House, 1991, 639–40.

5. Hodge, Charles. "I Stand Amazed"—IBC Workshop, Florence, AL, September 23, 1994, Audiocassette.

6. Bowen, Roland. "Kneeling in His Presence"—Austin Avenue Church of Christ, Brownwood, Texas, October 11, 1998, Audiocassette.

Debbie Isham, the Activities Director at a retirement center, was asked if there was **kneeling** in the church where she attended. She said, "O yes, we **kneel** during our time of praise and **worship.** There is such a *presence* of the Lord that people just feel that they have to **kneel**."[7]

David Young: "Real '**worship**' begins when we recognize that God is here. When I really recognize that God is here, I will **fall down** in adoration."[8]

Keith Brooks: "The man who **bows the lowest** in the *presence* of God stands the straightest in the *presence of sin*."[9]

Jack Reese: "In the *presence* of God, you can encourage one another as you live in a pagan world. You can encourage one another, rather than have a divisive spirit as the pagans surely will be able to see. You will be able to experience this kind of encouragement, because you are able to **bow down before** God and **worship** Him."[10]

Fuchsia Pickett, in the book *Worship Him*, says, "He asked me what I would do if I looked up and saw Jesus for the first time. I said that 'I would **bow at His feet, kiss His nail-scarred hands** and *wash His feet* with my tears.'"[11]

Robert Webber explains how to bring the congregation into the *presence* of God in his book, *Planning Blended Worship: The Creative Mixture of Old and New*. He says, both contemporary and traditional **worship** seek to "Gather the people into the *presence* of God and prepare them to hear the word of God." He details the process step by step until, "Finally, the congregation becomes very reserved as the approach is made into the Holy of Holies. Now the people may assume a posture of *humble* **kneeling**, and perhaps some of the **worshipers will be prostrate** on the floor as

7. Isham Debbie. Activities Director at a retirement center, and member of Rose Heights Church of God

8. Young, David. "Rethinking Worship"—Jubilee Seminar, Nashville, TN, 1996, Audiocassette.

9. Brooks, Keith L. *The Cream Book of Sentence Sermons*. Chicago: Moody Press, 1974, 158.

10. Reese, Jack. Harding University Annual Preacher's Forum, Searcy, AR, April 1994, Audiocassette.

11. Pickett, Fuchsia. *Worship Him*. Lake Mary: Creation House Publishing, 2000, 4.

songs are sung to God such as 'I Love You, Lord' by Laurie Klein or 'Father, I Adore You' by Terrye Coelho."[12]

Clarence DeLoach tells how a life lived in the *presence* of God is a life of acceptance. He says, "When Job learned that all was gone—his children, his possessions, and his health, the Bible says, 'Then Job arose, tore his mantle, shaved his head, and **fell down upon the ground and worshiped"** (Job 1:20). That was **worship** of unquestioned acceptance."[13]

Rubel Shelley: "To encounter God, through, is to be overwhelmed by His wholeness and judgment, by His grace and forgiveness, by His sovereignty and love. These experiences of confrontation force us **to bow down** and **worship**—whether by a well in Mesopotamia, where one man '**bowed down** and **worshiped**' (Geneses 24:26), or around the heavenly throne, where the four living creatures and the twenty-four elders '**fell down** and **worshiped**' (Revelation 5:14). Encountering God produces the awareness of His awesome *presence* which can only be acknowledged with **worship**."[14]

Lynn Anderson asks, "What other appropriate response is there when we have come face to face with the holiness of God? In Matthew 17:5, is the transfiguration. Jesus was still speaking, and a voice in the cloud said, 'This is My beloved Son.' Verse 6 says, 'When the disciples heard this, they **fell face down** to the ground.' In Matthew 26:39, this is Jesus now going to pray in the garden. 'He **fell with His face to the ground**'. Jesus Himself **fell face down** and prayed, 'My Father, if it's possible, let this cup pass from me.' It's not just human beings, but also Christ in the *presence* of His Father. And in Acts 26:14, when the people see the glory of God, they **fall down** to **worship** Him."[15]

Roland Bowen: "We need to come into Jesus' *presence*, realize who He is, and **fall down before** Him and **worship**. In the book of Revelation,

12. Webber, Robert. *Planning Blended Worship*. Nashville: Abingdon Press, 1998, 59.

13. DeLoach, Clarence. "Principles for Worship" FHU Lectures, Henderson, TN, 1994. 56.

14. Shelley, Rubel and Randall J. Harris. *The Second Incarnation*. West Monroe: Howard Publishing Company, 1992, 119–29.

15. Anderson, Lynn. Harding University Annual Preacher's Forum, Searcy, AR, April, 1994, *Audiocassette*.

chapter 1, and verse 9, the apostle John has come into the *presence* of the resurrected Lord again, and what did he do? He heard a voice and when he turned around he comes into Jesus' *presence*, and when he sees Him he **falls down at His feet** and **worships** Him."[16]

Robert Webber says that his aim for writing the book, *Worship—Journey into His Presence*, was "to develop how God becomes *present* in our lives and to reflect on how we are to respond to the *presence* of God." He visited an Episcopal church where the service is ordered by the *Book of Common Prayer*. He says, "As I entered the church, I **knelt** and began to pray with others. Following this time of individual preparatory prayer, the prelude was played, and then a great and marvelous procession of minister and choir joyously marched to the altar area. Following the procession I heard the *call to worship*. In the *Book of Common Prayer*, this call begins, 'Blessed *be God: Father, Son, and Holy Spirit.*' Right the Trinitarian nature of **worship** has been expressed. (We come to *praise* the Father, and *thank* the Son, and *invoke the presence* of the Holy Spirit among us.)"[17]

Chris Bullard: "We need to give attention to being in His *presence* without ceasing, because that will empower us with confidence to go into His *presence* with ceasing, and **get down on our knees** and say, 'God here it is. This is what I need.'"[18]

Marvin Phillips: "If I had longer I'd pursue the way people felt when they saw God or perceived His *presence*. Very, very often they **fell at His feet.** They **bowed.** They **fell upon their face before** the Lord. In Matthew 17, Peter was astounded. He was **bowing before** an awesome God. There was Jesus transfigured and a voice out of heaven said audibly, 'This is my beloved son in whom I am well pleased, whom I love. Listen to him.' And they **fell face down on** the ground."[19]

16. Bowen, Roland. "Kneeling in His Presence"—Austin Avenue Church of Christ, Brownwood, Texas, October 11, 1998, Audiocassette.

17. Webber, Robert. *Worship—Journey into His Presence*.Mansfield: Kingdom Publishing, 1999, 34–35.

18. Bullard, Chris. "Disciplines for Growing Closer to God"—ACU Lectureship, Abilene, TX, 1995, Audiocassette.

19. Phillips, Marvin. "Bowing Before an Awesome God"—Jubilee Seminar, Nashville, TN, 1994, Audiocassette.

Harold Taylor, referring to Psalms 139:13–16, said, "Only God understands this language, but I **bow in reverence before** Him in awe of God's power as well as His wisdom. I would to God that we could see His power tonight. If we could really begin to understand just an inkling of His power and His wisdom and His *presence*, **all of us would fall on our faces before** Him and praise and laud and magnify by prayer and song the greatness of God."[20]

Ken Neller asks, "What would you do if suddenly you were transported into the very *presence* of God? The reaction we would have determines to a great extent how we are going to **worship** God. One of the most frequently used words in the Old Testament is the word *shachah* which means **to bow one's self down** or **to worship**. The Hebrew OT was translated into Greek, which we call the Septuagint. *Shachah* and words that are similar to *shachah* that emphasize the **bowing down** and **worship** are translated by the Greek word *proskuneo*, and *proskuneo* is also very similar in meaning. It means to **bow down** or to **prostrate one's self** or **to worship**."[21]

Lynn Anderson: "In the Old Testament, Psalm 95:6: 'Come and let us **worship** and **bow down**. Let us **kneel down before** the Lord, our Maker'. Or as Daniel, the prophet, said in Daniel 6:10, 'All the people **knelt down** in the *presence* of God and they **worshiped** God.' Now, that's true in the New Testament as well."[22]

Jimmy Jividen: "God is God, and we are human. God is pure spirit, we are flesh and blood. God is creator, and we are creatures. God is good, and we are sinful. As humans, we **prostrate ourselves before** Him in *humility* because of His power and majesty. **Worship** is the natural response when we, as his creatures, come into His *presence*."[23]

Robert Webber, in his videocassette of *Ancient-Future Worship*, skillfully introduced the gathering protocol for **worshipers** in the assembly.

20. Taylor, Harold. "The Wonder of God"—West Erwin Church of Christ, Tyler, Texas, June 19, 1993, Audiocassette.

21. Neller, Ken. "Revelation and Christian Worship"—Harding University Lectures, Searcy, AR, 1992, Audiocassette.

22. Anderson, Lynn. Harding University Annual Preacher's Forum, Searcy, AR, April, 1994 Audiocassette.

23. Jividen, Jimmy. *More Than a Feeling—Worship That Pleases God*. Nashville: The Gospel Advocate Company, 1999, 34–35.

He quoted Matthew 18:20 which says, "Where two or three are gathered together in My name, there am I in the midst of them." Then he says, "We begin with a glorious procession and we end **on our knees.** Through these actions we are brought into the presence of God and ready to hear the word of the Lord." As the gathering concludes, he says, "Let us **kneel** to *confess* our sins with open hands and hearts."[24]

Roland Bowen: "Each of these three men came into Jesus' *presence* and all three reacted just the same way. You and I have come today to **worship** Him and what does **worship** mean? **'Worship'** comes from those two words. It means **to kiss.** It means **to fall down before** Him. And I hope as we read these things and as we have seen these individuals, it might rekindle in some small way the fire in us that wants to **worship** Him. The word **'worship'** literally means to **fall down**—showing *humility* and showing submission to our Lord and our Savior as we come to **worship** Him."[25]

A. W. Tozer: "To adore God means we love Him will all the powers within us. We love Him with fear, and wonder, and yearning awe. The admonition to 'love the Lord thy God with all thy heart and with all thy mind' (Matthew 22:37) can mean only one thing. It means to adore Him. In no other *presence*, and before no other being can I **kneel** in reverent fear, and wonder, and yearning, and feel the sense of possessiveness that cries 'Mine, mine!' Consecration is not difficult for the person who has met God."[26]

Jay Lockhart: "In Revelation when the Apostle John saw the Lord, he **fell at His feet**... When confronted with deity that's what people did."[27]

Billy Graham: "I **knelt** by my bed and experienced an overwhelming sense of God's *presence*."[28]

24. Webber, Robert. *Ancient-Future Worship*, Wheaton: Institute for Worship Studies, 1999, Videocassette.

25. Bowen, Roland. "Kneeling in His Presence"—Austin Avenue Church of Christ, Brownwood, Texas, October 11, 1998 Audiocassette.

26. Tozer, A. W. "Genuine Worship Involves Feeling." Grand Rapids: *Classic Sermons on Praise*, ed. Warren W. Wiersbe, Kregel Publications, 1994, 146–47.

27. Lockhart, Jay, "You Have Life—Now Grow!" West Erwin Church of Christ, Tyler, TX, July 16, 1995, Audiocassette.

28. Graham, Billy. Dallas: *Unto the Hills—Words of Hope and Comfort*. Dallas: Word Publishing, 1986, 19.

Joseph Carroll: "I simply **knelt down** and quietly mediated upon the fact that I was in the *presence* of the Lamb of God and **worshiped** Him."[29]

Charles Hodge: "At the name of Jesus **every knee should bow.** I **kneel** amazed in His *presence*. Every time in the Bible when people thought someone was God or an angel of God **they hit the floor**, and they were told if it was a man, or if it was an angel to get back up and **worship** God."[30]

Helen Keller wrote a poem:

"In the Garden of the Lord"

At last I come where tall lilies grow,
Lifting their faces like white saints to God.
While the lilies pray, I **kneel** upon the ground;
I have strayed into the holy temple of the Lord.

—*Helen Keller*

Earnest Gentile recorded what Peter Brunner said about *presence*: "Because the risen Lord is really *present*, It behooves the congregation to **drop to its knees**—even now before the King of Kings and the Lord of Lords, as it lauds and glorifies Him."[31]

Roland Bowen: "In Luke chapter 5, this is Simon, who was also later called Peter. Those nets came up so full, they're breaking, and fish fill both boats, and both boats are about to sink. Then and only then, does Simon Peter **fall down at Jesus' knees**. He came into Jesus' *presence* and he **fell at his knees** to **worship**."[32]

Edwin White: "My belief is that hunger and thirst for God is lost to the Churches of Christ in this generation. The awareness of God is lost to the Churches of Christ in this generation."[33]

29. Carroll, Joseph F. *How to Worship Jesus Christ,* Chicago: Moody Press, 1984, 19.

30. Hodge, Charles. "I Stand Amazed", IBC Workshop Florence, AL, September 23, 1994, Audiocassette.

31. Gentile, Earnest B. *Worship God.* Portland: City Bible publishing, 1994, 198.

32. Bowen, Roland. "Kneeling in His Presence"—Austin Avenue Church of Christ, Brownwood, Texas October 11, 1998 Audiocassette.

33. White, Edwin. *A Sense of Presence.* IBC Lectureship, Florence, AL 1994, Audiocassette.

2. What can be accomplished for God through kneeling?

Rick Atchley: "I believe that God wants to accomplish great things for His glory through His churches and I think the key is going to be that we resurrect the power of prayer. Consider this morning a call to arms—**upon our knees.**"[34]

Martin Lloyd-Jones: "I am convinced that nothing can avail, except churches and ministers **on their knees** in total dependence on God. As long as you go on organizing, people will not **fall on their knees** and implore God to come and heal them."[35]

Jay Lockhart: "If I am going to be a disciple maker, I will need God's help, and it will **drive me to my knees**!"[36]

D. L. Moody: "Every work of God can be traced to some **kneeling** form."[37]

Joseph Garlington: "Our battle weapons consist of an odd collection of tears, shouts of joy, and prayers **on bended knee**."[38]

Charles Swindoll: "For a ministry to be effective, it must be a ministry **on its knees**."[39]

Armin Geswein: "To this day the prayer level is the power level of the church. Our prayer meetings give us away. When the **knees are not often bent** the feet soon slide!"[40]

34. Atchley, Rick. "Resurrecting the Power of Prayer"—Up from the Grave—Jubilee Seminar, 1998, Audiocassette.

35. Lloyd-Jones, Martin. Wheaton: *Prayer, Powerpoints.* Victor Books, 1995, 25.

36. Lockhart, Jay. "Make Disciples"—West Erwin Church of Christ, Tyler, TX, April 27, 1997, Audiocassette.

37. Moody, D. L. Wheaton: *Prayer, Powerpoints.* Victor Books, 1995, 56.

38. Garlington, Joseph L. *Worship: The Pattern of Things in Heaven.* Shippensburg: Destiny Image Publishers, Inc., 1998, 86.

39. Swindoll, Charles. "Excellence in Ministry," Insight for Living, KBJS, Jacksonville-Tyler-Longview, Texas, June 24, 1996, Audiocassette.

40. Geswein, Armin. Wheaton: *Prayer, Powerpoints.* Wheaton: Victor Books, 1995, 45.

3. Should we kneel to *confess Jesus as "Lord?"*

The apostle Paul tells us to *confess* Jesus as Lord: "Wherefore God also hath highly exalted him, and given him a name which is above every name: that at the name of Jesus **every knee should bow**, and that every tongue should *confess* that Jesus Christ is Lord, to the glory of God the Father" (Philippians 2:9, 10a, 11 KJV).

"At the Name of Jesus"

At the name of Jesus **every knee will bow**,
He is Lord, He is Lord.
At the name of Jesus every tongue will shout,
He is Lord, He is Lord.

—*Dennis Jernigan*

Quote from *Current Thoughts and Trends*: "You must make your choice. Either this man was, and is, the Son of God: or else a madman or something worse. You can shut him up for a fool, you can spit on Him and kill Him as a demon; or you can **fall at His feet** and call Him 'Lord and God.' But let us not come with any patronizing nonsense about His being 'a great human teacher.'"[41]

Mike Warner is a devout Bible scholar and preacher who effectively communicated the importance of obeying Philippians 2:10, 11. He began a recent article in his weekly church newsletter with the following quote: "*at the name of Jesus* ***every knee should bow*** *and that every tongue should confess that Jesus Christ is Lord.*" He continued by telling of the first century Roman emperors who became obsessed with their own divinity and demanded to be acknowledged by everyone, including Christians, as "Lord and God." Christians, however, acknowledged "Only Jesus as Lord and God." When the Christians refused to **kneel** before Caesar, they "suffered horribly and died as a result."

Mike Warner then emphasized why the command to **kneel** and *confess* Jesus as Lord is essential: "We are told we must **get on our knees** and *confess* openly that 'Jesus Christ is Lord.' It is not a ritual or a law that must

41. Unknown author: *Current Thoughts and Trends*, Quoted from *Mere Christianity*, Escondido, CA, February 1999, 8.

be fulfilled. It's a statement of faith, and surrender, and commitment, and loyalty. It IS a big deal, and you DO have to mean it with all your heart, soul, mind, and strength. It's the acknowledgment that you recognize Jesus as YOUR Lord. Everything else about being a Christian stands on that."[42]

Max Lucado: "My prayer for this book—without apologies—is that the Divine Surgeon will use it as a delicate surgical tool to restore sight, that we will **lay our faces at His pierced feet** and join Thomas in proclaiming, 'My Lord and my God.'"[43]

T. W. Hunt wrote a best-selling book called *The Mind of Christ.* He said, "We will all **bow** to Christ and *confess* His Lordship over our lives (Philippians 2:10, 11). If we are going to do that ultimately, would it not be intelligent to get ahead of the crowd and do it now? It is at the *name* of Jesus that **we will bow.**"[44]

Chuck Kraft proclaims, "He is Lord! He is Lord! He is risen from the dead, and He is Lord! **Every knee shall bow** and every tongue *confess* that Jesus is Lord. We are proclaiming that Jesus is our Lord, not Satan or some human being. We are siding with and enabling in the work of the victorious One to whom **every knee will bow.** We are aligning ourselves voluntarily in His *presence* with 'all who will openly proclaim that Jesus Christ is Lord to the glory of God the Father'" (Philippians 2:10–11 GNB).[45]

The late John Osteen was a very popular preacher at Lake-Wood Church in Houston, Texas. He said, "I tell you there is one *name* that we exalt here, and that is the *name* of the Lord Jesus Christ, and at that *name* **every knee must bow.**"[46]

42. Warner, Mike. "The Big Deal," *Shiloh Family Chronicle* from Shiloh Road Church of Christ, Tyler TX February 4, 2004.

43. Lucado, Max. *God Came Near.* Portland: Multnomah Press, 1987, 17.

44. Hunt, T. W. *The Mind of Christ.* Nashville: Broadman and Holman Publishers, 1995, 144.

45. Kraft, Chuck. "How Acts of Worship Help to Defeat the Devil," *Worship Leader*, June–July 1993, 44.

46. Osteen, John. Lake Wood Church, Houston, TX, INSP, 1992, Audiocassette.

"Your Call is Clear"

I kneel before you, Jesus crucified,
My cross is shouldered and my self denied.
I'll follow daily, closely, not refuse
For love of you and man, myself to lose.

—*John Stott*

Richard Leonard: "Paul, commending to the Philippians Christ's *humility*, declares that his obedience even to death on the cross led to His exaltation; God 'gave Him the *name* that is above every *name*, that at the *name* of Jesus **every knee should bow**, and every tongue *confess* that Jesus Christ is Lord, to the glory of God the Father' (Philippians 2:9–11)."[47]

Tyler Morning Telegraph: "After 11 years of portraying Jesus in Rose Height's Church of God's Easter Pageant, Doug Anderson said 'this would be his final year of playing the part.' After the crucifixion, people representing all races and all walks of life **kneel** at the cross, said Anderson. 'His sacrifice was for all mankind.'"[48]

Johnny Ramsey: "God has given Jesus a *name* that is a above every *name*, and one of these days '**every knee shall bow**, and every tongue shall *confess* Jesus Christ as Lord to the glory of God the Father.' God gave the Son a *name* greater than any other (Philippians 2:8–11). Christ has all authority in heaven and earth (Matthew 28:18). He is verily King of kings (Revelation 17:14) with a kingdom that transcends all others (Revelation 11:15–16). Never has anyone else spoken as He did (John 47:6). Christ Jesus is the Master Teacher of all time (John 3:2). He truly 'hath done all things well' (Mark 7:37). He is 'the blessed and only Potentate, the King of kings, and Lord of lords.' Christ was raised to reign (Romans 15:12). We must take our own wills from the pedestal and joyously **bow before** the Redeemer (Philippians 2:8–11). Christ is our High Priest (Hebrews 7:26), seated on David's throne (Acts 2:30). He alone is worthy to receive blessing, honor and glory (Revelation 5:12). Most of the problems in the

47. Leonard, Richard C. "New Testament Vocabulary of Worship" *The Biblical foundations of Christian Worship*, Robert E. Webber, ed., Nashville: Star Song Publishing Group., 1993, 19–23.

48. "From Death to Life", *Tyler Morning Telegraph*, Tyler, Texas, Sec. 5, March 26, 1999.

church, as well as in our personal lives, would be solved if we realized that Jesus was the ruler of our lives."[49]

Rubel Shelley: "The name of Jesus is an honorable *name*; it is a worthy *name*, and a *name* at which **every knee should bow**."[50]

"All Hail the Power of Jesus' Name"

All hail the power of Jesus' name! Let angels **prostrate** fall!
Bring forth the royal diadem, and crown Him Lord of all.
O, that with yonder sacred throng we **at His feet may fall**!
We'll join the everlasting song, and praise Him Lord of all.

—Edward Perronet, et al.

Mike Warner tells who Jesus is, and what our response should be. He says, "Jesus IS the Lord and King whether a person wants Him to be or not. Paul says, 'God exalted Him to the highest place and gave Him the *name* that is above every *name*, that at the *name* of Jesus **every knee should bow**, in heaven, and on earth, and under the earth, and every tongue confess that Jesus Christ is Lord, to the glory of God the Father" (Philippians 2:9–10). You honor Him, and serve Him, and pay tribute to Him, and you are loyal to Him. You treat Him like a King, Your King! Otherwise, you are a traitor. We all have a King! A Christian is one who acknowledges Jesus as Lord, and King of his life."[51]

Frederick Kubicek gives several facts about Jesus with Scripture references. He says, "The choice, as in all things is ours, but His direction to us is clear. We are to **worship** Him—we are to physically **prostrate ourselves before** Him. Is not He the Author and Finisher of our faith (Hebrews 12:2), the Rock of our salvation (1 Corinthians 10:4), the Lion of the tribe of Judah (Revelation 5:5), the Brightness of the Father's glory (Hebrews 1:3), the Bright and Morning Star (Revelation 22:16), the Light of the World (John 1:9), the Messiah (John 1:41), Mighty God (Isaiah 9:6), the Deliverer (Rom. 11:26), the Holy One of God (Mark 1:24), the Judge (Acts

49. Ramsey, Johnny. "The Master Teacher," *The Restorer*, Mesquite, TX, September/October 1999, 9–10.

50. Shelley, Rubel. *I Just Want to be a Christian*. Nashville: 20th Century Christian, 1986, 219.

51. Warner, Mike. "Reflections," *Shiloh Family Chronicle*, Shiloh Road Church of Christ, Tyler, Texas, July 12, 1998, 1.

10:42), the Great High Priest (Hebrews 3:1), our Mediator (1 Timothy 2:5), the Purifier (Malachi 3:3), the Head of the Church (Colossians 1:!8), the Desire of All Nations (Haggai 2:7), the very Word of God (Revelation 19:3)? 'Worthy is the Lamb who was slain to receive power, and wealth, and wisdom, and strength, and honor, and glory, and praise' (Revelation 5:12). 'Ascribe to the Lord the glory due His name. **Worship** the Lord in the splendor of His holiness. Tremble before Him, all the earth. The Lord reigns' (1 Chronicles 16:29).'"[52]

In summary, God says, "**Fall down before** his son and **kiss his feet** before his anger is arroused and you perish. I am warning you—his wrath will soon begin. But oh, the joys of those who put their trust in him." (Psalm 2:12—The Living Bible).

"O Holy Night"

O holy night! The stars are brightly shining,
It is the night of the dear Savior's birth;
Fall on your knees! Oh hear the angel voices,
O night divine, O night when Christ was born!

—*John S. Dwight*

4. Should we kneel to *confess sins* before God?

Dr. Jay Lockhart is a devoted disciple of the Lord, a diligent student of the Bible, and a dedicated preacher. In a sermon on "**Worship**", he brought to our attention that, "Seeing the invisible allows us to see God. *It allows us to be transformed*—It's true. In I Corinthians 14:24–26, Paul said that when the unbeliever is in your assembly and you are **worshiping** right, in the correct way, the way God wants us to, that the unbeliever **will fall down and worship** God. He will become a believer. We will see God. We will be transformed. We will evangelize. We ought to **bow our heads before** God **and fall on our faces** and *repent of our sin. The reason that we do not see our sin* and; therefore, there is no repentance *and there is no confession* is because we have not seen a Holy God. The heavenly hosts **fell before** God. Have we?"[53]

52. Kubicek, Frederick C. "Worship Him Now" Accessed 1/15/01. Website: www.unlimitedglory.org/needful.

53. Lockhart, Jay. "Worship is the Solution: What is the Problem?"—West Erwin Church of Christ, Tyler, TX, October 9, 1994, Audiocassette.

R. A. Torrey: "It is through prayer that *my sin is brought to light, my most hidden sin.* As I **kneel before** God and pray, 'Search me, Oh God, and know my heart: Try me, and know my thoughts: And see if there be any wicked way in me' (Psalm 139:23–24). God shoots the penetrating rays of His light into the innermost recesses of my heart, and *the sins I never suspected are brought to view.* In answer to prayer, *God washes me from my inequity and cleanses me from my sin* (Psalm 51:5)."[54]

Rick Atchley: "I was reading recently of the famous Cane Ridge revival in Kentucky in 1803, where 25,000 people came out to hear preaching, where preachers just stood up on stumps and started preaching. And some people just **fell down** *because of their conviction over sin.* How do you explain things like this? The interesting thing is that the Cane Ridge revival was led by Barton W. Stone, considered to be one of the founders of the Churches of Christ in America."[55]

Bill McCartney: "We'll be **on our knees** in *humility*, and on our feet in unity, *confessing* the *sins* of our nation, and seeking heaven's throne for an outpouring of the Holy Spirit in revival, it is called 'Stand in the gap—a sacred assembly of men.'"[56]

Jimmy Chalk Hooper prayed, "May each of us get **down on our knees** *and confess our sins,* and rejoice that the tomb was empty on that day."[57]

Kay Arthur asks, "What do we need to do? I believe we need to call the people into the churches. I believe that we need to assemble our congregations. I believe we need to sanctify ourselves, to set ourselves apart and cleanse ourselves, and to *confess our sins.* I believe we need to get **on our knees** and cry out to a holy God."[58]

54. Torrey, R. A. *How to Pray.* New Kensington: Whitaker House Publishing, 1961, 20–27.

55. Atchley, Rick. "If My People will Humble Themselves"—Richland Hills Church of Christ, Ft. Worth, Texas, 1998, Audiocassette.

56. McCartney, Bill. Quoted by David Brandt in "Positioning Yourself for Revival Prayer" *Pray Magazine,* Issue 2, Sept/Oct 1997.

57. Hooper, Jimmy Chalk. Personal notes, Saturn Road Church of Christ. Garland, TX, September 24, 1995.

58. Arthur, Kay. *The Day of the Lord* Presentation of *Precept Ministries,* Chattanooga, TN, May, 1995 Audiocassette.

"He is Lord"

He is Lord, He is Lord!
He is risen from the dead, and He is Lord!
Every knee shall bow, every tongue *confess*
That Jesus Christ is Lord.

—*Alton Howard*

Jeff Christian: "One of the main things that I think we have neglected over all else, is the act of *confession*. One of the ways we as Christians avoid God is by talking about God, and study prayer without actually **falling to our knees**. It is one thing to acknowledge the beauty of a summer sunset without ever acknowledging the Creator of that sky."[59]

Jay Lockhart: "**Worship** must be a time of *confession*, and repentance, and renewal, because we are in the *presence* of a God who has *no tolerance of sin* or of evil. And we are seeking to be God's people. And we are seeking to be like God. And consequently, we must **prostrate ourselves before** Him."[60]

Dan Flournoy: "When Isaiah saw the Lord God, he was **driven to his knees** in prayer, and was caused to recognize his own weak and *sinful* condition."[61]

Ancil Jenkins, in the *Synoptic Gospels,* tells about Peter's initial encounter with Jesus. He said, "There were so many fish, both boats would not hold them and they were in danger of sinking. Peter **fell to his knees before** Him and *confessed his sins*. This is the normal reaction of men who come into God's *presence* (Gen. 18:27; Exodus 20:19; Job 42:6; Isaiah 6:5)."[62]

59. Christian, Jeff. "Making Theology Practical"—ACU Lectures, Abilene, TX, 1997 Audiocassette.

60. Lockhart, Jay. "The Kingdom's Growth"—West Erwin Church of Christ, Tyler, TX Audiocassette, Dec. 19, 1993.

61. Flournoy, Dan. "A Vision of God," Nashville: *The Gospel Advocate*, Feb. 2000, 6.

62. Jenkins, Ancil. "This is My Son," Miami: *Synoptic Gospels*, Gospel Advocate's 1998-1999 Bible Study Lessons, 1998, 22.

"Jesus, Worship Jesus"

As You wash the stains of my *guilty heart*,
Till I'm clean in every part,
I **kneel down**, I **kneel down**.
Wash away my shame, my pain, my pride,
Every *sin* that I once denied.
I **kneel down**, I **kneel down**.

—*Graham Kendrick*

5. Should we kneel to *ask forgiveness and cast our cares* upon Him?

Larry Lea offers this advice: "Stop trying to think your problem through or wait it through. Only when you are desperate enough to get **down on your knees**, *confess* your needs to Him, and call on His name, will He speak peace to you and your problems. That's your next step. Take it now, my friend. Take it now."[63]

Pat Boone: "I got **down on my knees** and prayed for God to *forgive* me and to restore not only my marriage and family, but my relationship with Him."[64]

We **kneel**—and all around us seems *lower* . . .
We **kneel**: how *weak*! We rise: how full of power!

—*Trench, Richard C.*

Rick Atchley: "I will never forget the day I got **down on my knees** in my office and said, 'God *forgive* me. I want You more than I want to be recognized as an outstanding preacher.' Two things happened: First, I started growing again. Second, I became a better preacher."[65]

James Watkins recommends, "Get **on your knees**, take it to God and *leave it*."[66]

63. Lea, Larry, *Could You Not Tarry One Hour*. Lake Meary: Creation House Strang Communications Company, 1996, 15.

64. Boone, Pat. *Article Title unknown, (The National Enquirer?)* April 1995.

65. Atchley, Rick. "Personal Spiritual Growth." West Monroe: *Image Magazine*, 1995.

66. Watkins, James. "Giving God our Best in Worship." FHU Lectures, Henderson, TN, 1994, Audiocassette.

Jeff Christian: "It is one thing to read passages in the Bible about prayer, and another thing entirely different to actually pray. And it takes true grit to **fall to your knees** in praise and thanksgiving to God, begging His *forgiveness.* "[67]

Bill Streckert, M.D: "To 'walk in Him', I think it helps to start the day **on your knees.**'" (Quoted from Wednesday morning physician's Bible study—Personal communication).

Max Lucado offers this advice when we feel troubled: "The next time a stone seals shut your *exit to peace*, think about the empty, musty tomb outside of Jerusalem. And when you see it, **bow down**, enter quietly, and look closely, for there on the wall, you may see the charred marks of a divine explosion."[68]

"Anxious Prayers"

We **kneel** down in sheer desperation.
Just trust on the Lord and believe,
For whatever you ask in faith and love,
In abundance you are sure to receive.

—*Helen Steiner Rice*

Charles Stanley says he learned this from "Daniel in the lion's den": "To find God during your hardship, *go to the portal* Daniel knew best: **Go to your knees.**"[69]

Jack Reese: "When we see who we are; when we see ourselves in our *sinfulness*; when we see ourselves in relation to God as utterly unworthy, then all we can do is surrender: surrender our will, surrender our lives, surrender our future, surrender our conversations, surrender our marriages, surrender our homes, surrender our cars, surrender our thoughts, and all those things to **lay ourselves before** God. So, as the psalmist said

67. Christian, Jeff. "Making Theology Practical." ACU Lectures, Abilene, TX, 1997, Audiocassette.

68. Lucado, Max. "The Hidden Tomb." *Wineskins Magazine* 1993, 12.

69. Stanley, Charles. "Mighty in Spirit," *In Touch magazine*, Atlanta, GA, July 1998, 13.

in 95:6, 'Come, let us **worship** and **bow down**, let us **kneel before** the Lord our Maker.'"[70]

The Dallas Morning News: "Reggie White, a licensed minister, is finally realizing a dream this week in New Orleans: to reach the Super Bowl and use the stage to spread the word of God to a world-wide audience. When White decided to sign with Green Bay prior to the 1993 season, he was ridiculed for citing a conversation with God as the reason for his move . . . "I was really confused, White says, 'I went down in my basement, and I prayed half the night. I prayed and I cried, because I wanted to make the right decision. I'd been saying, 'I want to go to a team that's going to win the championship. I knew then that when I got **off my knees**, this was the right decision."[71]

The Kneeling Christian, written by an unknown Christian, says, "I read in eager tones St. Matthew 21:21–22. 'If ye have faith and doubt not, all things whatsoever you ask in prayer, believing, ye shall receive.' I **fell on my knees**, and as I **bowed before** my Lord, what thoughts surged through my mind, what hopes and aspirations flooded my soul! God was speaking to me in an extraordinary way. This was a great call to prayer."[72]

Byron Hanspard, the professional football player, said, "The decision that I have made has come through much prayer, much seeking, just really **on my knees**."[73]

Wyatt Fenno has learned that, "Many of these people have been converted to 'the Church', rather than to Christ. For 40 years, many have heard a gospel that has been off-balance. These experiences have forced me **to my knees** more than once."[74]

70. Reese, Jack. Harding University Annual Preacher's Forum, Searcy, AR, April 1994, Audiocassette.

71. Caldwell, Dave. "*Reggie White Talks the Gospel Like He Plays—With Heart,*" *Dallas Morning News*, January 24, 1997, Section B, 8.

72. *The Kneeling Christian.* Author: (An Unknown Christian) Grand Rapids: Zondervan Publishing House, 1945, 17.

73. Hanspard, Byron. "All-American running back on entering the NFL," *Tyler Morning Telegraph*, Tyler, TX December 31 1996, Section 4, 1.

74. Fenno, Wyatt E. "Forty Years of Preaching 'the Church'," *Image Magazine*, Kingfisher, OK, May/June 1996, 40.

"Kneel at the Cross"

Kneel at the cross,
Leave every care,
Kneel at the cross,
Jesus will meet you there.

—*Charles E. Moody*

Dale Evans Rogers, wife of Roy Rogers said, "An indescribable peace washed over my heart. As I got **up from my knees,** I felt as though a crushing burden had fallen from my back and shoulders. How great it was to be alive and free. "How great Thou art!"[75]

The *Tyler Morning Telegraph* had these headlines: "Woman found frozen at home out of hospital" Chicago (AP)—Victoria Moryn, a widow who lived alone was discovered Jan. 17 in her unheated home, and **kneeling** barefoot in an inch-thick layer of ice from leaking pipes. Police who found her thought she was dead until one touched her and she moaned, 'Oh, God' in Polish, her native language. Moryn was released Tuesday and is staying with friends."[76]

Major Ian Thomas: "One night in November, I got down **on my knees before** God, *and I just wept in sheer despair*. God that night; simply focused upon me the Bible message of 'Christ who is our life.' I got up the next morning to an entirely different Christian life."[77]

Larry Lea: "If you do not consistently pray one full hour every day but would like to learn how, take the prayer secrets the Holy Spirit has taught me **on my knees** and begin to practice them. As you learn to pray the way Jesus taught us to pray, your prayer *life will no longer be a frustrating, hit-or-miss experience*; instead, tarrying with the Lord an hour in prayer will actually become easy and natural."[78]

75. Evans, Dale. *The Woman at the Well*, Tappin: New Jersey: Fleming H. Rebell Company, 1970.

76. Chicago (AP) *Tyler Morning Telegraph*, Tyler, TX, February 11, 1994.

77. Thomas, Major Ian M. *The Saving Life of Christ*. Grand Rapids: Zondervan Publishing House, 1964, 6–7.

78. Lea, Larry. *Could You Not Tarry One Hour*? Lake Meary: Creation House Strang Communications Company,1996, 7.

Charles Stanley shares this: "*Every time I find myself in a strain*, I know what to do: Get **on my knees**, *confess* unto God, and just reaffirm who I am in Him and who He is in me."[79]

"Every Time I Kneel to Pray"

Every time I **kneel** to pray
I open up my heart to the Lord.
Every time I close my eyes
I feel the sweet embrace of my Lord.

—Phillip Organ

Gene Barron: "*When life knocks you **to your knees***, you're in a perfect position to pray."[80]

Dryden Sinclair tells this about a friend: "He pledged himself to pray a half an hour every morning and a half an hour every night. He said the first night he was able to get away by himself, he got **down on his knees**, took a look at his watch, and started to pray. He prayed and thought about everything he should pray for. He looked at his watch, and he'd prayed only 12 minutes."[81]

Corrie Ten Boom says, "As a camel **kneels before** his master to have him remove his burden at the end of the day, *so **kneel** each night and let the Master take your burden*."[82]

Edwin White: "One of the things that has helped me tremendously in working for an inner-city church—we're not an inner-city church anymore—but *for twenty-three years I struggled just to keep it alive*—due to things that I could not control, that kept slipping. And many years ago I came to the conclusion that if God doesn't build a house, they labor in vain who build it, so I **fell upon my knees** and prayed. The work that I've

79. Stanley, Charles. "The Spirit Filled Life—The Abiding Life." *In Touch Ministries*, Atlanta, GA, 1992, Audiocassette.

80. Barron, Gene. *Invited into His Presence*. Joplin: College Press Publishing Company, 1997, 122.

81. Sinclair, D. W. Dryden. *Increasing Our Faith*. Wichita Falls: Published by Western Christian Foundation, Inc., 1980, 143.

82. Ten Boom, Corrie. *Don't Wrestle, Just Nestle*. Old Tappan: Fleming H. Rebell Company, 1978, 79.

done has taught me humility and has been so hard, but one of the benefits is, I have drawn closer to God."[83]

Charles Stanley asks, "What is it that results in the greatest qualities of our life? What is it that produces those characteristics that are most Christ-like? It isn't ease, comfort, pleasure, and plenty. It is hardships, trials, difficulties, and adversities of every type. *Those things that drive us to the word and* ***drive us to our knees*** *drive us to God.*"[84]

"The House of Prayer"

The house of prayer is no farther away
Than the quiet spot where you **kneel** and pray
For all of our errors and failures
That we made in the course of the day
Are freely forgiven at night time,
When we **kneel** down and earnestly pray
The first thing every morning
And the last thing every night.

—Helen Steiner Rice

6. What about kneeling to *commune* with God and Jesus?

Robert Webber says, "And finally, *the body becomes an expression of* ***worship*** *as we walk to the communion table,* and then **kneel** to receive the bread and the wine. This is a powerful act symbolic of our desire to receive Christ. Any and all body gestures in **worship** should be done with intention and purpose. They are not mere external trappings, but are ways of bringing external actions in line with internal feelings."[85]

Charles Holbrook *humbly shared this at a men's Wednesday noon Bible study* in Tyler Texas: "We feel close to God when **we kneel** at the altar, and remember His sacrifice as we partake of the bread and the wine."[86]

83. White, Edwin. "A Sense of Presence, Part III." IBC Annual Workshop, Florence, AL, September 24, 1994, Audiocassette.

84. Stanley, Charles. "The Spirit Filled Life—The Abiding Life". *In Touch Ministries*, Atlanta, GA, 1992, Audiocassette.

85. Webber, Robert E. *Worship is a Verb.* Nashville: Star Song Publishing Group, 1992, 104.

86. Holbrook, Charles "Trying to be a Christian" Men's Wednesday noon Bible study, @ Marvin UMC, Tyler, Texas May 1, 1996.

Gary Selby asks, "When we pray, what if we invited any who wished - **to kneel before** the Lord? And when we celebrate the Lord's invitation to 'come to the table, what would happen if we actually got out of our seats and came to the table?"[87]

Mike Cope explains it well. He said, "*Jesus came to deal with the sin that clogs the arteries of all of our hearts.* With that word of Christian *confession* we come today to the communion table, asking God to bring tears to our eyes, to bring us **to bended knee**, to do whatever He needs to do to create in us pure hearts. As we pass the bread and as we pass the cup today, it is a reminder that God has actually delivered us."[88]

Mike Dent made a wonderful comparison when he said, "Like the woman at the well, *He welcomes us today to satisfy that spiritual thirst.* He invites us to come to this table and to **kneel**, to bring our thirst for *forgiveness*, our need for love, our thirst for hope, and our thirst for a new beginning. Our Lord wants to fill our cup today to make us whole. Our Lord invites us to eat and drink and then go to work as a witness."[89]

Fanny Crosby wrote "I Am Thine, O Lord" to help us surrender and commune with God.

"I Am Thine, O Lord"

O the pure delight of a single hour
That before Thy throne I spend
When I **kneel** in prayer,
And with Thee my God,
I *commune* as friend with friend!

—*Fanny J. Crosby*

7. What about kneeling in *humility* before God?

Charles Hodge tells us how to awaken worship: "Beloved, today if you want to awaken **worship**, get your heads back in the Book, get **your knees**

87. Selby, Gary. "Journey To Worship: A Personal Journey," *Image Magazine*, 1994, 32.

88. Cope, Mike. "Heart Surgery—Part I." Highland Church of Christ, Abilene, TX, May 11, 1997, Audiocassette.

89. Dent, Mike. "A Wild Woman is Won." Marvin UMC, Tyler, TX, March 7, 1999, Audiocassette.

down on the floor, get your hearts into the lost, and may God help us to *humble* ourselves before our King."[90]

Denny Boultinghouse explains our need for brokenness. He said, "When people truly understand that they are unworthy before God, they do not stand before Him stressing their works. Instead, they **fall to their knees** confessing their brokenness."[91]

Speaking of "*humility,*" remember: the word *"humble"* in 2 Chronicles 7:14 is from the Hebrew word *kana*', which means "**to bend the knee.**" In his book, *Worship: The Pattern of Things in Heaven*, Joseph Garlington quotes the verse: "If My people who are called by My name will **humble themselves** and pray, and seek My face and turn from their wicked ways, then I will hear from heaven, will forgive their sin, and will heal their land."[92]

Richard Foster, in his book *Celebration of Discipline*, says, "**Kneeling, bowing the head, lying prostrate** are postures consistent with the spirit of adoration and *humility*."[93]

Keith Brooks: "Man is the only created being who **bows in *humility*** and adoration."[94]

"All to Jesus I Surrender"

All to Jesus I surrender,
Humbly at His feet I bow;
Worldly pleasures all forsaken,
Take me, Jesus, take me now.

—*J. W. Van de Venter*

90. Hodge, Charles, "I Stand Amazed." IBC Workshop, Florence, AL, September 23, 1994, Audiocassette.

91. Boultinghouse, Denny. "A Broken and Contrite Heart," *Image Magazine*, Vol. 12, No. 2, March–April 1996, 5.

92. Garlington, Joseph L. *Worship: The Pattern of Things in Heaven*. Shippensburg: Destiny Image Publishers, Inc., 1998, 8–10.

93. Foster, Richard J. *Celebration of Discipline*. San Francisco: A Division of Harper Collins Publishers, 1988, 169.

94. Brooks, Keith L. *The Cream Book of Sentence Sermons*. Chicago: Moody Press, 1938, 159.

Rick Atchley expressed it very clearly: "God is not moved by men of standing. God is moved by men of **kneeling**—that pray, and seek His face."[95]

Don Crawford presented a very inspiring sermon that *humbled* the hearers when he described the "city of the living God" as recorded in Hebrews 12:18–24 and in Revelation. He also pointed out in verse 24 that, "You have come to Jesus, the mediator of a new covenant." Before reading the last part of the verse regarding the blood of Jesus, he said, "We're standing in the center of the city of God and what we see next . . . this is what's going to make us **fall down on our knees** and praise God." Don Crawford then read about the blood that was shed by Jesus and what it means to all of us. With deep *humility* and emotion he said, "I **fell on my face** as I was reading this. I am not worthy of one drop of this blood."[96]

Dick Sztanyo: "We must never forget that before we can stand before men, we must **kneel before** God."[97]

Ralph Gilmore: "Each of us needs to encounter God as fully as is humanly possible because of the strength and encouragement which it brings to each **worshiper** of God. In this series of lectures, I intend to examine what it means that God is sovereign, or Absolute Ruler. Let me hasten to claim my own fragility. I **bow my knees before** him who is the subject of these lectures. *I am aware of my own relative insignificance* in comparison to his Majesty."[98]

Dan Dozier: "**Bowing down** indicates reverence, awe, *humility, and submission* to the great, powerful, and majestic God Almighty. When the Israelites, for instance, realized that God was at work to deliver them from Egyptian captivity and bondage, they **bowed down and worshiped.** After the Lord talked in front of Moses at Mount Sinai, Moses **bowed to the**

95. Atchley, Rick. "If My People Will Humble Themselves—Revive Us Again #2", Richland Hills Church of Christ, Ft. Worth, TX, June 21, 1998, Audiocassette.

96. Crawford, Don. "Recapturing New Testament Awe." West Erwin Church of Christ, Tyler, TX, November 16, 2003, Audiocassette.

97. Sztanyo, Dick. "Praying as Elijah Prayed," *The Restorer*, Mesquite, TX January 1994, 8.

98. Gilmore, Ralph. "Sovereignty of God," FHU Lectures, Henderson, TN, 1997, 159.

ground at once and **worshiped.** Just before his death, Moses said to the Lord, '**At Your feet,** they will **all bow down.**'"[99]

When Robert Webber hears the Scriptures read he wants to **bow before** God. He says, "Nehemiah (chapter 8) tells how the people listened, raised their hands, **bowed down**, and wept. When I hear the scriptures read, I want to respond in faith to the God of the covenant. I want to **bow before** Him **and worship** Him as my Lord and Savior."[100]

Jim Goll: "Try posturing yourself **on bended knees** in dependency, *humility*, brokenness, and **worship before** the Lord. Join with me in asking the Lord to anoint us to be His velvet warriors—those who come forth in unity and brokenness, **on bended knees**, resolved in their hearts to take territory for the King."[101]

Gordon McDonald: "**Worship** is, above all, submission to God. **Worship** is best understood by those who appreciate majesty, submission, and *humility.* Rather, **worship is a bowing**, a saluting, if you please, in recognition of an absolute Power, and one's unconditional submission to it. The (worship leader's) objective should be singular: help the people **to bow** and then draw them to the living God."[102]

Walter Scott, in *The Gospel Restored* wrote, "Sir Frances Bacon was a man who, for his greatness of genius and compass of knowledge, did honor to his age and country. We find him **prostrating himself before** the great mercy-seat, and *humbled* under afflictions which at that time lay heavy upon him, and we see him supported by the sense of his integrity, his zeal, his devotion, and his love to mankind."[103]

99. Dozier, Dan. "Worship is a Verb." The Church That Connects III Seminar, San Antonio, TX, August 6, 1994, Audiocassette.

100. Webber, Robert. *Worship is a Verb*, Nashville: Star Song Publishing Group, 1992, 73.

101. Goll, Jim W. *Kneeling on the Promises*. Grand Rapids: Chosen Books, 2000, 34.

102. McDonald, Gordon. "The Constance of Worship," *Worship Leader*, October–November 1992, 25–26.

103. Scott, Walter. *The Gospel Restored.* Joplin: College Press Publishing Company, 1836, 105.

Jimmy Jividen: "Because of the glory, the majesty, the power, the holiness and the nature of God, we **worship**. We stand in awe. We hide our face in *humility*. We **fall before** His *presence* in submission. He is God."[104]

"Have Thine Own Way Lord"

Whiter than snow Lord,
Wash me just now,
As in Thy presence **humbly I bow**.

—Adelaide A. Pollard

Joseph Garlington: "When you **worship**, you are **prostrating yourself before** God. You are submitting your intellect, your future, and your arrogance to God. You are literally submitting your sense of superiority to God."[105]

Bob Hackler, the creative architect who designed the Saturn Road Church of Christ in Garland, Texas, wrote, "As you walk into the assembly area the ceiling drops to eight feet above the floor. If I had my preference the ceiling would have dropped to about five feet above the floor. We should **humble ourselves** with **bowed head** and **bowed heart** as we enter to **worship**. 'Come let us **bow down** and **worship**.' (Psalm 95:6). '**Bow down then before** the power of God now, and He will raise you up on the appointed day' (1 Peter 5:6 Jerusalem Bible). Be reminded as you walk under the 'low' ceiling of the *humble* service we are to bring to one another and to God. '*Humble* yourselves before the Lord and he will lift you up' (James 4:10)."[106]

Richard Foster: "**Kneeling, bowing the head**, and **lying prostrate** are postures consistent with the spirit of adoration and *humility*."[107]

104. Jividen, Jimmy. *More Than a Feeling—Worship That Pleases God*. Nashville: The Gospel Advocate Company, 1999, 85.

105. Garlington, Joseph L. *Worship: The Pattern of Things in Heaven*. Shippensburg: Destiny Image Publishers, Inc., 1998, 10.

106. Hackler, Bob. Architect of The Saturn Road Church of Christ, Garland, TX *To Be Reminded pamphlet* given at the Open House.

107. Foster, Richard J. *Celebration of Discipline*. San Francisco: Harper Collins Publishers, 1988, 169.

E. M. Bounds, speaking of the apostle Paul, says, "He **kneeled down** and prayed. **Kneeling** in prayer was Paul's favorite attitude, *humility*, and intensity before Almighty God."[108]

Stafford North emphasizes that, "True **worship** springs from submission. After all, that's the nature of **worship**, isn't it? Didn't we talk yesterday about how **worship** is **kissing**? How **worship** is honoring by submission and **prostrating oneself**? So we **worship** because we are submissive to God. If we aren't *humble* in His sight, if we don't have a spirit of **prostrating ourselves** in His *presence*, of **throwing ourselves on the ground at His feet**, it's going to be vain, isn't it? We must submit to God. We have to have a sense of His *presence*, a sense of God being with us."[109]

Daniel Morgan prepared the congregation by saying, "God is our God and we are His people. Let us **bow before** Him. 'Lord, we surrender and submit to Your will.'"[110]

Charles Hodge says, "It's the glorious privilege of the church to embrace God and to preach the sovereignty of God. I **kneel** amazed! I **kneel** amazed at the creative power of God Almighty. Our text says he *humbled* himself. Oh, how we need to *humble ourselves*. No wonder God raised Him King of Kings and Lord or Lords. No wonder when we're **down on our knees,** every tongue should *confess* Jesus to the glory of God. I **kneel** amazed tonight, beloved, because of what all this has done for me."[111]

Joseph Garlington: "If you're going to please God, then be prepared to be *humiliated* **before** your peers at some point. Why? Because the word '**worship**' doesn't mean just 'to sing'. It also means 'to **prostrate yourself**' and '**to bow down.**'"[112]

108. Bounds, E. M. *Prayer and Praying Men*. Chicago: Moody Press, 1980, 257.

109. North, Stafford. "Training for Worship Part II". International Bible College, Florence, AL, September 23, 1994, Audiocassette.

110. Morgan, Daniel. "Missionary who gave main prayer." West Erwin Church of Christ, Tyler, TX May 17, 1998, Audiocassette.

111. Hodge, Charles. "I Stand Amazed," IBC Workshop: "Worship Styles of the 90's," Florence, AL, September 23, 1994, Audiocassette.

112. Garlington, Joseph L. *Worship: The Pattern of Things in Heaven*. Shippensburg: Destiny Image Publishers, Inc., 1998, 120–21.

8. What do Bible scholars say about *kneeling and the heart* ?

Jack Reese is a gifted Bible professor who expressed it well. He says, "Growing up in the Fifties, I remember times that Godly men and women would **kneel** in prayer in the assembly. I believe there is a direct connection between *the knee and the heart.*"[113]

Gary Thomas: "*Walking is good for the heart*—**kneeling** is better."[114]

Jack Lewis points out that, "This concept of **worship** begins with the physical gesture that shows homage, but the body can be **prostrated** *while the heart remains unbowed. It is the broken and contrite heart* that God does not despise (Psalm 51:7). The physical gesture is only of value when accompanied by a true, *humbling* of the spirit which seeks above all else to do the will of the Lord. The Lord is near to the broken-hearted and saves the crushed in spirit." (Psalm 34:18).[115]

Jeff Clark: "I think *the man's heart is not right before* God unless when he comes to **bow down** and offer service and **worship** unto Jehovah, that he is ready to say, 'Lord, not my will, but thine be done.'"[116]

Tommy King reveals that **kneeling** helps shape who we are. He says, "When we get into **kneeling** and when we get into raising of hands, those things can be formational issues that shape who we are and what we do and how we express ourselves."[117]

This quote by Mike Cope also occurs with **kneeling** to "commune with God," but it is very appropriate also with "**kneeling** and the heart." He says, "*Jesus came to deal with the sin that clogs the arteries of all of our hearts.* With that word of Christian *confession* we come today to the communion

113. Reese, Jack. Preston Road Church of Christ, Dallas, TX, January 2, 1994, Audiocassette.

114. Thomas, Gary: Marquee at Lane Chapel UMC, Tyler, TX, October 11, 1995.

115. Lewis, Jack P. "Old Testament Word Studies in Worship,"—FHU Lectures, Henderson, TN, 1994, 232–36.

116. Clark, Jeff. "Worship: Unauthorized Acts." Twenty-third Annual Florida School of Preaching Lectureship, Lakeland, FL, 1998, 400–401.

117. King, Tommy. "Evangelistic Worship." ACU Lectureship: Behold He Comes!, 1999, Audiocassette.

table asking God to bring tears to our eyes, **to bring us to bended knee**, to do whatever He needs to do to *create pure hearts in us*."[118]

"Lord, We Come Before Thee Now"

Lord, we come before Thee now:
At Thy feet we **humbly bow**.

—*W. Hammond*

Pope John Paul II, referring to sermons preached in the early part of the twentieth century exclaimed, "It could be said that these sermons, which correspond perfectly with the content of Revelation in the Old and the New Testaments, 'they went to the very heart of man's inner world. They stirred his conscience. They **threw him to his knees**.'"[119]

Jay Lockhart asks, "Isn't it true that the greater our faith, the greater our dependence on prayer? And isn't it true that the greater our dependence on prayer, the greater will be our faith? The learning of the word of God will produce faith. And, yes, the Word of God in our hearts **brings us to our knees** in prayer: Faith and prayer!"[120]

Gene Barron: "**Bowing** and **kneeling** are common practices for Christians today. **Bowing, kneeling**, and lifting holy hands are mentioned in the imperative verb tense in Psalm 95:6, 'Come let us **worship** and **bow down**; let us **kneel before** the Lord our Maker.'"

In I Timothy 2:8, "Therefore, I want the men in every place to pray, lifting up holy hands, without wrath and dissention."[121]

John Scott suggests letting God control your heart. He said, "Perhaps, you have never really *handed Him those controls of your heart*, and **bowed** in acquiescence to Him."[122]

118. Cope, Mike. "Heart Surgery—Part I." Highland Church of Christ, Abilene, TX, May 11, 1997, Audiocassette.

119. Pope John Paul II. *Quoting the Threshold of Hope*, Rome: Italy, 1994.

120. Lockhart, Jay. "From the Heart of Tyler." Vol. 27. No. 48 Tyler, TX, Dec. 5, 1996, 1.

121. Barron, Gene. *Invited into His Presence*. Joplin: College Press, 1977, 120.

122. Scott, John. "The Mystery of Worship"—Saturn Road Church of Christ, Garland, TX, June 13, 1993, Audiocassette.

"Into the Heart of Jesus"

Bowing in full surrender
Low at his blessed feet,
Bidding Him take, break me and make,
Till I am molded and meek.

—Oswald J. Smith

Denny Boultinghouse: "*Broken and contrite hearts* are the basis for the radical lifestyle to which we are called. And such *hearts* must begin with self-examination and such examination will force us **to our knees before** our righteous and holy God."[123]

Lynn Anderson: "**Worship** is the primary business of the Church: To **fall on our knees** and to adore God, to hug Him, **to kiss** Him, to listen to Him, to honor Him, to reach for Him. And somehow, in **worship**, we are sensitized to God and we are reoriented to the invisible, the real world. *Who can look into the eyes of God and his heart not be changed.* **Worship** *changes our hearts, and when our hearts are changed our character changes.*"[124]

Charles Sibert made several good points that are worth remembering. He began by asking, "*Does He rule and reign in our hearts?* Does He rule and reign in this church as King ascended on His throne? Do our **knees humbly bow** and **do our hearts bend** and break into submission? That's the challenge. It may be the day of declaring that He is the one, in fact, who has all authority and, therefore, **you must bow**. And for those of us who have already **bowed the knee** but have dared to get up in proud defiance again, perhaps it is time for us **to come to our knees** again. The only appropriate response in His presence is to confess that He is Lord and He is King!!"[125]

Henry Blackaby tells how studying Scripture, praying **on your knees**, communicating with fellow church members, and the awareness of God working in the circumstances of your life—can help you to experience

123. Boultinghouse, Denny. "A Broken and Contrite Heart." *Image Magazine*, Vol. 12, No. 2, March–April, 1996, 5.

124. Anderson, Lynn. Harding University Annual Preacher's Forum, Searcy, AR, April 1994, Audiocassette.

125. Sibert, Charles. An Elder in the Highland Church of Christ—Abilene, Texas, September 12, 1993, Audiocassette.

God and to know the will of God. He says, "In your life personally, God has provided the Holy Spirit who will guide you in your life as you open the word of God. He will begin to tell you, from the word of God, what God is doing. When you go to pray, the Holy Spirit again is your enabler. He will use the word of God, but He'll also enlighten and cause your heart to begin to pray in the direction of the activity of God.

"When you get up **off your knees** and out of the quiet time and you start to walk out into the circumstances, you're going to see some things that only God can do. You're going to see people drawn to the Lord. You're going to see people who are feeling the impact of the call of God on their life. And what God said to you in the closet, He's starting to unfold in the life of the church, in the people you are meeting, the places you are going, and in the circumstances that begin to surround your life.

"And the spirit of God will take the circumstances, and cause your heart to know that this is something only God can do. And then when you function in the life of the people of God, the spirit of God is going to begin to equip the people of God, and as they share with you, you begin to know the will of God."[126]

Jack Hayford, author of the song "Majesty", says, "God reveals Himself to **those who bow before** Him and seek Him. *If you seek Him with all your heart, you will find Him.*"[127]

Kay Arthur: "It is fitting to develop **calluses on your knees**—*but never on your heart.*"[128]

Daniel Morgan prayed, "Father, although our physical facilities don't permit us to **kneel**, *our hearts are* **bowed before** you and **our spirits are laid prostrate before** You."[129]

David Dykes preached on Ephesians 3:14–21: He said, "As Paul is dictating this letter, right there in that prison cell on that rough stone floor, the

126. Blackaby, Henry. *Experiencing God: Knowing and Doing the Will of God.* Sunday School Seminar, Atlanta, GA, 1990, Videocassette.

127. Hayford, Jack. *Worship His Majesty.* Ventura: Regal Books, 2000, 9.

128. Arthur, Kay. "Love That Lingers—An Interview with Kay Arthur," *In touch Magazine*, May 1999, 10.

129. Morgan, Daniel. "Missionary—Main prayer." West Erwin Church of Christ, Tyler, TX, August 24, 1997, Audiocassette.

apostle Paul **goes to his knees** and prays this prayer. You know, there is something special about **kneeling** when you pray. Sometimes the attitude of your heart is demonstrated by your body language. How many of us can **kneel**, but simply refuse to do so? The posture of Paul's prayer ought to teach all of us something **about bowing before** the Lord."[130]

John Burton summarizes:

"Kneeling and the Heart"

I may as well **kneel down** and **worship** gods of stone
As offer to the living God a prayer of words alone.
For words without the heart, the Lord will never hear;
Nor will He to those lips attend whose prayer is not sincere!

—Burton, John

9. What about kneeling to *pray for revival*?

Ken Joines told an interesting story about how to start a revival. He said, "The famed evangelist, Gypsy Smith, gave this advice to someone who asked, 'Gypsy, how do you start a real revival?' Gypsy said, 'Take a piece of chalk and **get down on your knees** and draw a circle all the way around you. Then throw the chalk away and pray this to God: 'Dear God, send a revival to everyone in this circle.' And don't leave until He answers your prayer.' He said, 'that's how you start a revival meeting.' And you know, some of that is true when it comes to worship. How do you produce worshiping people? It starts with me. Unless you realize that you are face to face with the Father, none of those mechanical things matter very much."[131]

Rick Atchley has concluded that, "Revival never starts by organizing. It always starts by agonizing. *Revival* happens when people get **on their knees**, humble themselves, seek God, and ask Him to come."[132]

The *Dallas Morning News* headline read, "Millions forego food, **hit their knees** for *revival*." "More than 1,000 people got on **their knees** in

130. Dykes, David. "Prayer that Moves Heaven." Green Acres Baptist Church, Tyler, TX, April 30, 1995, Audiocassette.

131. Joines, Ken. "Worshiping God." 55th Annual Pepperdine University Bible Lectures, Anaheim, CA, 1998, Audiocassette.

132. Atchley, Rick. "And Pray and Seek My Face." Richland Hills Church of Christ, Ft. Worth, TX, 1998, Audiocassette.

a Houston hotel ballroom last week to pray and fast for a national, *spiritual revival.* Meanwhile, people from all over North America, representing at least 60 denominations, joined them on the Internet and at 4,100 satellite sites in churches, homes and civic centers. They were part of a movement called Fasting & Prayer, started by Campus Crusade for Christ founder, Bill Bright. Organizers estimate that 1 million to 2 million people participated."[133]

Ron Owens, in his book *Return to Worship*, says, "*The motto of the Welch Revival* of 1904-05 was '**Bend the church** and save the world.'" This motto apparently inspired him and his wife to write the words of the song: "Bend me Lower":

"Bend Me Lower"

Bend me lower,
lower down at Jesus' feet,
Holy Spirit, **bend me**
till you work's complete.

—Ron & Patricia Owens[134]

The Kneeling Christian, authored by an unknown Christian, says, "The Lord Jesus, now in the Heavenlys, beckons us to **fall upon our knees** and claim the riches of His grace. All *revivals* have been the outcome of prayer."[135]

Kay Arthur: "After I had spoken at "Prayer and Fasting '97", Jack and I were **on our knees** in a circle with Bill Bright, Senator Sam Brownback of Kansas, Peter Marshall, and other leaders who were praying that the church would return to the Word of God and, thus, to the fear of God, and walk in truth. What would happen if we first **got on our knees** and asked God to show us how to reach our friends, and neighbors?"[136]

133. Stewart, Marcus, Kovach Caldwell, and Reese Dunkin. "Hungering for God—Word and Deed," *Dallas Morning News*, November 21, 1998, 2G.

134. Owens, Ron. *Return to Worship.* Nashville: Broadman and Holman, 1999, 68.

135. Unknown. *The Kneeling Christian.* Grand Rapids: Zondervan Publishing House, 1945, 26.

136. Arthur, Kay. "A Message from Kay Arthur," *Precept Ministries*, January 1998, 1–3.

Ron Floyd asks, "What if *God is raising up a mighty spiritual revival* right here in this fellowship that could be used in bringing America once again **to its knees**?"[137]

An *Austin Avenue Church Newsletter* read, "The theme for this year's retreat was 'LIGHT THE FIRE,' which is the title to a song that is popular to our teens. Note the words to the song: 'I stand to praise You, but I **fall on my knees**.' This HAS to change us!"[138]

10. What do Bible scholars say about kneeling in *1 Corinthians 14:25* ?

(The only time the word "**worship**" is used in 1 Corinthians—Does it include **bowing the knees**?)

Jay Lockhart asks, "Didn't Paul emphasize in I Corinthians 14 that when the unbeliever is in the assembly, where Christians are **worshiping** God in the right way, didn't he emphasize that the church would be edified, and the unbeliever would **fall down** and **worship** God saying, 'Surely, God is among you?'"[139]

Harold Taylor, with great insight, says, "**Worship**, then, is not just a window through which we see God. **Worship** is a mirror by which I see myself. No wonder in 1 Corinthians, Chapter 14, Paul says that when the pagan comes into the assembly and he understands what is going on he will see himself as God sees him, and he will recognize that he must give an account of himself. God will reveal the secrets of his heart. He will **fall on his face** and **worship** God and say that 'God is in your midst.' These people are having an encounter with God, and are doomed and lost, and need forgiveness. That is the power that comes through the actions of **worship**."[140]

137. Floyd, Ron. "Being Filled with the Holy Spirit." First Baptist Church, Spring Hill, AR, 1995, Audiocassette.

138. Austin Avenue Church of Christ *Newsletter*, Brownwood, Texas, May 3, 1998.

139. Lockhart, Jay. "Rediscovering the Dynamics of Worship—Part III". Florence, AL, September 24, 1994, Audiocassette.

140. Taylor, Harold. "Worship: The Missing Jewel." IBC Annual Workshop, Worship Styles of the 90's, Florence, AL, September, 1994, Audiocassette.

Carl Holladay wrote a good commentary on 1 Corinthians 14:25. He says, "The missionary intent of the assembly is clear. The church should realize that its **worship** is actually proclamation, and if effectively done, will result in the conversion of unbelievers: **falling on his face**, he will **worship** God. Paul's hope is that the unbeliever will actually see that 'God is among you,' a proclamation of God's presence."[141]

Larry Bridgesmith: "We must remain vigilant to use **worship** forms consistent with Biblical freedoms which connect with God-seekers who are not familiar with 'the way we have always done it.' Those traditions may feel good to us but lack any capacity to bring unbelieving outsiders **to their knees** and exclaim, 'God is really among you!' (1 Corinthians 14:24–25). With expectant hearts, anticipating a holy encounter with the Creator, let us enter into **worship** defined only by the Holy One who is the sole focus of our **worship**."[142]

Richard Oster also explained 1 Corinthians 14:25: He said, "And the secrets of his heart will be laid bare. So he will **fall down and worship** God, exclaiming, 'God is really among you!' Paul's description in 1 Corinthians 14:25 portrays unbelievers whose hearts are touched in such a way by the words of God that they are led to **fall down** and **worship** God."[143]

When Everett Ferguson commented on 1 Cor.14:25, he said, "After the secrets of the unbeliever's heart are disclosed, that person will **bow down before** God and **worship** Him, declaring, 'God is really among you.'"[144]

John Frame: "An unbeliever should be able to understand what is taking place, so that he will **fall down** and **worship**, exclaiming, 'God is really among you'" (1 Corinthians 14:25).[145]

141. Holladay, Carl. *The First Letter of Paul to the Corinthians—The Living Word Commentary*. Austin: Sweet Publishing Co., 1979, 184.

142. Bridgesmith, Larry. "Putting the 'Meaning' in Meaningful Worship," *Wineskins*, October 1997, 10–11.

143. Oster, Richard E. Jr. *The College Press NIV Commentary of I Corinthians*. Joplin: College Press Publishing Company, 1995, 331.

144. Ferguson, Everett. "Some Contemporary Issues Concerning Worship in the Christian Assembly," *Inman Forum*, 1998, 23.

145. Frame, John M. *Worship in Spirit and Truth*. Phillipsburg: Presbyterian and Reformed Publishing Company, 1996, 8.

Jay Lockhart wrote, "Paul argued that when an unbeliever attends our assemblies and understands the teaching, 'He is convicted', 'The secrets of his heart are disclosed, and so he will **fall on his face** and **worship** God, declaring that God is certainly among you.' He will become a believer (1 orinthians 14:24–25).[146]

Lynn Anderson: "I guess one of my favorite verses in the NT is in 1 Corinthians—Chapter 14, verse 25. 'But if an unbeliever comes in he will be convinced by all that he is a sinner and the secrets of his heart will be laid bare, so he will **fall down** and **worship** God exclaiming, "God is really among you.""""[147]

"His Name is Wonderful"

Love and adore Him,
bow down before Him,
His name is Wonderful,
Jesus my Lord.

—*Audrey Mieir*

Lindsey Garmon: "In 1 Corinthians 14:24, 25 the word *proskuneo* is used. The stranger **fell down** and **worshiped**—*proskuneo*. And he said, 'God is really among you.' We know He is here with us in our assembly, and we can be aware of His *presence by faith*. We should **bow before** Him and offer **worship** and praise to His name."[148]

Henry Halley quoted the apostle Paul who said, "the unbeliever will **Fall down on his face** and **worship** God" (1 Corinthians 14:25). "Power to make unbelieving visitors **fall down on their faces** and **worship** God; O for such today, instead of dead formalism on one hand, and irreverent monkey-business on the other!"[149]

146. Lockhart, Jay. "What Happens in Church," *The Visitor*, West Erwin Church of Christ, Tyler TX August 18, 1988, 1.

147. Anderson, Lynn. Harding University Annual Preacher's Forum, Searcy, AR, April 1994, Audiocassette.

148. Garmon, Lindsey. "Worship and the Assembly"—Church of Christ South, Corpus Christi, TX, 1995, Audiocassette.

149. Halley, Henry H. *Bible Handbook*, Grand Rapids: Zondervan Publishing House, 1927, 549.

Jay Lockhart: "I've mentioned recently to you on more than one occasion, that in 1 Corinthians 14, right in the middle of the **worship** passage, I am intrigued by the fact that the Apostle Paul gives instruction to the church, and right in the midst of that he says, 'And if there be an unbeliever in your midst, 'he will **fall down** and **worship** God.' I take that to mean he'll be converted. Why? Because of what he sees."[150]

Jack Reese is convinced that **bowing the knees** was practiced in the first century by everyone in the Corinthian assembly, because the unbeliever who **falls down** and **worships** God is reflecting what he sees the others doing. Dr. Reese says, "I believe the critical verse is 1 Corinthians 14:25. Paul says, 'The unbeliever will see what's going on, and will hear what is being said, and will experience what's being experienced in these assemblies. After the secrets of the unbeliever's heart are disclosed, Paul says, that person is going to reflect what he sees. That person will **bow down before** God and **worship** Him, declaring 'God is truly in your midst.' It is the same expression that we've seen in the Old Testament: 'God is truly in our midst.'"

Jack Reese then clarifies a very important issue. He recalls someone saying, 'Well yes, but that **worship** word *proskuneo* there refers only to the outsiders.' "It is as if Paul was saying that the outsiders can **worship**, but the Christians cannot. No, the outsiders are reflecting what they see and experience. And like the Christians, as they see the secrets of their hearts revealed, they will **bow down** and **worship,** because they recognize that God has met them there. There has been an encounter with God, and in that context, encouragement can go on, and then edification takes place."[151]

Furman Kearley agrees with Jack Reese that the "unbeliever" at Corinth who **falls down** and **worships** God is reflecting what he sees the others doing. He says, "Now, in terms of the situation in 1 Corinthians, Chapter 11, 12, 13, and 14, it is true that you do not have a '**worship**' word used with respect to the specific activities that were done there, but you have the specific activities required to be done in this particular situation. You

150. Lockhart, Jay. "The Assembly." West Erwin Church of Christ, Tyler, TX, December 4, 1994, Audiocassette.

151. Reese, Jack. Harding University Annual Preacher's Forum, Searcy, AR, April, 1994, Audiocassette.

have, of course, in I Corinthians 14:25, '**falling down on his face**, he will **worship** God,' which describes the unbeliever. Seeing and understanding what is being said, he will **fall down** and **worship** God. This would seem to reflect that others who were there would have the same reaction—So this would seem to indicate that what he would do in the Corinthian assembly, is what the others were doing in the Corinthian assembly."[152]

11. Should we kneel before God for *spiritual preparation* ?

Mike Warner **kneels** for spiritual preparation. He says, "I go to my office before I come in here to worship and preach, and I spend some time **on my knees**."[153]

J. R. Baxter, Jr. quotes Jesus at Gethsemane as He prepared Himself for the cross: "Thy will not mine."

"I Love My Savior Too"

Kneeling to him I pray,
'Thy will not mine,'
I love my Savior too.

—J. R. Baxter, Jr. (1933)

Robert Webber **kneels** for spiritual preparation. He says, "As I prepare to **worship**, I **kneel** in silence and pray the Lord's Prayer. I savor each line and apply its meaning to my own life. I need time to lay my burdens **at the feet of Jesus**. I need to be still and know that God is God. I need to hear Him say 'You are forgiven. You are my child. I love you.'"[154]

Jack Hayford, the preacher who wrote the popular song "Majesty", had a big decision to make early in his ministry and he was able to make it after he and his wife went **to their knees** in prayer. "'Honey,' I said to my wife,

152. Kearley, Furman. "Is All of Life Worship?" IBC Annual Workshop, Florence, AL, September 22, 1994, Audiocassette.

153. Warner, Mike. "Acceptable Worship." Shiloh Road Church of Christ, Tyler, TX, 1993, Audiocassette.

154. Webber, Robert E. *Worship is a Verb*. Nashville: Star Song Publishing Group, 1992, 46–47.

'you stay here with the baby and **kneel**. I'm going by myself to pray. If we don't pray right now, this will beat us.'"[155]

"Waiting on the Lord" can be an act of spiritual preparation. Stuart Hamblen wrote:

"Teach me Lord, to wait"

Teach me Lord, to wait **down on my knees,**
Till in your own good time you will answer my pleas.
Teach me not to rely on what others do,
But to wait in prayer for an answer from you.

—*Stuart Hamblen*

Chris Bullard asks, "Can the physical impact the spiritual? Sure! What is baptism except a physical act with a spiritual dimension? What is communion except a physical act with a spiritual dimension? What is **kneeling in prayer,** except a physical act with a spiritual dimension?"[156]

Marilyn Connelly: "*Resolve each day to converse with no person until you have talked to God and to do nothing with your hands until you have been* **on your knees.**"[157]

Zig Ziglar: "If you already know Him as Lord and Savior, it is my prayer you will make the total commitment to serve Him in everything you do, so you will enjoy more of what God has to offer in this world. Where ever you are, and what ever you are doing, just quietly close your eyes and if possible, get **down on your knees.**"[158]

Billy Graham: "I was *called to preach* one day when I was on the golf course. I **knelt down** and prayed, 'Lord, I'll do what you want me to do, and I'll go where you want me to go.'"[159]

155. Hayford, Jack. "Preparing Myself," *Mastering Worship.* Portland: Multnomah Press, 1990, 36.

156. Bullard, Chris. "The Physical Side of Being Spiritual." ACU Lectureship, Abilene, TX, No. 208, 1996, Audiocassette.

157. Connelly, Marilyn. "Pray Without Ceasing—Ongoing Know Your Bible," *The Gospel Advocate*, August 1999, 11.

158. Ziglar, Zig. *Confessions of a Happy Christian.* Gretna: Pelican Publishing Company, 1978, 194.

159. Graham, Billy. *Larry King Live.* CNN, June 26, 2005.

Billy and Ruth Graham's daughter, Anne Graham Lotz, wrote a book called *The Vision of His Glory*. She quotes the apostle John as our example: "John said, 'When I saw him, I **fell at his feet** as though dead' (Rev 1:17). To **fall at the feet** of Jesus as though dead means there is no more argument about His will, no more rationalization of your behavior, no more excuses for our sin! **Falling prostrate** means you are silent before Christ—dead silent. As John **lay prostrate at the feet** of Jesus, silent and still, he was surrendered for service. Then God gave him his assignment: 'Write, therefore, what you have seen, what is now, and what will take place later (Revelation 1:19).'"[160]

"The Purpose in Gethsemane"

All those who journey, soon or late,
Must pass within the garden's gate;
Must **kneel** alone in darkness there,
And battle with some fierce despair,
'Not my will but Thine.'

—*Ella Wheeler Wilcox*

Darlene Matthews spoke from the Garden of Gethsemane on Easter morning in 1987. She told how Jesus prepared Himself for the cross at Gethsemane. She also pointed to a large rock and said, "When Jesus went to **bow down** at that rock, He went determined not to get up until His will was surrendered. There was a battle that went on at this place. It was a battle between the Father's will and Jesus' will. There is no other way for you to live for God except for you to give Him your will. You will have to have a Gethsemane in your life. You must get **down on your knees** and forever give your will to the Father. You must make up your mind. Jesus did not need to pray for Himself at the cross. He prayed at Gethsemane."[161]

Florence Littauer is a popular speaker who is convinced that, "We need some kind of experience that has brought us **to our knees**, a power point in our lives when we said, 'Lord, I can't do it. You're going to have to do it through me.'"[162]

160. Lotz, Anne Graham. *The Vision of His Glory—Finding Hope through the Revelation of Jesus Christ.* Dallas: Word Publishing, 1996, 39–41.

161. Matthews, Darlene. Live broadcast from the Garden of Gethsemane, KLTV Channel 7, Tyler, TX, April 3, 1987.

162. Littauer, Florence." Counseling the Depressed." Personality Plus Seminar, 1984, Audiocassette.

R. A. Torrey: "I dropped **upon my knees** and cried to God for help. It seemed as if God stood right there and had put out his hand and touched me."[163]

Jack Hayford usually **prostrates himself before worship**: "King David wrote, 'Search me O Lord and know my heart. Try my thoughts, and see if there be some wicked way in me, and lead me in the way everlasting.' When it comes to preparing myself for **worship**, that's my desire as well. I usually **prostrate myself** and 'call on the Lord,' as the Psalms put it, I'm ultimately looking for a new perspective on myself, a revelation of pride or self-centeredness, or an insight into what God would have me do next in ministry."[164]

William Ayer: "The quickest way to get a church on its feet is to get it **on its knees**."[165]

Preparation for Gethsemane:

"Night With Ebon Pinon"

When Christ, the Man of Sorrows,
In tears, and sweat, and blood,
Prostrate in the garden,
Raised His voice to God.

—*L. H. Jameson*

Dale Evans Rogers, or Mrs. Roy Rogers, wrote a book called *Finding the Way*. She said, "A friend of mine gave me an old-fashioned **kneeling** bench, and many a time, when the pressure becomes almost more than I can bear, that hallowed little altar has been a place of refuge and a re-fueling station. I always find God there, waiting for me to come. Of course, the whole house is His—but that little altar and **kneeling** bench are especially set aside for Him and for me, and for our quiet communion together."[166]

163. Torrey, R. A. *How to Pray*. Chicago: Old Landmark Publishing 1961, 16.

164. Hayford, Jack. "Preparing Myself," *Mastering Worship*. Portland: Multnomah Press, 1990, 39–40.

165. Ayer, William. *The Complete Speaker Source Book*. Grand Rapids: Zondervan Publishing House, 1996, 59.

166. Evans, Dale. *Finding the Way*. Old Tappan, NJ: Fleming H. Revell Company, 1969, 120–21.

12. Should we kneel before God for *healing*—physically and spiritually?

Betty Davis says, "Jairus, the ruler of the synagogue, came and **fell at Jesus' feet**, earnestly pleading with Him to come and heal his dying daughter. Jairus said, 'My little daughter is dying. Please come and put your hands on her so that she will be healed and live.' Jesus got up and went with him and so did His disciples."[167]

Ed Glasscock wrote, "The leper approached Jesus in an attitude of **worship** and faith in His ability to heal him." He explains that, "The leper **'bowed down'** (*prosekunei*, imperfect of *proskuneo*), indicating either an act of **worship** or a demonstration of respect. Unlike some other commentators, this writer will assume the first."[168]

Jim Goll: **Worship is about bending the knee.** In Matthew 8:2–3, we are given the account of the leper whom Jesus cleansed: 'Behold, a leper came in to Him, and **bowed down.** We find **prostration** coming once again before petitioning. I do not believe that this was just cultural and ethnic protocol."[169]

Charles Stanley makes a good point. He says, "The distance between spiritual defeat and victory is about 12 inches. This is the distance for us to **drop to our knees** in prayer to God. When we take our frustrations and disappointments to the Lord in prayer, we acknowledge our need for Him. We *confess* that we cannot solve life's problems on our own."[170]

Betty Davis says, "The woman came up behind Him and touched the hem of His garment. Immediately, her bleeding stopped. And He turned to the crowd and asked, 'Who touched me?' And Jesus turned and He saw the woman. Then, seeing that she could not go unnoticed, the woman came, trembling, and **fell at His feet.** Then He said to her, 'Take heart daughter.

167. Davis, Betty. Harding U.—Women's Student Lecture, Searcy, AR, 1995, Audiocassette.

168. Glasscock, Ed. *Moody Gospel Matthew Commentary*. Chicago: Moody Press, 1977, 184.

169. Goll, Jim W. *Kneeling on the Promises*. Grand Rapids: Chosen Books, 2000, 23.

170. Stanley, Charles. *In Touch Ministries,* August 1999, 1.

Your faith has healed you.' We need to put our faith into action. Being patient and waiting on the Lord is an action."[171]

Jeff Berryman: "And what do we do on these Sundays? Why do we come? To respond: We **fall on our knees, and on our faces**. We come to be loved. We come in all our ugliness, in soiled lives, in sin-filled moments—to find God finding us."[172]

"Come to the Savior Now"

Come to the Savior now,
He gently calleth Thee;
In true repentance **bow,**
Before him **bend the knee.**

—John M. Wigner

Bill Crouch, a Bible Study Fellowship teacher, asked, "Where are we going to find our strength? We are going to find it **on our knees**." (Personal Communication 1995).

Jim Goll: "The Amplified Bible says, 'She came **kneeling**, and **worshiped** Him, and kept praying, "Lord, help me!"' Yes, she got what she came for. But she came **on bended knee**. Does Jesus deserve anything less?"[173]

When we **kneel down** to pray
The Lord understands
And He gives us new strength
By the touch of His hands

—Helen Steiner Rice

171. Davis, Betty. "The Sick Woman." Harding U. Women Student Lecture, Searcy, AR, 1995, Audiocassette.

172. Berryman, Jeff. "Confessions of a Song Leader," *Wineskins*, September 1992, 26.

173. Goll, Jim W. *Kneeling on the Promises*. Grand Rapids: Chosen Books, 2000, 24.

13. Some are ***not physically able*** to kneel before God. If we are able, we should!

David Dykes shares with us that, "Janette Davis was in her early 40's and was stricken with severe rheumatoid arthritis. Her poor knees were so enlarged and swollen that she was seldom able to come to church. She was in such constant pain. And I remember one afternoon I went by their home to visit. I came to the back and was getting ready to knock on that sliding glass door when I couldn't help but look in there and see, to my surprise, that she was **kneeling** on those arthritic knees."[174]

In a personal communication with "Doc" Wright, he said: "I'm glad to see you men still get **on your knees** to pray. I do too, and I'm 92!"

James LeFan: "Stephen, in Acts 7:59, was praying while they stoned him to death. As the stones fell he said, 'Lord Jesus, receive my spirit.' Then he **fell on his knees** and cried with a loud voice, 'Lord, lay not this sin to their charge', and he fell asleep. The body died, and the soul went to be with the Lord."[175]

James Hobson reminds us that, "By faith Jacob, when dying, blessed each of the sons of Joseph, **bowing in worship** over the head of his staff (Heb. 11:21 RSV). The statement that Jacob **bowed in worship** over the head of the staff is from the Septuagint in Genesis 47:31. The Hebrew text says, 'Israel **bowed himself** over his bed.' The Septuagint translators rendered the Hebrew for 'bed' as 'staff.'"[176]

David Dykes, in his sermon "Prayer that Moves Heaven," tells this very inspiring story about a lady who wishes she could kneel, but is not physically able. He began by asking, "Have you ever heard of Joni Eareckson Tada? When she was 17 years old, she was a beautiful, active teenager. But she had a diving accident, and she broke her neck, and was paralyzed. She's a quadriplegic today, and many of you have seen the painting of Joni where she puts a paintbrush in her mouth and paints beautiful scenes and calligraphy. Each takes her many, many hours to do. She's a delightful

174. Dykes, David. "Prayer that Moves Heaven." Green Acres Baptist Church, Tyler, TX, April 30, 1995, Audiocassette.

175. LeFan, James. "Taking Care of Your Soul." West Erwin Church of Christ, Tyler, TX, October 4, 1998, Audiocassette.

176. Hobson, James. *The Letter to the Hebrews*. Austin: R. B. Sweet Co., 1952, 154.

Christian and she speaks at many, many conferences. And I was reading recently where she was at a conference, and the speaker at the conclusion of his message asked everybody there to get **on their knees** before God. And, everybody went **to their knees**, except of course Joni Erickson Tada. She could not. And commenting on that night, she said it broke her heart and she literally wept because she could not go **to her knees.**

She prayed a prayer that night and these are the words that she said: 'Lord Jesus, I can't wait for the day when I will rise up on resurrected legs. The first thing that I will do then is to **drop on grateful, glorified knees** and **worship** you.' Here's a woman who cannot **kneel** but wishes she could."[177]

Scotty Ratliff reassured everyone by saying, "If you are physically able, and you would like to, I want to invite you to join me. You can just **kneel** in front of the pew where you are sitting. If you are not physically able or would feel uncomfortable, it's O.K. You don't have to. Now, with *humble* hearts, let us go to our Heavenly Father in prayer."[178]

Dan Dozier appropriately said, "I realize that that there are some who cannot **kneel** because of physical weakness or infirmity. Also, age sometimes creates health problems that make it impractical for us to **kneel.** But if we are able, the Biblical perspective is that we **kneel.**"[179]

14. *Does God care* whether we kneel or not? What do Bible scholars say?

Mike Warner asks, "How do we come to God? 'God opposes the proud but gives grace to the *humble.*' (1 Pet. 5:5). We come to God **on our knees**, or not at all."[180]

James LeFan: "What are you doing for the health of your soul? Do you study your Bible regularly? Do you pray often, and sometimes a long time

177. Dykes, David. "Prayer that Moves Heaven" - Green Acres Baptist Church, Tyler, TX, April 30, 1995, Audiocassette.

178. Ratliff, Scotty. Worship Leader & Youth Minister, Austin Avenue Church of Christ, Brownwood, TX, November 29, 1992, Audiocassette.

179. Dozier, Daniel A. "Worship is a Verb." The Church That Connects III Seminar, San Antonio, TX August 6, 1994, Audiocassette.

180. Warner, Mike. "Words of Life," *Tyler Morning Telegraph,* September 2, 1994, Sec. 2.

to God? Not two minutes, but do you **get on your knees**, and struggle in prayer with Him? I hope, beloved, you're taking care of your soul. If you don't take care of it, it will be forever lost."[181]

John Frame: "To **worship** God is also to **bow before** His absolute, ultimate authority."[182]

Robert Webber, in his book *Worship is a Verb*, recorded an interesting quote from St. John Chrysostom, a fourth-century bishop from Constantinople. He said, "We insult God when we do not recognize Him and His transcendent majesty. What of the angels, the cherubim, and seraphim? Do they reason about the nature of God? No, **they fall down** and **worship** Him with great trembling."[183]

David Sain: "Do you recall the scripture that Jay Lockhart read? 'That God has exalted Him and given Him a *name* above every *name*, that at the *name* of Jesus **every knee should bow** and every tongue should *confess*.' Think about it as we sing this song. You are going to *confess* His name and **you are going to bow** and honor Him as Lord, some time—either now, while there's time and it counts, or when He comes and it's too late!"[184]

In a personal communication with Henry Blackaby, he said, "It is difficult to walk into the presence of God and not **kneel**. If we just strut into the presence of God and not **kneel**, that's arrogance, and He is not pleased."

J. Cleo Scott: "A person may deny God now but will confess Him later. 'As I live, says the Lord, **every knee shall bow** to Me and every tongue shall *confess* to God' (Rom. 14:11)."[185]

181. LeFan, James. "Taking Care of Your Soul." West Erwin Church of Christ, Tyler, TX, October 4, 1998, Audiocassette.

182. Frame, John M. *Worship in spirit and Truth*. Phillipsburg: Presbyterian and Reformed Publishing Company, 1996, 4.

183. Webber, Robert. *Worship is a Verb*. Nashville: Star Song Publishing Group, 1992, 111.

184. Sain, David. "Jesus is the Pre-eminent One." West Erwin Church of Christ, Tyler, TX, November 3, 1994, Audiocassette.

185. Scott, J. Cleo. "Are We Fools?" *The Restorer*, Mesquite, TX, March/April 2000, 3.

Alan Redpath: "Before Him, **every knee shall bow**, and every life in the process of time must either bend or break. It must either **bend before** the throne or be broken before the justice of an almighty God."[186]

Mike Warner: "The Creator, Father-God, demands that Jesus, His son, be acknowledged as Lord by every creature in heaven and on earth. **Every knee is to bow** and every tongue is to *confess* Him as Lord to the glory of God (See Phil. 2:9–11)."[187]

John Scott: "Some one said, 'God loves a broken heart, a wet eye, and **a bent knee.**'"[188]

Kevin Eltife: "We must live every day, every hour, every minute in a manner that would make God proud. We must get **down on our knees** and pray for God's help."[189]

Poem from pamphlet, "My Statue of Liberty" *One Nation Under God*: "On lonely Golgotha stood a cross with my Lord raised to the sky, and all who **kneel** there live forever as the saint can testify."[190]

The Kneeling Christian: "Shall we get **on our knees before** God and allow His Holy Spirit to search us? Are we sincere? Do we really desire to do God's will? Do we really believe His promises? If so, will it not lead us to spend more time **on our knees before** God?"[191]

Adam Clark: "Quoting from Ephesians 3:14, Paul says, 'I **bow my knees** to the Father.' The apostle prays to God the Father that they may not *faint*; and he **bows his knees** in this praying. What can any man think of

186. Redpath, Alan. *Blessing Out of Buffetings*. Old Tappan: Fleming H. Revell Company, 1965, 90.

187. Warner, Mike. "Words of Life," *Tyler Morning Telegraph*, Dec. 11, 1992.

188. Scott, John. Saturn Road Church of Christ, Garland, TX, 1995, Audiocassette.

189. Eltife, Kevin. *Mayor's Prayer Breakfast.* Harvey Hall Convention Center, Tyler, TX May 4, 2000.

190. "My Statue of Liberty," *One Nation Under God Pamphlet*, Printed and distributed by Churches of Christ in Tyler, TX 1991.

191. Unknown. *The Kneeling Christian.* Grand Rapids: Zondervan Publishing House, 1945, 27.

himself, who, in his addresses to God, can either *sit* on his seat or *stand in the presence of his Maker, and Judge of all men*?"[192]

Garland Elkins: "They forsook the Lord God of their fathers who brought them out of the land of Egypt, and followed other gods - the gods of the people round about them, and **bowed themselves** unto them and provoked the Lord to anger."[193]

Dan Dozier reminds us that, "Psalms 95:6 says, 'Come, let us **worship and bow down**. Let us **kneel before** the Lord, our maker.' And God Himself declares, 'Before Me, **every knee will bow**.' That's in Isaiah 45:23 and Paul picks it up in Romans, Chapter 14, verse 11. God said, '**All mankind will come and bow down before** Me.'"[194]

Brenda Terrell asks, "Isn't it past time for us, those of us who profess to believe, to **bow down before** Him literally, physically, to **bow down on our knees** to the King of Kings? As Romans 14:11 declares, "'As surely as I live,' says the Lord, '**every knee will bow** to me; every tongue will *confess* to God.'"[195]

Rick Atchley: "The Bible says that one day **the knee will bow**. That is not the issue. The only issue is when. We're not talking today about whether or not you'll be *humbled* before God. We're just talking about when."[196]

Gene Barron: "A lot of **kneeling** keeps one in good standing with God."[197]

Roland Bowen: "In **falling before** Jesus **and worshiping** Him they knew what it meant to be in His *presence*, because they saw Him as He is, the all powerful Creator, the Almighty One. It is time to come into His presence

192. Clark, Adam. *Clark's Commentary, Vol. VI Romans/Revelation*, New York: Abingdon Press, January 9, 1832, 446.

193. Elkins, Garland. "What the Bible Says About Restoration." Cane Ridge Restoration Lectureship, Harrodsburg, KY. 1998, Audiocassette.

194. Dozier, Daniel A. "Worship is a Verb." The Church That Connects III Seminar, San Antonio, TX, August 6, 1994, Audiocassette.

195. Terrell, Brenda. "Bow Down Before Him." *Heartlight Magazine*, Austin, TX, 1998, Online: http://www.heartlight.org/feature/sf_98071_bow.html. Accessed 2000.

196. Atchley, Rick. "If My People Will Humble Themselves." Richland Hills Church of Christ, Ft. Worth, TX, June 21, 1998, Audiocassette.

197. Barron, Gene. *Invited Into His Presence* Joplin: College Press Publishing Company, 1997, 122.

in *humility.* God can change your life. He can make the difference in your life. But He can't make that difference in your life - He will not - until you **bow the knee** to Him, until you **fall before** Him."[198]

"On Zion's Glorious Summit"

Shout vic-t'ry now and hail the Lamb,
And **bow before** the great I AM,
And **bow before** the great I AM.

—John Kent

Larry Lea: "Abraham knew God's longsuffering, compassionate nature, 'Would the Lord destroy the city if He found 10 righteous there?' May the pledge of God, Himself, echo in our ears and **drive us to our knees**: 'I will not destroy for 10's sake!'"[199]

15. *Yes, God cares*: God has sworn by Himself, "Unto Me every knee shall bow"

In Isaiah 45:22–23, God took an oath regarding "**every knee shall bow**," and He swore by Himself that He will never change the "pattern." He said, "Look unto me, and be ye saved, all the ends of the earth: for I am God, and there is none else. I have sworn by myself, the word is gone out of my mouth in righteousness, and shall not return, that unto me **every knee shall bow**" (KJV). He swore by Himself because there was no greater to swear by.

The apostle Paul brings the oath forward in Romans 14:10b–12 and emphasizes that we shall all be standing before the judgment seat of Christ when we "give account" regarding "**every knee shall bow**." Romans 14:10b–12 says, "For *we shall all stand before the judgment seat of Christ.* For it is written, As I live, saith the Lord, **every knee shall bow** to me, and every tongue shall *confess* to God. So then every one of us *shall give account* of himself to God."

The only change in the NT is that the oath now includes His Son, Jesus who has been "highly exalted" and given "a name which is above every

198. Bowen, Roland. "Kneeling in His Presence." Austin Avenue Church of Christ, Brownwood, Texas, October 11, 1998, Audiocassette.

199. Lea, Larry. *Could You Not Tarry One Hour?* Lake Meary: Creation House Publishing, Strang Communications Company, 1996, 184–88.

name that at the name of Jesus **every knee should bow** . . . and that every tongue should confess that Jesus Christ is Lord to the glory of God the Father" (Phil. 2:10–11).

16. Does the *main "worship" word* in the NT include bowing the knees?

(What do Bible scholars say? To properly answer this question, a quote used previously may be placed here, but most quotes are displayed for the first time).

Jay Lockhart: "It is difficult for people who feel self-sufficiency to come into a place where they are **going to bow down**, which is what **'worship'** means, remember, before God."[200]

James Pullin: "John 4:23–24 declares that we must **worship** God in spirit and in truth. In doing so, we must reverence His glory, **fall prostrate before** Him, expose all our faults and errors to Him and repent of them. It is during these times that we realize we are very insignificant, yet God loves and cares for us all as unique individuals."[201]

John Scott: "**Worship** is an attitude of *humbleness*, brokenness, awe, fear, and reverence, but it is also coupled with an action—A physical action of **bowing low**, of **kissing toward**—and *using my lips to praise* God Almighty. It is attitude and action."[202]

Howard Norton: "It seems to me that one of the best ways to discover what **worship** means is to go to the original language and look at the words that have been translated from the Greek into the English, and find out what those original words meant, *literally*. And, as I went to those original words, I found out that there is a word used, for example, in the temptation of Jesus which literally means, 'blowing a **kiss** to one of higher

200. Lockhart, Jay. "Worship: In Church and in Life." West Erwin Church of Christ, Tyler, TX, September 1, 1996, Audiocassette.

201. Pullin, James. "The Spiritual Preparation for Leading Worship," *Worship Leader*, June–July 1992, 12.

202. Scott, John. "The Mystery of Worship" Saturn Road Church of Christ, Garland, Texas, June 13, 1993, Audiocassette.

rank, **kissing the hand or the ground toward** God, **prostrating oneself** in the *presence* of a great person or a deity.'"[203]

Ronald Bridges and Luther Weigle wrote *The King James' Bible Word Book.* Regarding *proskuneo,* it says, "In the New Testament, the Greek verb *proskuneo* means to **kneel** or **prostrate one's self** in honor or supplication."[204]

Richard Leonard wrote, "*Setting the pattern* for the **worship** of the creator are the twenty-four elders. They interject their commentary in the form of powerful declarations of praise, **falling down to worship** God (*proskuneo,* Revelation 5:14; 11:16; 19:4)."[205]

John Sloper: "In today's world, we dislike the idea of **bowing down before** anyone. But true **worship** must acknowledge our **lowly state before** the holy creator. So, when is a **'worship service'** not a **'worship' service?** It is when we have not prepared ourselves to come before a holy and righteous God with *humble* and contrite hearts. Until we are willing to **fall down before** the living God, we will never experience true **worship**, and all our efforts and enthusiastic services will only be 'filthy rags' (Isaiah 64:6)."[206]

Mike Root: "The word that Jesus uses for **worship** is the Greek word *proskuneo*, which means 'to **bow down, kiss**, and do obeisance to.' Jesus says, 'Believe me, an hour is coming when neither in this mountain, nor in Jerusalem, **shall you worship** the Father' . . . (See John 4:7–30; especially verses 23–24)."[207]

J. D Douglas wrote the *New Bible Dictionary.* He said, "To offer this **'worship'** to God, His servants **must prostrate themselves**—Hebrew:

203. Norton, Howard. "User Friendly Worship", Part I. IBC Annual Workshop, Florence, AL. September 22, 1994, Audiocassette.

204. Bridges, Ronald and Luther A. Weigle. *The King James' Bible Word Book,* Nashville: Thomas Nelson Publishers, Inc., 1994.

205. Leonard, Richard C. "New Testament Vocabulary of Worship" *The Biblical foundations of Christian Worship*, Robert E. Webber ed., Nashville: Star Song Publishing Group, 1993, 19–23.

206. Sloper, John. "When is a 'Worship Service' not a 'Worship' Service?" *Worship Leader*, April–May 1993, 44.

207. Root, Mike. *Unbroken Bread.* Joplin: College Press, 1997, 99.

histahwah or Greek: *proskyneo*—and thus manifest reverential fear and adoring awe and wonder."[208]

Brian Kenyon: "The most common Greek word translated **'worship'** is '*proskyneo*'. In classical Greek literature the basic meaning of '*proskyneo*' meant '**to kiss**'. Pre-Christian Greeks considered this verb a technical term for 'the adoration of the gods, meaning to **fall down, prostrate one's self, adore on one's knees**'"[209]

Rubel Shelley and Randall Harris wrote, "The Gonypeteo (**to bend the knee**) word group in the New Testament points to *an attitude of respect and adoration* that shows itself in a physical gesture. Therefore, one may **kneel** to pray (Luke 22:41), to make a petition of Jesus (John 4:23), it is an activity of submission on our part. **Worship** is the *adoration* of God for who He is. It is the *awe, wonder, and reverence* for a creature to give his creator."[210]

Lindsey Garmon: "The word *proskuneo* means '**to fall down before** an object or a person worthy of adoration and **worship**. You **fall down before** a person deserving of **worship** and praise. This is the word too that the Samaritan woman used in John 4, when Jesus conversed with her at the well. She is thinking of **worshipers bowing down** in holy places where there was the presumption of a divine presence."[211]

Earnest Gentile helps us to visualize "The basic meaning of *proskuneo*." He says, "Picture a person **falling on his knees** to **kiss someone else's feet. Worship** in the Bible includes appropriate body action and *humility*"[212]

208. Douglas, J. D. *New Bible Dictionary*. Downers Grove: Intervarsity Press, 1992.

209. Kenyon, Brian. "True Worship: A Word Study." *Florida School of Preaching*, Vol. XIX, No. 9, April 1999, 1.

210. Shelley, Rubel and Randall J. Harris. *The Second Incarnation*. West Monroe: Howard Publishing Company, 1992, 119–29.

211. Garmon, Lindsey. "Worship and the Assembly." Church of Christ South, Corpus Christi, TX, 1995, Audiocassette.

212. Gentile, Earnest B. *Worship God*, Portland: City Bible publishing, 1994, 68.

Frederick C. Kubicek: "The Greek word for **"worship"**, *proskuneo*, "is used to designate the custom of **prostrating oneself** and **kissing another's feet**. Will you wait, or will you **bow your knee** to Him now?"[213]

Cecil May: "Some of the Greek and Hebrew words for **worship** suggest **'kiss the ground toward'** or **'bow the knees to'**. The English **'worship'** is from 'worth-ship'. **Worship** is given to One deemed to be 'worth' such adoration. Our God is worthy of **worship**."[214]

Zondervan Expository Dictionary of Bible Words: "Both the Hebrew (*shachach*) and Greek (*proskuneo*) words for **worship** indicate **falling down** and **prostrating one's self before** the Almighty. *Reverence* and *humility* are vitally linked to acceptable **worship**."[215]

The New Unger's Bible Dictionary says, "*Proskuneo*, properly **to 'kiss the hand to (toward)** one', in token of *reverence*; also by **kneeling** or **prostration** *to do homage*."[216]

Jack Lewis: "**Worship is bowing before** the divine king. The fact that Westerners do not **bow before** any person is perhaps a part of the cause of their failure to grasp the essence of the **worship** of God. The psalmist calls: 'O come, let us **worship** and **bow down**. Let us **kneel before** the Lord our Maker' (Psalm 95:6). This verb *chawah* is used in the prohibitions of **worship** of other Gods (Exodus 20:5). The Greeks found *proskynein*, which most scholars assume means **'to kiss'**, as their nearest equivalent."[217]

John Frame: "To **worship** God is also to **bow before** His absolute, ultimate authority."[218]

213. Kubicek, Frederick C. Accessed 2001. Online: www.unlimitedglory.org/needful.

214. May, Cecil Jr. "Worship—An Overview," FHU Lectures, Henderson, TN, 1994, 252.

215. Richards, Lawrence O. *Zondervan Expository Dictionary of Bible Words*. Grand Rapids: Zondervan Publishing House, 1991, 639–40.

216. Unger, Pearl C. *The New Unger's Bible Dictionary*. Chicago: The Moody Bible Institute, 1993, 1371.

217. Lewis, Jack P. "Old Testament Word Studies in Worship," Freed HU Lectures, Henderson, TN, 1994, 232.

218. Frame, John M. *Worship in spirit and Truth*. Phillipsburg: Presbyterian and Reformed Publishing Company, 1996, 4.

Stafford North summarizes the "essentials" of **worship** as follows: "John 4:24 capsules the essentials of **worship**: (1) God is spirit, (2) those who **worship**, (3) must **worship** in spirit, and (4) in truth. The word '**worship**' means for me **to prostrate myself before** the object of my **worship**. I would do this only to send a very strong message of *submission* and *reverence* to my God."[219]

Joseph Carroll: "Revelation 5 is one of the great chapters, if not the greatest chapter on **worship** in all the Bible. Notice again the order in verse 8. First **they fall down**: "And when he had taken the book, the four beasts and four and twenty elders **fell down before** the Lamb, having each one of them harps, and golden vials full of odours, which are the prayers of the saints. And they sang a new song."[220]

Jim McGuiggan: "All healthy **worship** has at its heart a sense of *awe* and *reverence*—has a central feeling of dependence—*humbles* us and deepens our *humility*—strengthens our trust in Him whom we can't see—leads us to acknowledge the majesty of the Lord God. The **bowed head** and **bent knees in the presence** of the unseen, anchors us more firmly in the realities beyond this life of tangible and visible things."[221]

Welton Gaddy wrote *The Gift of Worship*. He says, "*Proskuneo* means literally '**to kiss toward**' or '**to bow down**'. Immediately obvious is the sense of *humble adoration* so important to each **worshiper** and so vital in a **worshiping** congregation."[222]

Ted Waller emphasizes that, "**Worship** is to call all to **fall before the feet** of God."[223]

Joseph Garlington: "***Worship*** speaks of **bent knees** and **bowed faces pressed to the ground** in His awesome *presence*."[224]

219. Stafford North, "Unlocking Our Hearts to God is Key to Making Our Worship Meaningful," *Christian Chronicle*, May 2000, 31.

220. Carroll, Joseph S. *How to Worship Jesus Christ*. Chicago: Moody Press, 1984, 37.

221. McGuiggan, Jim. "Worship: The Oxygen of the Soul," *Image Magazine*, July/August 1994, 38.

222. Gaddy, C. Welton. *The Gift of Worship*. Nashville: Broadman Press, 1992, XVI.

223. Waller, Ted. "Worship that Leads Men Upward." Nashville: *20th Century Christian*, 1970, 17.

224. Garlington, Joseph L. *Worship: The Pattern of Things in Heaven*. Shippensburg: Destiny Image Publishers, Inc., 1998, 8.

W. T. Allison: "What is **worship**? The Greek word carries with it the idea **to fall down before**, to do *reverence* unto—Genuine **worship** changes a worthless church member into a worthwhile servant." He then quotes William Temple, the Archbishop of Canterbury: '**Worship** is to quicken the conscience by the holiness of God, to feed the mind with the truth of God, to purge the imagination by the beauty of God, to open the heart to the love of God and to devote the will to the purpose of God.'"[225]

Ken Neller: "The Greek word *proskuneo* means **to bow down** or **to prostrate one's self** or to **worship**. This is the word that is used most often in the NT to describe the **worship** activity. **Prostrating one's self** indicates *reverence and humility.*"[226]

Larry Bridgesmith: "We must remain vigilant to use **worship** forms consistent with Biblical freedoms which connect with God-seekers who are not familiar with 'the way we have always done it'. Those traditions may feel good to us but lack any capacity to bring unbelieving **outsiders to their knees** and exclaim, 'God is really among you!' (1 Corinthians 14:24–25). With expectant hearts, anticipating a holy encounter with the Creator of the universe, let us enter into **worship** with the clear understanding that meaningful **worship** is defined only by the Holy One who is the sole focus of our **worship**."[227]

Ralph Gilmore: "**Worship** should have these motivations: (1) Making obeisance to someone greater (proskyneo); (2) Feeling awe in His *presence* (sebomai); (3) *Reverently* **bowing our knees before** Him (gonupeteo); (4) *Humbly* offering our lives in sacrificial service to Him (latreuo); and (5) Establishing a pattern of life consistent with our **worship** (leiturgeo) . . . Perhaps one of the most significant missing elements in many of our assemblies is the *awe* that should be felt or the *penitent* **bending of the knees in the presence** of God."[228]

225. Allison, W. T. "Worship—Power" Freed Hardeman University Lectures, 1994, Audiocassette.

226. Neller, Ken. "Revelation and Christian Worship." Harding U, Lectureship, Searcy, AR, 1992, Audiocassette.

227. Bridgesmith, Larry. "Putting the 'Meaning' in Meaningful Worship," *Wineskins*, Nashville, TN Oct., 1997, 10–11.

228. Gilmore, Ralph. "The Meaning of Worship," *Gospel Advocate*, August 1995, 13–14.

When Earl Edwards presented "Focus on God's plan for **worship**", he said, "The word most frequently used for **worship** in our NT is the Greek word, *proskuneo*. It means **kiss**, literally, **kiss toward**. In fact, Ardnt and Gingrich's Greek Lexicon on page 723 says it means '**fall down before**', even **touching your forehead to the ground**, do obeisance, do *reverence*, to **kiss one's hand and feet**.' In other words, you would **bow down before** that king and say, 'I am at your complete disposition. Do with me whatever you desire.' That's the word from which we get our main term for **worship**."[229]

Hal Hougey asks, "What is **Worship**? The English word comes from an Anglo-Saxon background, where the word was 'worth-ship,' or 'worthiness.' It referred to showing *reverence* and honor to one who was worthy of such honor. The most worthy One is God himself, to whom we show the supreme level of *reverence* and honor. The Greek word which best conveys this concept is *proskunesis*. Literally, it means '**to kiss toward**.' The idea is that when man comes into the Presence of God, he **falls down before** him, sinful and unworthy, to do obeisance before the Worthy One. The ancient practice was **to fall down before** a conquering king and **kiss his foot**, **or the ground** on which that foot stood, as a pledge of obedience and loyalty to the conquering master. Regrettably, translators have seriously damaged the whole concept of **worship** by rendering several different Greek words as '**worship**' when that is not what they mean."[230]

Perry Cotham: "*Proskuneo* means literally '**to kiss forward**' or '**to kiss toward**' and was understood as **falling down in worship**, doing obeisance, **prostrating oneself before** another, demonstrating *reverence*, showing *humility*, or welcoming respectfully."[231]

Dennis Lindsay: "It is significant that the expression '**bowing down to**' (Hebrew: *hishtahavah* = LXX; *proskuneo*) is reflected by *proskuneo* in John 4:20 ff."[232]

229. Edwards, Earl. "Focus on God's Plan for Worship." Hartsville Pike Church of Christ, Lectureship, 1995, Audiocassette.

230. Hougey, Hal. *The Quest for Understandable Hermeneutics*. Concord: Pacific Publishing Company, 1997, 460–61.

231. Cotham, Perry C. *Ceasefire: Ending Worship Wars with Sound Theology & Plain Common Sense*. Orange: New Leaf Books, 2002, 37.

232. Lindsay, Dennis R. "What is Truth? (Altheia) in the Gospel of John," *Restoration Quarterly*, Abilene, Texas, Vol. 35 No. 3, 1993, 136.

Ken Neller spoke at the Harding Lectures in 1992 on "Revelation and Christian **worship**." He said, "*Proskuneo* is the word that is used most often in the NT to describe the **worship** activity, and this word *proskuneo*, this word for **bowing one's self** or **prostrating one's self**, is the word Jesus uses in a very important passage on **worship** found in John 4, and just for emphasis sake, I want to read this passage to you substituting instead of our word **worship** the literal phrase '**prostrating one's self**', and you can kind of get an idea of what **worship** is all about. The woman says, 'Sir, I can see you are a prophet. Our fathers **prostrated themselves** on this mountain before God, but you Jews claim that the place where we must **prostrate ourselves** before God is in Jerusalem.'"

"Jesus declared, 'Believe me woman, a time is coming when you will **prostrate yourself** before the Father, neither on this mountain nor in Jerusalem. You Samaritans **prostrate yourselves** before what you do not know. We **prostrate ourselves** before Him whom we do know. For salvation is from the Jews. Yet, a time is coming and is now come when the **true prostraters** will **prostrate themselves before** Him must do so in spirit and in truth.' It gives you the idea of what God seeks. God seeks people who *humbly* come before Him. And such obeisance, such *humility*, such respect, and such devotion belongs to God and God alone."[233]

Jack Lewis wrote in the *Gospel Advocate* that, "One of the most common words in the New Testament for **worship** is p*roskynein*, and its basic meaning is to **prostrate oneself** in the presence of a superior. In a democracy, we do not **prostrate ourselves before** superiors, and that attitude carries over into our relationship with God. The idea of **prostration**, even when taken *figuratively* and emotionally, comes hard for us."[234]

David Young spoke on "Rethinking Worship." He said, "When preachers and teachers talk to you about '**worship**', they tell you that the Greek word *proskuneo* means what? Or in the Hebrew it was *histahawah*. They said it means to '**get down on your knees**.' Well, if it means to **get down on your knees**, it means '**get down on your knees**.' It doesn't mean '**worship**.' It means 'get **down on your knees**.'"[235]

233. Neller, Ken. "Revelation and Christian Worship." Harding U Lectures, Searcy, AR, 1992, Audiocassette.

234. Lewis, Jack P. "Time for Worship," *Gospel Advocate*, April 1998, 34–35.

235. Young, David. "Rethinking Worship"—Jubilee Seminar, Nashville, TN, 1996, Audiocassette.

Joseph Carroll: "Here is true **worship**, and the order is significant. The first thing in Revelation 4, verse 10, is that **they fall down.** 'The four and twenty elders **fall down before** Him that sat on the throne.' That is first, and that is always first. The **falling down** speaks of submission to the one **worshiped,** for here we find that they '**fall down before** Him that sat on the throne, and **worshiped** Him that liveth forever and ever, *and cast their crowns before the throne.*'"[236]

Jim Goll prefers to say it this way: "Yes, we are **kneeling** on the promises of God our Savior; **kneeling** on the promises of God! The Lord is searching for His dependent warriors to find those who know how to **worship** Him in Spirit and in truth."[237]

17. Does the *main "worship" word in the OT* include bowing the knees?

Frederick Kubicek reminds us that, "God Himself directed them **to bow down to** Him when they brought in the grain offering (Deut. 26:10). The Hebrew word for '**worship**' used here and elsewhere, like it's Greek counterpart means **to prostrate oneself** and **bow down before** God."[238]

Bailey McBride, editor of the *Christian Chronicle,* says, "The Bible speaks about **worship.** The following are some key guidelines for **worship**: 'O come, **let us bow down and worship, let us kneel before** the Lord our Maker' (Psalm 95:1–6). 'And the twenty-four elders who were seated on their throne before God, **fell on their faces** and **worshiped** God' (Revelation 11:16)."[239]

Spiros Zodhiates says that, "*proskuneo* (NT) and *shachah* (OT) were not used in the Bible for "**worship** in general." He emphasizes that, "*Shachah* was not used in the general sense of **worship**, but specifically to **bow down, to prostrate one's self** as an act of respect before a superior being.' The equivalent' in the New Testament is '*proskuneo*'."[240]

236. Carroll, Joseph S. *How to Worship Jesus Christ.* Chicago: Moody Press, 1984, 36.

237. Goll, Jim W. *Kneeling on the Promises.* Grand Rapids: Chosen Books, 2000, 32.

238. Kubicek, Frederick C. Accessed 2000, Online: www.unlimitedglory.org/needful.

239. McBride, Bailey, "Can worship be improved and still be biblical?"—*The Christian Chronicle,* Oklahoma City, OK, February 1993, C-17.

240. Zodhiates, Spiros. and Warren Baker. *The Complete Word Study Old Testament.* Chatanooga: AMG Publishers 1994, 2372.

Richard Leonard: "The word usually translated '**worship**' (*shahah*, in the reflexive form *hishtahvah*) means '**to bend down** or **prostrate one's self**.' **Worshipers** are invited to **bow down** (*kara'*, Psalm 95:6; Isaiah 45:23) to the Lord, **to kneel** or **bend the knee** (*berekh*, Psalm 95:6) **before** Him."[241]

Chris Smith: "I just want you to pay attention to the emotion in the Psalms—Chapter 5, Verse 7: 'But I, by your great mercy will come into your house, and in *reverence* will I **bow down toward** your holy temple.'"[242]

Jack Lewis: "The word which is primarily the '**worship**' word in the OT is that of **bowing one's self** in the *presence* of a superior. The gesture is that of unconditional surrender. I think that we not only have rejected the gesture, but also the **bowing of the spirit** to a larger extent, in the presence of the Lord. That is, we pretty well have thrown out the baby along with the bath in this situation. I do think we need to ask ourselves if we really have gotten across to our people—the concept that **you do bow yourselves** in *unconditional surrender* to the great King, in this act that we call **worship.**"[243]

Welton Gaddy: "Psalm 95:6–7a says, 'Oh come, let us **worship** and **bow down**, let us **kneel before** the Lord, our Maker! For he is our God.'"[244]

Dan Dozier gives several examples of **kneeling** in the OT: "'O come, **let us bow down** and **worship, let us kneel before** the Lord our Maker' (Psalm 95:6). When Solomon was dedicating the temple, 'he stood on the platform and then **knelt down before** the whole assembly of Israel and spread out his hands toward heaven' (2 Chronicles 6:13) and prayed. After Solomon's prayer, God sent fire down from heaven and consumed the offerings and sacrifices and filled the temple with His glory. 2 Chronicles 7:3 records, 'when all the Israelites saw the fire coming down and the glory of the Lord above the temple, they **knelt** on the pavement **with their faces to the ground**, and they **worshiped** and gave thanks to the Lord, saying 'He

241. Leonard, Richard C. "Old Testament Vocabulary of Worship," *The Complete Library of Christian Worship*, Vol. 1, *The Biblical Foundations of Christian Worship.* Robert E. Weber, ed., Nashville: Star Song Publishing Co. 1993, 5.

242. Smith, Chris. "A People of Depth: Learning to Pray, III." Jubilee Seminar, Nashville, TN, 1998, Audiocassette.

243. Lewis, Jack. "OT Word Studies in Worship." FHU Bible Lectureship, Henderson, TN, 1994, Audiocassette.

244. Gaddy, C. Welton, *The Gift of Worship*. Nashville: Broadman Press, 1992, XVII.

is good; His love endures forever.'Years later, after King Hezekiah purified the temple, and 'the offerings were finished, the King and everyone present with Him, **knelt down** and **worshiped**' (2 Chronicles 29:29)."[245]

Jack Lewis calls to our attention that, "**Kneeling** is also an OT gesture of *submission* used in prayer. And so you see, **"Every knee shall bow** to the Lord" (Isaiah 45:23). And often times prayer is **on bended knee** (Daniel 6:10). Solomon **knelt** in his prayer at the dedication of the temple. The Psalmist then says, 'O come, and let us **worship** the Lord and **bow down,** and let us **kneel before** God our maker.' That's Psalm 95:6."[246]

Ralph Martin: "*To worship God is to ascribe to Him—supreme worth,* for He alone is worthy. Who can refuse to **bow down** and acknowledge that He is God alone?"[247]

W. T. Allison tells us, "Again, the psalmist says in Psalm 95:6, 'Oh come, let us **worship** and **bow down.** Let us **kneel** before the Lord our maker.' That's the kind of attitude that must be prevalent in our acceptable worship unto God."[248]

Jimmy Clark: "It is a marvelous privilege to **worship** the true and living God. David wrote, 'I was glad when they said unto me, "Let us go unto the house of the Lord."'" (Psalm 121:1). David also wrote of **worship,** "O come, let us **worship** and **bow down**: Let us **kneel** before the LORD our maker" (Psalm. 95:1–7).[249]

245. Dozier, Daniel A. *Come Let Us Adore Him*, Joplin: College Press Publishing Co, 1994, 287.

246. Lewis, Jack. "OT Word Studies in Worship"—FHU Bible Lectureship, Henderson, TN, 1994, Audiocassette.

247. Martin, Ralph P. *Worship in the Early Church*. Grand Rapids: William B. Erdsman's Publishing, 1964, 10.

248. Allison, W. T. "Worship—Power"—FHU Lectures, 1994, Audiocassette.

249. Clark, Jimmy. "Expediencies in Worship," Florida School of Preaching Lectureships, Lakeland, FL, 1998, 377.

"Come, Let Us Worship and Bow Down"

Come, let us **worship** and **bow down**;
Let us **kneel** before the Lord our God our Maker.
For He is our God, and we are the people of His pasture
And the sheep of His Hand.

—Dave Doherty

Jim Mankin quotes a portion of Psalm 95 that has been put to music. He said, "One other passage that I want us to look at just for a minute is Psalm 95. And if you're into contemporary music, you may know that they have used this particular Psalm that has been put it to music. I mean they just used the words right out of the NIV: 'Come, let us sing for joy to the Lord. Let us shout aloud to the rock of our salvation. Let us come before Him with thanksgiving and bestow Him with music and song. For the Lord is a great God, the great King above all Gods. In His hand are the depths of the earth and the mountain peaks belong to Him. The sea is His, for He made it, and His hands formed the dry land. Come, let us **bow down** and **worship**. Let us **kneel before** the Lord our Maker. For He is our God, and we are the people of His pasture.'—So, there you have it."[250]

H. H. Rowley makes a very important point. He says, "The first element in **worship** is *adoration*. 'O come, let us **worship** and **bow down**; let us **kneel** before the Lord our Maker' (Psalm 95:6–7). They did not come with an easy familiarity into the *presence* of God, but were aware of his greatness and majesty with a sense of privilege to His house."[251]

Willard Tate tells about "the glad and the sad." He says, "Jehosephat **bowed with his face to the ground** and all the people of Judea and Jerusalem **fell down** and **worshiped** . . . Job looked up to God, tore his robe and shaved his head. Then he **fell to the ground** and **worshiped**. Whether blessings or disasters come, there is only one response if we have faith. The glad and the sad, they all **bow before God**."[252]

250. Mankin, Jim. "Come Let Us Adore Him—Intimacy with God." Spiritual Growth Workshop, Orlando, FL, 1996, Audiocassette.

251. Rowley, H. H. *Worship in Ancient Israel*. Philadelphia: Fortress Press, 1967, 257.

252. Tate, Willard. "Area Praise Service." Austin Avenue Church of Christ, Brownwood, Texas, December 1, 1996, Audiocassette.

18. What do Bible scholars say about kneeling for intercessory Prayer? (Kneeling to pray for others)

Charles Brent: "Intercessory prayer might be defined as loving our neighbor **on our knees.**"[253]

The Kneeling Christian, authored by an unknown Christian, says, "Let everyone of us ask **on our knees** this question: 'If no one on earth prayed for the salvation of sinners more fervently or more frequently than I do, how many of them would be converted to God through prayer?'"[254]

Tracey Hanson: "One last note on intercessory prayer is that it should be persistent. Let's not become spiritual couch potatoes. Let's stay **on our knees.**"[255]

Charles Hodge preached a sermon called "The Power of Prayer." He said, "The greatest thing that Jay can do for this church is not in the pulpit on Sunday, but it is when he is **down on his knees** during the week. Amen? Amen!"[256]

Jerry Rushford shares this marvelous story: He says, "I am here tonight because of those times I have walked into my Grandfather's study and found him **on his knees** in prayer. And I would leave knowing full well, that who he was praying for, was leaving the room. And so here I am tonight. My Grandfather's hope has been realized. I stand on the stage at ACU in Moody Coliseum, the home of my Grandpa's alma mater."[257]

Willie Nettle: "In verse 14 of Ephesians chapter 3, Paul comes back to the prayer: 'For this cause, I **bow my knees** unto the Father of our Lord Jesus Christ.' He's praying about some mighty things on behalf of these Christians."[258]

253. Brent, Charles H.—*Prayer, Powerpoints.* Wheaton: Victor Books, 1995, 150.

254. Unknown. *The Kneeling Christian.* Grand Rapids: Zondervan Publishing House, 1945, 23–4.

255. Hanson, Tracey. "Putting God on His Throne." 55th Annual Pepperdine University Bible Lectures, Anaheim, California, 1998, Audiocassette.

256. Hodge, Charles. "The Power of Prayer." West Erwin Church of Christ, Tyler, TX, October 22, 1995, Audiocassette

257. Rushford, Jerry. "Surrounded by a Great Cloud of Witnesses." ACU Lectureship: Behold He Comes!, 1999, Audiocassette.

258. Nettle, Willie. "Paul's Prayer." Harding U. Lectures, Searcy, AR, 1994, Audiocassette.

Begin the day with God;
Kneel down to Him in prayer
Lift up your heart to His abode,
And seek His love to share.

—*Anonymous*

James Dobson, author of *Focus on the Family*, wisely proclaimed that, "There is nothing that compares to winning our children to Christ. The culture is going to try to steal them from you. How are you going to cope with that? There is only one way. And that is to stay **on your knees** everyday for them."[259]

Luis Palau tells how Billy Graham "*humbled*" himself while interceding. He says, "This young man came up to Billy Graham and I after the meeting, and asked us to pray for his ministry. We all started out **on our knees**, and when we finished praying, I looked up and saw Billy **lying flat**, **face down**. Billy said, 'As I was praying, I felt that I really needed to *humble* myself before the Lord.'"[260]

John Scott said, "Hezakiah **dropped to his knees** in 2 Chronicles 30, and he's praying for the religious people that are doing the 'ritual', but somehow it has lost its vibrancy of meaning."[261]

"Prince of Peace"

Maker of all, we **kneel** interceding
Father of life,
Your children are pleading still.

—*Twila Paris*

Randall Roth: "I am an answer to prayer. My Grandpa Charlie told me that Grandma Ollie, both now with the Lord, would rise daily at 5:30 a.m., roll out of bed and **onto her knees**. I was on that prayer list. I am convinced

259. Dobson, James. "All That Matters." *ACU Today*, Abilene, TX, Winter Edition, 1996, 16.

260. Palau, Luis. Radio Broadcast. KGLY FM, Tyler, TX 1997.

261. Scott, John. "Evangelistic Praying" Saturn Road Church of Christ, Garland, TX, April 26, 1998, Audiocassette.

that I would not be where I am today, were it not for prayer. The question I asked myself is, 'who will be the beneficiary of my prayers?"[262]

David Dykes: "We have the great opportunity to participate in a special prayer of rededication for this missionary family. They will return to Argentina. I'm going to ask that they **kneel** here on the platform and I'm going to place my hands here on Karen and Richard and ask Mike to pray over their children, Micah and Christy. Will you join us as we pray?"[263]

Tex Williams recalls his mother **kneeling** in prayer. He said, "Before she went to bed, my mother always **kneeled down** and prayed out loud, and she prayed for us."[264]

Robert Webber: "I entered the Church and **knelt** with a person who was to lead the noon prayer service. Prayer requests were then read: 'A new van is needed for missionaries in Burma, India. Let us pray to the Lord.'" Dr. Webber responded to this and other requests with, "Lord, hear our prayer." He then says, "These and other ways may help us break through the passive practice of prayer to a more increased involvement of God's people in bringing their petitions before the Lord. I felt deeply involved in these prayers and in that whole service."[265]

Jim Clark wrote a book called *More than We Could Ask*. In Chapter 10, he tells about his three year old daughter Shannon, "who prayed fervently **on her knees** for the Lord to heal her six year old brother, Aaron, who was having a seizure. Aaron had developed a severe case of the flu, and when his fever shot up suddenly, he had a seizure or febrile convulsion. When the seizure began, the mother, Susan, immediately turned to the three year old and said, 'Start praying for your brother.'" Jim Clark goes on to say, "This miniature prayer warrior promptly leaped up, ran to our

262. Roth, Randall D. *Prayer, Powerpoints*. Wheaton: Victor Books, 1995, 11.

263. Dykes, David. "Prayer Dedication Service for the DeLeon Family" Missionaries to Argentina, Green Acres Baptist Church, Tyler, Texas, KLTV, January 23, 1993.

264. Williams, Tex. "Who Are We and Why Are We Here?" West Erwin Church of Christ, Tyler, TX, August 13, 1997, Audiocassette.

265. Webber, Robert E. *Worship is a Verb*. Nashville: Star Song Publishing Group, 1992, 146.

bedroom, got **on her knees** and began praying for her big brother. The brother fully recovered."[266]

The *Tyler Morning Telegraph*: "In an odd twist, a woman without an admission pass made her way into the courtroom and **knelt down** and prayed, 'Father, in Jesus' name, I ask you to open the heavens to give peace and strength to this court.'"[267]

Mike Gravois: "As we remember our missionaries and the hardships that they are going through, it causes us to be **down on our knees** as we pray to God on their behalf."[268]

The June 12, 1994 *Shiloh Family Chronicle* of the Shiloh Road Church of Christ in Tyler, TX included the following poem on intercessory prayer for our missionaries.

But I said, "Jesus, I can't go
To lands across the seas."
He answered quickly, "Yes, you can,
By traveling **on you knees.**"

—McDaniel, 1987

John Scott: "Let's get down to Verse 8 of our text in I Timothy, chapter 2. Paul doesn't say, 'I want'. What he really says is much more intense: 'I demand, I command that the men everywhere pray'. He knows the women are already praying. It is the men that need the exhortation to pray. We are the ones that need to be **down on our knees** with holy hands lifted. Paul doesn't have to exhort the women to pray; it is the men he is trying to drive **to their knees** in prayer for the lost."[269]

266. Clark, Jim. *More than We Could Ask*. Orange: New Leaf Books, 2001, 120–21.

267. Los Angeles (AP), *Tyler Morning Telegraph*, Tyler, TX May 2, 1995.

268. Gravois, Mike. Main Prayer at West Erwin Church of Christ, Tyler, TX April 8, 1998, Audiocassette.

269. Scott, John. "Evangelistic Praying." Saturn Road Church of Christ, Garland, TX, April 26, 1998, Audiocassette.

19. Does Satan value kneeling more than all the kingdoms of the world?

Joseph Carroll: "In the temptation of our Lord in the wilderness, we are introduced to the subtle attempt of the enemy to bring our Lord under his control. 'All these things will I give thee it thou wilt **fall down** and **worship** me' (Matthew 4:8–9). Notice that Satan has the correct order."[270]

Dan Dozier: "The devil himself knows that **bowing** is essential for **worship**. One of his temptations was when he took Jesus up on top of a high mountain and showed Him all the kingdoms of the world. And he said, 'Jesus, if you will **bow down and worship** me, I'll give you everything your eyes see.' Jesus realized immediately that to **bow down** before him would be to **worship** him and so Jesus' response was, 'Away from me Satan. For it is written, **Worship** the Lord your God and *serve* Him only.'"[271]

George Barna, in the book *Experience God in Worship,* brings to our attention that Satan, the tempter, "sought to be **worshiped** by the Son of God (Matthew 4:1–11). As soon as Satan uttered the words '**bow down** and **worship** me' the contest was over. Surely it's no mistake that the first commandment is that we must not worship any other deity (Exodus 20:3–6)."[272]

Charles Spurgeon: "When the tempter hissed in His ear that abominable offer, 'All these things will I give thee, if thou wilt **fall down** and **worship** me' (Matthew 4:9), it must have grieved the holy heart of Jesus intensely. He could not yield to temptation, but He did suffer from it."[273]

The Kneeling Christian: "We allow the Devil to persuade us to neglect prayer! He makes us believe that we can do more by our own efforts than by our prayers. How dare we work for Christ without being much **on our knees**?"[274]

270. Carroll, Joseph S. *How to Worship Jesus Christ.* Chicago: Moody Press, 1984, 39.

271. Dozier, Daniel A. "Worship is a Verb." The Church That Connects III Seminar, San Antonio, TX, August 6, 1994, Audiocassette.

272. Barna, George et all. *Experience God in Worship.* Group Publishing, Inc. Loveland, CO, 2000, 13–15.

273. Spurgeon, Charles, *The Power of Christ's Tears.* Lynwood: Emerald Books, 1996, 143–44.

274. Unknown. *The Kneeling Christian.* Grand Rapids: Zondervan Publishing House, 1945, 22.

Ken Neller: "To remind you again of what Jesus said to Satan, 'Thou shalt **worship**,' that is, 'Thou shalt **prostrate yourself**, before the Lord thy God.' Remember, Satan was trying to get Jesus to **prostrate Himself** before him. But Jesus said, 'No, you shall **prostrate yourself** before the Lord Thy God and Him only shall you serve.'"[275]

Adron Doran: "Satan proposed that Jesus **fall down and worship** him (Matthew 4:9). However, Jesus rebuffed Satan by saying, 'For it is written, you shall **worship** the Lord your God and Him only you shall *serve*'" (Matthew 4:10).[276]

Keith Brooks: "Satan trembles when he sees the weakest saint **on his knees**."[277]

Jimmy Jividen: "The devil tempted Jesus and promised to give Him all the kingdoms of the world if He would **fall down and worship** him. Jesus responded by quoting from the law: 'You shall **worship** the Lord your God, and *serve* Him only' (Matthew 4:10)."[278]

Jim Goll: "Some of us today are taught to stand and shoot at the devil before we are taught to **kneel before** the Father. If we reversed the order, our aim would be better!"[279]

Keith Brooks: "Soldiers of the Lord are doing real fighting when they are **on their knees** . . . To whip the devil, **fall on your knees**."[280]

275. Neller, Ken. "Revelation and Christian Worship." Harding U Lectures, Searcy, AR, 1992, Audiocassette.

276. Doran, Adron. "A Lesson at the Well," *The Gospel Advocate*, September 1997, Vol. CXXXIX, No. 9, 39.

277. Brooks, Keith L. *The Cream Book of Sentence Sermons*. Chicago: Moody Press, 1974, 94.

278. Jividen, Jimmy. *More Than a Feeling—Worship That Pleases God*. Nashville: The Gospel Advocate Company, 1999, 79.

279. Goll, Jim W. *Kneeling on the Promises*. Grand Rapids: Chosen Books, 2000, 21.

280. Brooks, Keith L. *The Cream Book of Sentence Sermons*. Chicago: Moody Press, 1974, 95.

20. What about kneeling to *honor men and angels* compared to God?

Michael Wyatt: "Peter *refused* **worship** when Cornelius **bowed down before** him. He said, 'Stand up. I myself also am a man (Acts 10:26). You remember that the apostle John **fell at the angel's feet** to **worship** him and the angel said, 'See thou do it not, **worship** God' (Revelation 9:10). Only deity is to be **worshiped**."[281]

Charles Hodge: "In Revelation, John **fell down before** an angel twice. Each time the angel said, 'Get back up. I'm an angel, but I'm not God. **Worship** God.'"[282]

Earl Edwards: "We are not to **worship** men. In Acts 10:25–26, Peter said to Cornelius, who **bowed down before** him and **worshiped** him, 'Stand up, I too am a man.' Only God and Christ and the Holy Spirit are to be **worshiped**." [283]

21. Should we kneel to *give thanks* to God and Jesus?

Anita Donahue: "Great things happen while I'm **on my knees**. Forces of heaven are released when one person goes to God in prayer. The same power that raised my Lord Jesus from the dead is available for my needs. 'Thank You that when I **bow in prayer**, Your Son intercedes. In His purity, He raises each of my petitions to You.'"[284]

Max Lucado: "More than once the impact of my late-hour ponderings took me out of my swivel chair and put me **on my knees** in thankfulness. We serve a wonderful God!"[285]

In a personal communication with Dorothy Jewell Scott (My aunt and a Sunday School teacher), says, "The first thing I want to do when I get to

281. Wyatt, Michael. "Worship in Spirit and Truth". 1st Lubbock Lectureship, "The Faith Once for All Delivered," Southside Church of Christ, Lubbock, TX, 1998, Audiocassette.

282. Hodge, Charles. "I Stand Amazed" IBC Workshop, "Worship Styles of the 90's," Florence, AL, September 23, 1994, Audiocassette.

283. Edwards, Earl. "Focus on God's Plan for Worship" Lectureship at Hartsville Pike Church of Christ, Gallatin, TN, 1995, Audiocassette.

284. Donahue, Anita Corrine. *When I'm on My Knees*. Uhrichsville: Barbour & Company, Inc., 1997, 10.

285. Lucado, Max. *God Came Near*. Brentwood: Multnomah Press, 1987, 160.

heaven is to **bow my knees before** my Lord and Savior, and thank Him for all He's done for me—for answering my prayers, and for carrying me through the valleys to higher ground."

"More Love to Thee, O Christ"

More love to Thee, O Christ,
More love to Thee!
Hear Thou the prayer I make,
On bended knee.

—Elizabeth Prentiss

Dan Dozier: "Our chief aim in existence, and certainly the chief aim of praise, is to honor and magnify the Lord, to uphold and adore Him, to glorify and exalt the Savior, to thank Him, to **bow ourselves before** God's awesome mystery and might, to laud His love and grace, and to rejoice in His presence! That's what our praise is designed to do."[286]

John Glenn, a State Senator and former astronaut, says, "You should be **on your knees** every day of your life thanking God that there were some men who required a dedication to a purpose, and a love of country, and a dedication to duty—that was more important than life itself. And their self-sacrifice is what made this country possible."[287]

Betty Hamblen prayed, "Father, we **kneel** in awesome wonder at Your creation, and at Your goodness and at Your greatness. We're so grateful for the blessings that we have."[288]

Hillard Hughes: "We thank you Lord for allowing us to be in this place at this time, so that we may **bow down before** you."[289]

Manuel DeOliveira: "We receive so many things from God that my life is blessed. That makes me **fall on my knees** and give thanks to the Father

286. Dozier, Daniel A. "Spiritual Formation-Praise". ACU Lectures, Abilene, TX, 1994, Audiocassette.

287. Glenn, Senator John. Accessed 2004. Website: http://forums.speedguide.net/showthread.php?t=142504.

288. Hamblen, Betty. "Reach for your Spiritual Potential" IBC Workshop, Florence, AL, 1995, Audiocassette.

289. Hughes, Hillard. Prayer @ West Erwin Church of Christ, Tyler, TX, September 21, 1997, Audiocassette.

who first blessed us with the love of Jesus Christ. It makes me **fall on my knees** and *give thanks* to God who has blessed me with such a great family as you all. For more than 15 years you have supported me in Lisbon and in Africa. I am in debt to God and in debt to you."[290]

Jeff Christian is convinced that, "We as Christians would be better served and serve better if we concerned ourselves with encountering God. Yes, read your Bibles, but then do what it says. You read and then act. You read the beautiful words, *give thanks* to the Lord for He is good. But then, after that, you **fall to your knees** and you *give thanks*. It's time that we admit to ourselves as Christians that it is one thing to study theology, and an entire quantum leap to follow through and practice it. To Him be the glory forever, Amen! Let us be thankful and so worship God."[291]

Tyler Morning Telegraph: "Historic moment: Florence Griffith Joyner **falls to her knees** in a prayerful manner after setting the world record in the 200-meter finals in the 1988 Seoul Olympics. FloJo, as she was known, died Monday of an apparent heart seizure."[292]

22. Should we kneel before God's *throne in heaven*? And Jesus at His right hand?

A. W. Tozer: "Worship, I say, rises or falls with our concept of God. And if there is one terrible disease in the Church of Christ, it is that we do not see God as great as He is. We ought to have again the old Biblical concept of God which makes God awesome and that makes men **lie face down** and cry, 'Holy, Holy, Holy, Lord God Almighty.' That would do more for the Church than everything or anything else."[293]

290. DeOliveira, Manuel. "I Want to Know Christ" Richland Hills Church of Christ, Ft. Worth, TX, July 26, 1998, Audiocassette.

291. Christian, Jeff. "Making Theology Practical." *ACU Lectures*, Abilene, TX, 1997, Audiocassette.

292. AP Photo, *Tyler Morning Telegraph*, Tyler, TX, September 22, 1998, 1.

293. Tozer, A. W. *Worship: The Missing Jewel.* Camp Hill: Christian Publications, 1992.

"On Bended Knee"

On bended knee I come,
with a humble heart I come;
Bowing down before
Your holy throne.

—Robert Gay

Jack Lewis tells us that, "Old Testament physical acts have their counterpart in spiritual ones. Perhaps the most important of all is the idea of relationship. God is a great King over all the earth. His holiness, righteousness, faithfulness, mercy and wrath must be recognized. In the light of His majesty, I **must fall down (with Isaiah)** crying, 'Woe is me! I am a man of unclean lips in the midst of a people of unclean lips.'"[294]

Rubel Shelley: "The name of Jesus is an honorable name; it is a worthy name, and a name at which **every knee should bow**."[295]

John Gipson says submission to God is a present need. He says, "The four living creatures and the twenty-four elders **fall down before** the throne. Until then, God is no less on His throne and our need for submission is a present need, and not one that merely belongs to the future. 'Oh, that with yonder sacred throng, we **at His feet may fall**.'"[296]

"We Will Glorify"

Lord Jehovah reigns in majesty,
We will **bow before** His throne;
We will **worship** Him in righteousness,
We will **worship** Him alone.

—Twila Paris

Harold Taylor: "When I began to conjure up these qualities and hallmarks of God the Father, God the Son, and God the Holy Spirit, I was so

294. Lewis, Jack P. "Old Testament Word Studies in Worship," FHU Lectures, Henderson, TN, 1994, 235–36.

295. Shelley, Rubel. *I Just Want to be a Christian*. Nashville: *20th Century Christian*, 1986, 219.

296. Gipson, John. "God on His Throne." Harding U. Searcy, AR, 1992, Audiocassette.

overwhelmed. I won't be fidgeting in worship anymore. I'll want to **fall on my face** and *adore* Him."[297]

Dallas Morning News: "Joan Havala holds her 3-week-old son, Daniel, as **worshipers** and husband Paul, **kneel** for the Lord's Prayer during fellowship's Friday night service."[298]

Joseph Carroll: "I simply **knelt down** and quietly mediated upon the fact that I was in the *presence* of the Lamb of God and **worshiped** Him. We **kneel**, with our eyes closed in order to concentrate all our attention and affection on the Lamb of God, forgetting all else in order not to forget Him.'"[299]

Jim Mankin: "In Revelation 4, they're gathered around the great white throne, the four living creatures **bow down** and say, 'Holy, holy, holy is the Lord'. Back to the original Hebrew language, we are talking about a word that means to **bow down** in the presence of a king. If you go to the New Testament word, the Greek word, it is the word that means **to kiss**. You know, like we **kiss** something that's very important, very sacred. We are **bowing** and **kissing** in the *presence* of God."[300]

Lynn Anderson: "John sets the scene for an extravaganza of **worship** in Revelation 4 and 5. The angels, the heavenly beings, the creatures, and the elders are **falling down before** the throne. In verse 10 of chapter 4, the 24 elders **fall down before** Him who sits on the throne and they **worship** Him who lives forever and ever, and they lay their crowns before the throne and they say, 'You are worthy O Lord our God to receive *glory* and *honor* and *power* for You created all things, and by Your will they were created and have their being. You are worthy to take the scroll and open the seals.' The Apostle John said for them and for us, '**Worship** God.'"[301]

297. Taylor, Harold. "Worship in Spirit and Truth." FHU Lectures, Henderson, TN, 1994, Audiocassette.

298. Caldwell, Deborah Kovach. "Independent Churches Attract Big Crowds With Conservative Theology, User-Friendly Worship," *Dallas Morning News*, April 26,1997, Sec. G, 1.

299. Carroll, Joseph F. *How to Worship Jesus Christ*. Chicago: Moody Press, 1984, 19–76.

300. Mankin, Jim. "Come Let Us Adore Him—Intimacy with God," Spiritual Growth Workshop, Orlando, FL, 1996, Audiocassette.

301. Anderson, Lynn. Harding University Annual Preacher's Forum, Searcy, AR, April 1994, Audiocassette.

A. W. Tozer: "Moses had no hesitation in **kneeling before** the bush and **worshiping** God. It was God and His glory in the bush. When we **kneel before** Him and say, 'My Lord and my God, Thy throne, oh God, is forever and ever,' we are talking to God."[302]

"O Perfect Love"

O perfect Love,
All human thought transcending,
Lowly we **kneel** in prayer
Before thy throne.

—*Dorothy B. Gurney*

Willie Cato knew Marshall Keeble well. He says, "The world was not permitted to direct Marshall Keeble's life. He always told them, 'You don't have to get an education nor be rich in order to be recognized, but you do have to get Christ in you, and then **people will bow**, not to you, but to Christ.' Marshall Keeble lived a life of '**bowing** to Christ'. Whenever Brother Keeble and I had been out on an evening appointment and had arrived home, he was greeted at the door by his wife, the lovely Laura Keeble. Brother Keeble would proceed to tell how they never went to bed until each had **knelt** and prayed. He instructed me to get **down on my knees** and we prayed together."[303]

Joyce Myer told her audience, "Let's not forget the song we just sang: 'I **fell on my knees** and cried, Holy! Holy! Holy!' When we get before God in heaven, we're going to **kneel** and that's what we're going to say. 'Holy! Holy! Holy!'"[304]

Reuel Lemmons: "May some imprisoned soul on some lonely isle in the future write, 'After this I beheld a great multitude of all the nations, kindred, people, and tongues step before the throne. And they cried with a loud voice saying, 'Salvation to our God which sits on the throne and to the Lamb.' The angels, the elders and the four beasts **fell down before**

302. Tozer, A. W. *Whatever Happened to Worship.* Camp Hill: Christian Publications, 1985, 119–20.

303. Cato, Willie. *His Hand and His Heart, The Wit and Wisdom of Marshall Keeble.* Nashville: J. C. Choate Publications, 1990.

304. Myer, Joyce. "I Am Determined to Live in the Word," INSP Network, January 3, 1998.

the throne and **worshiped** God saying, 'Amen! Blessing, and glory, and wisdom, and thanksgiving, and honor, and power, and might be unto our God forever.'"[305]

T. J. Taylor, Jr.: "God delights when He sees people **fall down before** Him and begin to cry and begin to call upon the name of the Lord of Hosts. Hallelujah!"[306]

"Holy, Holy, Holy"

Holy, Holy, Holy! All the saints adore Thee,
Casting down their Golden crowns around the crystal sea;
Cherubim and seraphim **falling down before** Thee,
Who wast, and are, and evermore shall be.

—*Reginald Heber*

Ron Owens asks, "Why do you suppose John placed so much emphasis on the twenty-four elders '**falling down before**' Him who sits on the throne? They seem to be doing this over and over. If we were honest with ourselves, we'd know that there could be no other appropriate response or reaction to the sovereign eternal God than to **bend in submission before** Him. It seems there is a lot more *strutting* in American churches today than **stooping.**"[307]

Mike Warner: "They were wise enough to come a long way looking for Jesus. They were wise enough to **worship** Him when they found Him. They were apparently rich and influential men—tradition says 'kings', but they recognized One greater before whom they **bowed.**"[308]

Welton Gaddy: "**Worshipers** get **off their knees** with spirits pervaded by *awe* and minds filled with wonder."[309]

305. Lemmons, Reuel. "The Future of Our Heritage", ACU Lectureships, February 19, 1986, Audiocassette.

306. Taylor, T. J. "Message of Hope." First Assembly of God Church, Tyler, TX, 1995, Audiocassette.

307. Owens, Ron. *Return to Worship.* Nashville: Broadman and Holman, 1999, 67.

308. Warner, Mike. "Words of Life," *Tyler Courier Times,* Shiloh Road Church of Christ, December 15, 1995.

309. Gaddy, C. Welton. *The Gift of Worship.* Nashville: Broadman Press, 1992, 50.

Alton Howard: "As the people of God, we need to reflect this holiness and God's character in our lives since we are created anew in Christ Jesus. We need to **fall upon our knees, upon our faces**, and touch the heavenly."[310]

Ron White: "We know God as the creator. That's incentive enough to **fall down before** God repeatedly. **Worship** should acknowledge His majesty and our **lowliness**. When Simon Peter saw this (both boats filled with fish) he **fell at Jesus' knees** and said, 'Go away from me Lord. I am a sinful man'. The *reverence* we see there by recognizing that he was in the presence of God is the *reverence* we ought to feel when we **worship**. At some point, our worship must **bring us low before** we can be lifted up."[311]

Marvin Phillips prayed, "O God, you are an awesome God and we **bow before** you and praise your magnificent name."[312]

"Before thy throne, O God, we kneel"

Before thy throne, O God, we **kneel**:
Give us a conscience quick to feel,
A ready mind to understand
the meaning of thy chastening hand;
What'er the pain and shame may be,
Bring us O Father, nearer thee.

—*William Boyd Carpenter*

A. W. Tozer: "When a man **falls on his knees** and stretches out his hands and says, 'Our Father, which art in heaven,' he is doing what seems natural to him."[313]

Jim Schwantz admits, "I do **kneel** and pray before every kick-off and kick return to give glory to God that I'm even able to be on the football field in the first place."[314]

310. Howard, Alton. "Standing on Holy Ground." 55th Annual Pepperdine University Bible Lectures, Anaheim, CA, 1998, Audiocassette.

311. White, Ron. "Attitudes for Worship." FHU, Henderson, TN, 1994, Audiocassette.

312. Phillips, Marvin. "Bowing Before an Awesome God". Jubilee Seminar, Nashville, TN, 1994, Audiocassette.

313. Tozer, A. W. *Whatever Happened to Worship*? Gerald B. Smith, ed. Camp Hill: Christian Publications, 1985, 37.

314. Schwantz, Jim. All-pro linebacker for the Dallas Cowboys. *The Dallas Morning News*, January 12, 1997, Section A, 18.

Dean Merrill: "**Kneeling** is a way of saying; 'I fully understand who is boss here.'"[315]

23. Should we *kneel to seek God* & *Jesus* in all their glory & *see the unseen*?

Keith Brooks: "A child of God can see more **on his knees** than a philosopher on his tip toes."[316]

Sir Isaac Newton, who discovered the laws of gravity, made a very profound statement on **kneeling**. He said, "I can take my telescope and look millions of miles into space, but I can lay it aside and go into my room, shut the door, get **down on my knees** in earnest prayer, and see more of Heaven and get closer to God than I can assisted by all the telescopes and material agencies on earth."[317]

"We Saw Thee Not"

We walked not with the chosen few,
Who saw thee from the earth ascend
Who raised to heav'n their wond'ring view,
Then low to earth all **prostrate bend**.

—*Anne Rich*

Edwin White: "We say that if anyone is baptized he becomes a new creature. Why? Because we are baptized into Christ, and we have become floored on the coils of a serious logic that says: 'If in baptism you come in contact with Christ, we no longer have a need to seek Him.' Someone would have done me a great favor, if the day I was baptized they had said, 'Now Edwin, this is just the beginning,' so that I could have gone off to a quiet place and **fallen upon my knees** and said, 'Oh God, show me Thy glory!' Jesus is to be experienced. We are to seek Him, and pursue Him every, every day." [318]

315. Dean Merrill is quoted by Earnest B. Gentile, *Worship God*. Portland: City Bible publishing, 1994, 198.

316. Brooks, Keith L. *The Cream Book of Sentence Sermons*. Chicago: Moody Press, 1974, 93.

317. Newton, Sir Isaac. *Prayer, Powerpoints*. Wheaton: Victor Books, 1995, 36.

318. White, Edwin. "A Sense of Presence, Part II." IBC, Florence, AL, September 23, 1994, Audiocassette.

Lawrence Richards: "When one is afforded a vision of the glory of God, the response is always the same. When Ezekiel beheld God on the throne, he **fell on his face** (Ezekiel 1:28). When John saw the glorified Christ on Patmos, he '**fell at His feet**'" (Revelation 1–7). In a true **worship** experience, one sees the contrast between the glory of God and his own unworthiness."[319]

Jay Lockhart: "Our natural response is, because we are weak and sinful and undone, we **fall before** Him. Not only because of His holiness but in His love, He has dealt with our sin so we could have a *relationship* with Him. He is holy and, therefore, we **worship**."[320]

Jim McGuiggan: "All healthy **worship** strengthens our trust in Him whom we can't see. The bowed head and **bent knee** in the *presence* of the unseen, anchors us more firmly in the realities beyond this life of tangible and visible things."[321]

Jeffrey Dillinger: "We are a few thousand years from the time of Moses, but it is the same God. He must be treated with the same respect. To pray puts us on holy ground . . . In Nehemiah, verse 6 the people cried out, 'Amen, Amen!' They **bowed low** and **worshiped** God, with their **faces to the ground**. The time has come to teach our children the *reverence that is due only unto God.*"[322]

"Kneel at the Feet of Jesus"

I'm gonna **kneel at the feet** of Jesus in the morning,
I'm gonna leave this sinful world before the dawning.
Don't you worry and don't you moan,
It's just about time I was moving along.
I'm gonna **kneel at the feet** of Jesus in the morning.

—As sung by Willie Nelson

319. Richards, Lawrence O. Grand Rapids: *Expository Dictionary of Bible Words*, Zondervan Publishing House, 1991, 639–40.

320. Lockhart, Jay. "We Have Been Raised with Christ, Now What?" West Erwin Church of Christ, Tyler TX, March 14, 1993, Audiocassette.

321. McGuiggan, Jim. "Worship: The Oxygen of the Soul," *Image Magazine*, July/August 1994.

322. Dillinger, Jeffrey. "What is This Holy Ground on Which Moses and All of Us Stand?" *Christian Chronicle*, November 1995, 21.

Charles Hodge offers this sound advice: "If you want to awaken **worship** where you are, come and **kneel before** the Maker. Come to God. You see God, and you **worship**."[323]

Joni Eareckson Tada is a quadriplegic and not physically able to **kneel**, but here is what she says: "Spending time with the Master will elevate your thinking. The more you pray, the more will be revealed. You will understand. You will smile and nod your head as you identify with others who fight long battles, and find a great joy **on their knees.**"[324]

Ted Waller: "We must keep in mind the purpose of it all—letting the glory of the invisible God come into our awareness and **bowing before** Him. Without this there is no **worship**, even if the temple is magnificent and the ritual activities are totally correct."[325]

Denny Boultinghouse: "Some in our fellowship know exactly what I mean when I talk about brokenness. When they have been confronted with the glory of God, they understand their own imperfection, and they **fall to their knees before** Him.[326]

24. Is kneeling before God a gesture that *speaks without words*?

Ron Thomlinson: "In the Garden of Gethsemane when Jesus was becoming aware of His imminent death, He fell **on His knees** to pray (Luke 22:41). Bodily actions matched a sentiment *too deep for words*. Wouldn't it help us if we allowed our bodies to pray our emotions: **kneeling** *in penitence* or **lying prostrate**, offering ourselves totally to Him?"[327]

Ralph Harris: "There will be times when words cannot fully express your feelings, and you can only say praise words like 'glory' or 'hallelujah.' You

323. Hodge, Charles, "I Stand Amazed." IBC Workshop, "Worship Styles of the 90's," Florence, AL, September 23, 1994, Audiocassette.

324. Tada, Joni Eareckson. *Prayer, Powerpoints*. Wheaton: Victor Books, 1995, 85.

325. Waller, Ted H. *Worship: Bowing at the Feet of God*. Nashville: 20th Century Christian, 1994, 21–22.

326. Boultinghouse, Denny. "A Broken and Contrite Heart," *Image magazine*, Vol. 12, No. 2, March–April 1996, 5.

327. Thomlinson, Ron. "Praying with the Body on Bended Knee," *The War Cry*. Alexandria: National Publication of the Salvation Army, June 8, 1996, Vol. 116, No. 12.

may even become silent as you **kneel,** overwhelmed at how great God is. How can I pray effectively? **Worship!**"[328]

Lynn Anderson: "When we **kneel** we are physically saying to God that, 'I have no right to stand in Your presence. I am **falling before** you, and I am recognizing my humility before you'. The act itself, says what words can't say to God. And the act itself creates in us an experience that *words themselves cannot create*."[329]

"The Mystery of Prayer"

If we **kneel** in prayer in His presence
We'll find no need to speak,
For softly in quiet communion,
God grants us the peace that we seek.

—Helen Steiner Rice

Pope John Paul II prayed, "We adore You, Jesus Christ, we adore You. We get **down on our knees.** *We do not find words enough* or gestures to express the veneration with which Your cross fills us, with which the gift of the redemption penetrates us, offered to all mankind once and for all through the total and unconditional subjection of Your will to the will of the Father."[330]

Burke Brack asks, "Can you imagine what those 1,500 souls on the Titanic's massive main deck were thinking after all the lifeboats had been launched? Many **fell to their knees** in *humility, faith, and prayer* as they knew they were about to meet their Maker."[331]

Abraham Lincoln: "I have been driven many times **to my knees** by the overwhelming conviction that I had no where else to go. My own wisdom, and that of all about me, seemed insufficient for the day."[332]

328. Harris, Ralph W. *Now What? A Guidebook for New Christians.* Springfield: Gospel Publishing House, 1995, 13.

329. Anderson, Lynn. Harding University Annual Preacher's Forum, Searcy, AR, April 1994, Audiocassette.

330. Pope John Paul II. *Prayers and Devotions.* St Paul: Penguin Highbridge, 1994, Audiocassette.

331. Brack, Burke. "To the Point," *Shiloh Family Chronicle*, Shiloh Road Church of Christ, Tyler, TX, April 26, 1997.

332. Abraham Lincoln, *Christian Chronicle*, July, 1998, 22.

25. Are there *examples of kneeling* in the New Testament?

Lynn Anderson: "Luke 22:41 is when Jesus goes out to pray in the Garden of Gethsemane. He goes out a few more paces beyond His disciples and it says, 'He **knelt down on the ground** and He prayed.'"[333]

Ken Neller: "People were coming to the earthly Jesus, and they **prostrated themselves before** Him. The leper in Matthew 8:2 **bowed before** Jesus. Jairus in Matthew 9:18 pleaded with Jesus that He might heal his daughter and **bowed before** Him. Jesus' companions, when He was in the boat, **bowed before** Him. The Canaanite woman in Matthew chapter 15, verse 25 **bowed before, prostrates herself before** Jesus. And the mother of James and John also **bowed before** Jesus, and asked a special favor. 'Let my sons sit on your right hand.'"[334]

"Adoration"

Worship the Lord in the beauty of holiness!
Bow down before Him, His glory proclaim;
With gold of obedience and incense of lowliness,
Kneel and adore Him: the Lord is His name!

—*John S. B. Monsell*

Mike Cope is an outstanding communicator, preacher, and co-editor of the religious journal called *Wineskins*. He recently brought to our attention that Mary, the sister of Lazarus, is mentioned in only three places in the gospels, and all three places have something in common. He says, "What I see in common in all three places is, when Mary is there with Jesus, she is **kneeling** at His feet. In Luke 10, she is **kneeling** at His feet soaking up His words. In John Chapter 11, she is **kneeling** at His feet sharing her grief with Him. And in John chapter 12, she is **kneeling** at His feet wiping His feet with her hair. Now that's not a bad place for us to be in 2004, is it—at Jesus' feet?" [335]

333. Anderson, Lynn. Harding University Annual Preacher's Forum, Searcy, AR, April, 1994, Audiocassette.

334. Neller, Ken. "Revelation and Christian Worship." Harding U, Lectureship, Searcy, AR, 1992, Audiocassette.

335. Cope, Mike. "Kneeling at Jesus' Feet." Highland Church of Christ, Abilene, TX, January 4, 2004, Audiocassette.

Charles Swindoll: "The servants are **bowing in worship** before their Lord in adoration and praise ascribing worth and honor to the one deserving of praise—the Lord God!"[336]

Harold Taylor: "In the New Testament when Jesus came with healing in His wings, the Son of Righteousness, when He donned human flesh, and He walked among men, and they beheld Him in all of His glory, and power, and deity, and splendor, and they **bowed** and **worshiped** Him."[337]

Dan Dozier: "Often, when people came to Jesus, they would **kneel** in His presence. Jesus also, was recorded to have **knelt** in prayer to God, especially in the Garden of Gethsemane. We see illustrations of the Apostle Paul **kneeling** when he is about to leave the elders of the church in Ephesus. They all **kneel** down and pray (Acts 20:36). In Acts 21, when he is leaving the city of Tyre, again Paul gets **down on his knees** together with the brothers and sisters."[338]

"We Fall Down"

We **fall down**, we lay our crowns at the feet of Jesus,
The greatness of mercy and love, at the feet of Jesus,
And we cry, "Holy, holy, holy!"
And we cry, "Holy, holy, holy!"
And we cry, "Holy, holy, holy is the lamb."

—*Chris Tomlin*

Lynn Anderson: "One of my favorites is in Acts 20. This is that wonderful farewell meeting when Paul is saying good-bye forever to the wonderful elders that he has worked with in Ephesus, and he's been with them about three years. In verse 26 of Acts 20, 'When Paul had said good-bye, he **knelt down** with all of them and prayed.' And they all wept as they embraced him and they **kissed** him and they grieved that they would never see his face again."[339]

336. Swindoll, Charles R. *The Finishing Touch*. Dallas: Word Publishing Co. 1995, 71.

337. Taylor, Harold. "Worship in Spirit and Truth." FHU Lectures, Henderson, TN, 1994, Audiocassette.

338. Dozier, Daniel A. "Worship is a Verb." The Church That Connects III Seminar, San Antonio, TX, August 6, 1994, Audiocassette.

339. Anderson, Lynn. Harding University Annual Preacher's Forum, Searcy, AR, April 1994, Audiocassette.

Hardeman Nichols: "In Acts chapter 21, Paul comes to Tyre. He meets with the church there and verse 5 says, 'We departed and went our way. And they all brought us on our way with wives and children until we were out of the city, and we **kneeled down** on the shore and prayed.' I read this passage and I think about those little children. Paul later dies, they're grown, and they think back on their youth, and they no doubt could say, 'You know the great Apostle Paul? I remember that the whole church met out at the sea shore and I saw them **kneel** and pray when he departed.' Now, think what that would have robbed from those children if they'd been left in a nursery back home."[340]

Chris Dempsey: "Luke records Jesus as being in agony as He '**fell down upon His knees.**' The prayer that He prayed was from His heart. His cries stemmed from His soul."[341]

Lindsey Garmon emphasized that the woman at the well is, "thinking of **worshipers bowing down** in holy places where there was the presumption of a divine presence."[342]

Richard Leonard: "Although Jesus had spoken of genuine worship of the Father as worship 'in spirit and in truth' (En pneumai kai aletheia, John 4:23). This did not mean that Christian **worship** was so spiritual that it was invisible. Within the assembly of believers, acts of **worship** were visible acts. The word translated '**worship**,' as noted above, means to **kneel**, **bow**, or **prostrate one's self**, and such actions must accompany the vocal expressions of praise and supplication. Paul, for one, expressed his faith in prayer, 'I **kneel** before the Father'" (Ephesians 3:14).[343]

340. Nichols, Hardeman. "Open Forum: Alternate Assemblies." IBC, September 23, 1994, Audiocassette.

341. Dempsey, Chris. "Teach Us to Pray." FHU Bible Lectures, Henderson, TN, 1994, Audiocassette.

342. Garmon, Lindsey. "Worship and the Assembly. #10-Word Study." Church of Christ South, Corpus Christi, TX, 1995, Audiocassette.

343. Leonard, Richard C. "New Testament Vocabulary of Worship," *The Biblical foundations of Christian Worship*, Robert E. Webber, ed. Star Song Publishing Group, Nashville, TN 1993,19–23.

"All Things Praise Thee"

All things praise Thee:
Heav'n's high shrine rings with melody divine,
Lowly bending at Thy feet,
seraph and arch-angel meet.

—*G. W. Conder*

26. Are there *examples of kneeling* in the Old Testament ?

Jack Lewis is an authority on the meaning of Bible words in the OT. He says, "In the Old Testament is the suggestion that physical acts precede your spiritual. Postures of prayer that are mentioned would include Moses **lying prostrate** 40 days and 40 nights at Sinai. Joshua **prostrated himself** in the conquest story. Ezra **prostrates himself** in Ezra chapter 10."[344]

Jack Reese: "When we come together as a people of God in **worship**, we come in surrender, in reverence, and in submission. It has always been this way. In Nehemiah 9, as the people give their lives in **worship**, as they return to the new land, Ezra blessed the lord and the people responded, 'Amen! Amen!' and **bowed to the ground** and **worshiped**."[345]

Leon Barnes: "We can get the old Elijah complex—where we think 'I'm the only one left.' And God said, 'Elijah, I have 7,000 people that have **not bowed the knee** to Baal that you don't know about.' And often we're that way. We begin to think that 'me and my congregation are the only ones and most of them are in trouble.'"[346]

Earnest Gentile: "The OT offers numerous illustrations of individuals and groups **kneeling, prostrating themselves, falling down**, or **bowing low**. The human form in **bent posture** best portrays reverential fear and dependence."[347]

344. Lewis, Jack. "OT Word Studies in Worship." FHU Bible Lectureship, Henderson, TN, 1994, Audiocassette.

345. Reese, Jack. Preston Road Church of Christ, Dallas, TX, January 2, 1994, Audiocassette.

346. Barnes, Leon. "Jesus and Prayer in Luke." Harding University Lectureship, Searcy, AR, 1995, Audiocassette.

347. Gentile, Earnest B. *Worship God*. Portland: City Bible publishing, 1994, 196.

Dan Dozier: "When Solomon was dedicating the temple, he stood up on the platform and then **knelt down before** the whole assembly of Israel and spread out his hands toward heaven. After Solomon's prayer, God sent fire down from heaven, consumed all the offerings that were there and the sacrifices and filled the temple with His glory and in 2 Chronicles 7:3 says this, 'When all the Israelites saw the fire coming down and the glory of the Lord above the temple, they **knelt** on the pavement with their **faces to the ground** and they **worshiped** and gave thanks to God saying, 'He is good and His love endures forever.'"[348]

Willard Tate: "Jehosephat **bowed with his face to the ground,** and all the people of Judea and Jerusalem **fell down** and **worshiped.** At this time, Job looked up to God, tore his robe and shaved his head. Then he **fell to the ground and worshiped.**"[349]

"When the Saints go Marching in"

O Lord I want to be in that number,
when the saints go marching in.
O **when they bow**, before the throne,
O **when they bow** before the throne,
O Lord I want to be in that number,
When they crown Thee Lord of Lords.

—As sung by Andy Griffith

A. W. Tozer: "When the prophets try to describe for me the attributes, the graces, and the worthiness of the God who appeared to them and dealt with them, I feel that I can **kneel down** and follow their admonition: 'He is thy Lord - **worship** thou Him.'"[350]

Jay Lockhart: "As David prepared to sacrifice to the Lord he 'saw the angel of the Lord standing between earth and heaven, having in his hand a drawn sword stretched out over Jerusalem' (I Chronicles 21:16).

348. Dozier, Daniel A. "Worship is a Verb." The Church That Connects III Seminar, San Antonio, TX, August 6, 1994, Audiocassette.

349. Tate, Willard. "Area Praise Service." Austin Avenue Church of Christ, Brownwood, Texas, December 1, 1996, Audiocassette.

350. Tozer, A. W. *Whatever Happened to Worship?* Camp Hill: Christian Publications, 1985, 120.

Immediately David and those with him **fell on their faces**, but Oran continued threshing wheat."[351]

Lynn Anderson: "In most concordances, they list in the Old Testament well over fifty passages that talk specifically about people **falling down** to **worship**."[352]

27. Should kneeling be *restored in worship* in the assembly?

(What do the Bible scholars say about **kneeling** in worship?)

James LeFan preached an excellent sermon on "Taking Care of Your Soul" that mentioned **kneeling**. Afterward, I asked him if **kneeling** was still appropriate. He said, "My favorite body position for prayer is **kneeling**, and I pray **on my knees** every day. My father always **kneeled** in the assembly during prayer—not some of the time, but always." (Personal Communication October 4, 1998).

Foxe's Christian Martyrs of the World: "Of James, the brother of the Lord, we read the following: 'James, being a just and perfect man, governed the church with the apostles. He would enter the temple alone, **fall on his knees**, and ask remission for the people, doing this so often that his knees lost their sense of feeling and became hardened, like the knees of a camel. Because of his holy life, James was called 'The Just' and 'The Safeguard of the People.'"[353]

"We Bow Down"

We **bow down**
And we worship You, Lord
Lord of all Lords You will be.

—*Twila Paris*

Mike Warner *humbly* admits, "I really, at times, want to raise my hands during a certain song that we sing and during prayer. It is absolutely scrip-

351. Lockhart, Jay. "But Oran continued threshing wheat" *From the Heart of Tyler*, West Erwin Church of Christ, Tyler, TX, October 7, 2004.

352. Anderson, Lynn. Harding University Annual Preacher's Forum, Searcy, AR, April 1994, Audiocassette.

353. John Foxe: "The Apostles," *Foxe's Christian Martyrs of the World*. Uhrichsville: Barbour and Company, Inc., 2001, 7.

tural. I really want to **kneel** sometimes. As a matter of fact, I'm going to *confess* something to you. Sometimes up there on the front pew, I **kneel** and you never know about it. The fact is, that doing any one of those—**kneeling**, or raising your hands, is decently and in order, and scriptural."[354]

Hal Hougey: "Father, have we forgotten how to adore and glorify You? Are our **knees so stiff** from *spiritual arthritis* that we may never **fall down before** You? God, forgive us!"[355]

Willard Tate: "A moment ago when we sang the song '**We Bow Down**', I started to physically **bow down**. In fact, the Hebrew word for praise is the **bowing down**. One of the things that is so great about the Psalms, is it brings us to a **bowing** and **worship** state. It is that one theme of God at the center, and man **bowing down** in praise and **worship** to Him."[356]

"Jesus, Hold My Hand"

When I **kneel** in prayer,
I hope to meet you there,
Blessed Jesus hold my hand.

—*Albert E. Brumley*

Marvin Phillips believes that we have lost something by not **kneeling in worship**. He says, "I got a chance to preach in a downtown Korean Church of Christ. When inside, the first thing they did was get **down on their knees**, and then **down on their elbows**, and then **down on their foreheads**. And it was their way of doing what you are reading about in Ezekiel chapter 44: 'The glory of the Lord is in the house and I **fell face downward**.' I think people have lost something through the years."[357]

Lynn Anderson vividly recalls **kneeling** in **worship**. He said, "I can remember many, many Church meetings in my family home in the winter, and when it came time to pray, everyone **knelt down** around the furniture.

354. Warner, Mike. "Acceptable Worship". Shiloh Road Church of Christ, Tyler, TX, July 11, 1993, Audiocassette.

355. Hougey, Hal. *The Quest for Understandable Hermeneutics*. Concord: Pacific Publishing Company, 1997, 462.

356. Tate, Willard. "Area Praise Service." Austin Avenue Church of Christ, Brownwood, Texas, December 1, 1996, Audiocassette.

357. Phillips, Marvin. "Bowing Before an Awesome God." Jubilee Seminar, Nashville, TN, 1994, Audiocassette.

In the summer, we met at the schoolhouse and **knelt** around the school desks. In fact, in my imagination, I can still smell the varnish on those old desks as we **knelt** to pray in that schoolhouse week after week."[358]

Jack Reese gives two excellent examples of **kneeling** in the book of Acts. He says, "In Acts 20, Paul prays for the last time with the Ephesian elders and they pray, **down on their knees**—Paul and the elders in prayer. And in Acts 21, he makes his way to the city of Tyre, and they go to the beach, men and women and children and Paul, **down on their knees** in prayer because an appropriate response of **worship** is to surrender."[359]

Mike Cope: "God is still waiting for people to **bow down** in *humility*, admitting their need for help—waiting for people to *confess* their inability to be good—waiting for people to see the dire need they have for a Savior."[360]

Dan Dozier: "**Kneeling** transcends time and place; it is not restricted to times long ago and lands far, far away. The real question is not 'shall we or shall we not **kneel** in our **worship** services?' Rather, the question is, 'shall we who *will* someday **bow the knee** in God's presence, **kneel** now as well'? Does it make sense that those who **kneel** as we **worship** God in heaven—get plenty of practice as we **worship** the Lord on earth?"[361]

Nelda Browning recalls, "Another memory, seldom seen anymore because of speaker systems, is the custom of men **kneeling** to pray. Many times men would **kneel** in the aisle, or up on the platform, they would **kneel** there to pray."[362]

Robert Webber: "With the congregation still **kneeling**, the choir sang 'The Lord's Prayer' in a simple and powerful Gregorian chant."[363]

358. Anderson, Lynn. Harding University Annual Preacher's Forum, Searcy, AR, April 1994, Audiocassette.

359. Reese, Jack. Preston Road Church of Christ, Dallas TX, January 2, 1994, Audiocassette.

360. Cope, Mike. "The Road to Canossa." Highland Church of Christ, Abilene, TX, April 4, 1993, Audiocassette.

361. Dozier, Daniel A. *Come Let Us Adore Him*. Joplin: College Press Publishing Company, 1994, 287–88.

362. Browning, Nelda. *From the Heart of Tyler A History of the West Erwin Church of Christ*. Tyler: Published by West Erwin Church of Christ, 1991, 10.

363. Webber, Robert E. *Worship is a Verb*. Nashville: Star Song Publishing Group, 1992, 14.

Alexander Campbell: "I know how reluctant men are to submit to God's government; and yet they must all **bow** to it. 'To Jesus, **every knee shall bow**, and to Him every tongue *confess*.' But, they object to **bowing now** and invent excuses."[364]

"Our King Immanuel"

Let us **bow down** and **worship** Him
Who doeth all things well,
All hail, all hail, our King, Immanuel!

—*James Rowe*

In a personal communication with Kenneth Chadwell, he said: "I remember that some older gentlemen in the congregation where I grew up would frequently **kneel down** when they prayed. Even though *proskuneo* lost its outward meaning to some over a period of time, does that mean that it lost it's meaning in the New Testament? I don't think so. I think restoration is an ongoing process."

Mother Teresa, regarding the Movement of "Nations for **Kneeling**", said, "God love you for your sincere desire to see Jesus. I fully support any organization which has **kneeling** as its aim, and I will be praying for you and all the intentions of 'The Movement of Nations for **Kneeling**.'"[365]

In a personal communication with Henry Blackaby, he said, "**Kneeling** is the deepest expression of humility. When your body **kneels**, it helps your heart to do the same. If there was ever a generation that needed to **kneel**, this is the one. This is a self-centered generation who refuses to **kneel** to anyone and its affecting the life of the Church. It is difficult to walk into the presence of God and not **kneel**. If we just strut into the presence of God and not **kneel**, that's arrogance, and He is not pleased." (Personal communication)

Dan Dozier: "I think the real question is, 'Shall we, who someday will **bow the knee** to the Lord, do it now or will we wait?' Paul said, '**Every knee**

364. Campbell, Alexander. *The Christian System*. Nashville: The Gospel Advocate Company, 1964, 209.

365. Mother Teresa—Re: Nations for **Kneeling**—she has pledged full support!

shall bow and every tongue will *confess'* (Romans 14:11). I would like to get a little practice here before I get there, wouldn't you?"[366]

"None of Self and All of Thee"

Day by day His tender mercy
healing, helping, full and free,
brought me lower while I whispered,
"Less of self, and more of Thee."

—*Theodore Monod*

Jack Reese longs for **kneeling in worship** to return. He says, "We find it difficult to image the symbol of the ancient words for **worship** that call for the **bowing down,** or the **kneeling in worship** in utter, devastated obedient submission to the One who is greater than we. Why we are not called **to our knees** to **worship,** I don't know. I can remember a time, and some of you can clearly remember times in the1940's and 1930's and earlier, where it was not an uncommon thing among Churches of Christ for Godly people to **kneel in worship,** and I long for those days to return."[367]

Leonard Pitts: "The church of my childhood was in a storefront in Los Angeles where the elders moaned exquisite songs and Deacon Dansby prayed **on bended knee.**"[368]

Harold Taylor: Following his excellent sermon that mentioned "**kneeling**", I asked Harold Taylor if he thought that **kneeling** was still appropriate. He said, "Oh yes! I think we've missed it. We've lost the *awe* and the *reverence* of who God is. When I was a kid, we had prayer **benches for kneeling** all across the front of the auditorium. Some of the young people don't think so, but I know what **true worship** really is."(Personal Communication).

Robert Webber: "If these creatures of heaven live before God in an unceasing **posture of praise** and adoration, how can we mortal beings act lightly and imprudently before Him in **worship**?"[369]

366. Dozier, Daniel A. "Worship is a Verb." The Church That Connects III Seminar, San Antonio, TX, August 6, 1994, Audiocassette.

367. Reese, Jack. Harding University Annual Preacher's Forum, Searcy, AR, April 1994, Audiocassette.

368. Pitts, Leonard. (AP) "Contract with the American Family," *The Dallas Morning News,* Dallas, TX, May 24, 1995.

369. Webber, Robert E. *Worship is a Verb.* Nashville: Star Song Pub, 1992, 111.

Jack Hayford, after writing the famous song, "Majesty", wrote the book called *Worship His Majesty.* On page 200 he says, "Many of us are learning to include another transaction in our **worship—the offering of our bodies as a living sacrifice,** *humbly* presented in **worship. Kneeling** was once avoided by evangelical Protestants as being too 'high church,' reserved only for a penitent at the altar following an invitation. Now it's practice is filling our **worship** services and prayer meetings. Such songs as 'Come Let Us **Worship and Bow Down,**' 'I Will Come and **Bow Down,**' and 'No Higher Calling' point the way and encourage us to do what we are singing."[370]

Friar Scanlan: "The act of **bending the knee before** Jesus Christ transcends culture because it is an act that has scriptural, traditional, and cosmic significance. If a person deliberately, and with full knowledge, discourages **kneeling,** he or she is 'anathema.'"[371]

"O God of Infinite Mercy"

O God of infinite mercy,
we come before Thee now.
Incline our hearts to worship,
as **all before Thee bow.**

—Tillit S. Teddlie

Jay Lockhart asked, "What would you do if we were in **worship,** and we were going to pray, and the person next to you got **down on their knees?** What would you do if the person next to you, when we pray, raised their hands? When Solomon dedicated the temple in I Kings chapter 8, he **kneeled** and lifted his hands to God. You say, 'Oh, but that is the Old Testament and that was Solomon.' 2 Timothy 2:8–10 says, 'I will that men pray everywhere lifting holy hands.' You see, when we are critical of somebody in their **worship** of God, let's make sure that it is a matter of Scripture and not of preference."[372]

Joseph Garlington: "Although the Bible is filled with rich references to exuberant praise in **worship** and **prostration before** God, countless mod-

370. Hayford, Jack. *Worship His Majesty.* Ventura: Regal Books, 2000, 200–201.

371. Scanlan, Friar. *Homiletic & Pastoral Review,* August 1994.

372. Lockhart, Jay. "The Shepherd King # 6—Standing on Holy Ground." West Erwin Church of Christ, Tyler, TX, December 31, 1995, Audiocassette.

ern church services are begun with the dry recitation of one scripture verse."[373]

Robert Webber, the well known author of *Worship is a Verb*, and editor of the *Complete Library of Christian Worship*, says, "**Worship** has a body language all its own, so why have we forgotten it? Scriptures tell us '**every knee shall bow** and every tongue confess that Jesus is Lord' (Phil. 2:10–11). 'He is Lord' is the earliest Christian creed implying **bending the knee**. So, the next time you gather to **worship, bow down**! For good **worship**, the inner person must intend what the outer person is doing."[374]

Dan Dozier emphasizes that, "It is altogether appropriate to **kneel**. And some of you are old enough to remember when that was not unusual, even in our fellowship."[375]

Jack Reese remembers **when congregations kneeled**. He says, "I don't know when it happened, but it happened sometime in this century, that in Churches of Christ we decided we don't need to **kneel** anymore. There was a time last century, and early in this century—as many of you will remember—when it was common in Churches of Christ for members to **kneel in prayer** and **worship**. It is sad to me that those days seem to be gone. I believe there is as a direct connection between the **knee** and the heart."[376]

373. Garlington, Joseph L. *Worship: The Pattern of Things in Heaven*. Shippensburg: Destiny Image Publishers, Inc., 1998, 27.

374. Webber, Robert, "Every Knee Shall Bow," *Worship Leader*, Vol. 7, No. 3, May–June 1998, 14.

375. Dozier, Daniel A. "Worship is a Verb." The Church That Connects III Seminar, San Antonio, TX, August 6, 1994, Audiocassette.

376. Reese, Jack. Preston Road Church of Christ, Dallas, TX, January 2, 1994, Audiocassette.

"Take the Name of Jesus with You"

At the name of Jesus **bowing**,
Falling prostrate at his feet,
King of Kings in heav'n we'll crown him,
When our journey is complete. (V. 4)

—*Lydia Baxter*

Rick Atchley is absolutely correct when he says, "Leaders, you have got to model it for our churches. **Kneeling** is the body position of Godly leadership. Check it out in your Bibles. 'The battle belongs to the Lord,' and prayer is our greatest weapon. Spiritual leaders do not view *prayer* as their last resort. It's their first priority."[377]

Charles Hodge is a gifted preacher who believes that, "As long as an old boy travels **on his knees** and has *reverence* for the word of God, we're going to be all right."[378]

A. W Tozer: "There must always be that awe upon our spirits that says, 'Ah, Lord God, Thou knowest!'—that stands silent and breathless—or **kneels** in the *presence* of that awesome Wonder, that Mystery, that unspeakable Majesty, before whom the prophets used **to fall**, and before whom Peter and John and the rest of them **fell down**."[379]

Frederick Kubicek: "God Himself directed them to **bow down** to Him when they brought in the grain offering (Deut. 26:10). The Hebrew word for **'worship'** used here, like its Greek counterpart, means to **prostrate oneself and bow down**."[380]

377. Atchley, Rick, "Resurrecting the Power of Prayer." Up from the Grave, Jubilee Seminar, Nashville, TN, 1998, Audiocassette.

378. Hodge, Charles, "The Power of Prayer." West Erwin Church of Christ, Tyler, Texas—1995, Audiocassette.

379. Tozer, A. W. *Worship: The Missing Jewel.* Camp Hill: Christian Publishing, 1992, 6.

380. Kubicek, Frederick C. Accessed 1/15/01 Online: www.unlimitedglory.org/needful.

"Father, Hear Thy Children's Call"

Father, hear Thy children's call:
Humbly **at Thy feet we fall.**

—*Thomas B. Pollock*

Stafford North accurately points out the meaning of the **"worship"** word *proskuneo* in John 4:24 that must be done in spirit and in truth. He says, "In John 4:24, Jesus tells the Samaritan woman the time has come for a change in **worship**. Jesus' word for **worship** here means '**to kiss.**' We **prostrate ourselves** to send God a message of *submission, adoration*, praise, or request.' For significant improvement in **worship**, then, we should teach what **worship** is—Changing the order, **kneeling**, or singing different songs might sometimes help us to think and feel more by taking us out of a routine."[381]

Dan Dozier: "We took the **kneeling benches** out, or never put them in, probably because some other religious groups did. And, frankly, part of the thing about **kneeling** is that it is difficult in most of our assembly halls, because the seats are so close together that you can't get down. If you do get down, you can't get up. I realize that sometimes there are health problems. Age sometimes creates kinds of health problems that make it impractical for us to **kneel**, But the Biblical perspective is still that we **kneel.**"[382]

Lynn Anderson has concluded that, "What we need today in the Church, is to be called back to **worship**." He illustrates his point with the worthiness of Jesus. He says, "Hear it again in the words of John, 'You are worthy to take the scroll and to open the seals because you were slain and with your blood you purchased men for God from every tribe and language and people and nation. Worthy is the Lamb who was slain to receive power and wealth and wisdom and honor and glory and praise. And to Him who sits on the throne and to the Lamb be praise and honor and glory and power forever and ever. And the four living creatures said, 'Amen!' And

381. North, Stafford. "The best way to improve our worship to God," *The Christian Chronicle*, Oklahoma City, OK, December 1994, 20.

382. Dozier, Daniel A. "Worship is a Verb." The Church That Connects III Seminar, San Antonio, TX, August 6, 1994, Audiocassette.

everybody fell down and worshiped Him.' What we need today in the Church is to be called back to **worship**."[383]

Mrs. T. J. (Wanda) Taylor personally shared this wonderful story to me: "Just before my husband died from cancer, I took him to church in a wheelchair. He had preached there for 20 years, and as I pushed him through the side door, he said, 'Push me to edge of the altar.' His body was racked with pain, but he was determined to get out of that wheelchair. When he was finally able to get **down on his knees**, he raised his hands toward heaven and just **worshiped** the Lord." (Personal communication).

"Let Every Heart Rejoice and Sing"

He bids the sun to rise and set:
In heav'n His pow'r is known:
And earth, subdued to Him,
shall yet **bow low before** His throne

—*Henry S. Washburne*

Charles Hodge: "We have taken awe and wonder out of our religion. The Bible says **every knee shall bow**. Beloved, nothing is as boring as trying to do church work without wonder. Going though the motions starves the soul and my brethren have just about worn themselves out. We need to restore the wonder! To **worship** God we have to have a sense of wonder. Ezekiel saw God and he **fell face down** to the ground repeatedly. Daniel saw God and **he collapsed**. And in Revelation the apostle John saw God and he **became as a dead man**."[384]

Randy Gill: "One of the side effects of the **worship** renewal movement is that people are feeling freer to express emotion in **worship**—to say 'Amen', 'Hallelujah', or to clap, or to **kneel** in prayer, or to lift up their hands when they sing."[385]

383. Anderson, Lynn. Harding University Annual Preacher's Forum, Searcy, AR, April 1994, Audiocassette.

384. Hodge, Charles. "I Stand Amazed." IBC Workshop: "Worship Styles of the 90's," Florence, AL, September 23, 1994, Audiocassette.

385. Gill, Randy. "Understanding Worship: Contemporary Perspective." Jubilee Seminar, Nashville, TN, 1998, Audiocassette.

Jim Goll believes that, "Some of us today are taught to stand and shoot at the devil before we are taught to **kneel** before the Father. If we reversed the order, maybe our aim would be better!"[386]

The Kneeling Christian by an unknown Christian says, "Gracious Savior, pour out upon us the fullness of the Holy Spirit that we may indeed become **Kneeling** Christians."[387]

Perry Cotham: "Your body is important in **worship. Worship** expressions during Biblical times include *humble* **kneeling** or **lying prostrate before** the Lord. Let's consider some of the scriptural evidence for these expressions of **worship**—kneeling *and* bowing: 'I **kneel** before the Father, from whom his whole family in heaven and on earth derives its name' (Ephesians 3:14–15); 'When he had said this, he **knelt down** with them all and prayed' (Acts 20:36). 'Come, let us **worship** and **bow down**, let us **kneel before** the Lord our Maker, for he is our God' (Psalm 95:6–7). Paul notes that in the right situation of assembly, even a sinner 'will **fall down** and **worship** God', exclaiming, 'God is really among you.' (1 Corinthians 14:25)."[388]

Earnest Gentile: "John Wesley's advice was to 'always **kneel** during the public prayer.' The motto of the Welsh Revival was: '**Bend the church**, and save the people.' Unfortunately, some churches find **kneeling** awkward and unnecessary. **Kneeling** enhances spiritual life. Many identify the praying hands as the true symbol of prayer. Actually, **bent knees** come closer to reality."[389]

"Jesus Paid It All"

O I hope to please Him now,
Light of joy is on my brow,
As **at His dear feet I bow.**

—M. S. Shaffer

386. Goll, Jim W. *Kneeling on the Promises*, Grand Rapids: Chosen Books, 2000, 21.

387. Unknown Author. *The Kneeling Christian*. Grand Rapids: Zondervan Publishing House, 1945, 28.

388. Cotham, Perry C. *Ceasefire: Ending Worship Wars with Sound Theology & Plain Common Sense*. Orange: New Leaf Books, 2002, 217–18.

389. Gentile, Earnest B. *Worship God*. Portland: City Bible publishing, 1994, 195.

Henry Wadsworth Longfellow wrote, "So, as I enter here from day to day, **kneeling** in prayer, and not ashamed to pray, while the eternal ages watch and wait."[390]

What about **kneeling** in the early church? Robert Webber's book, *Worship Old and New*, tells about **kneeling** in prayer in the early church as recorded by Gregory Dix. He is recognized as "one of the foremost liturgists of the twentieth century." He wrote, "First a subject was announced, and the congregation was bidden to pray. All prayed silently **on their knees** for a while; then, on the signal being given, they rose from their knees, and the officiant summed up the petitions of all in a brief collect. They **knelt** to pray as individuals, but the corporate prayer of the church is a priestly act, to be done in the priestly posture for prayer, standing. Therefore all rose for the concluding collect."

Gregory Dix also says the following scheme of the old Roman intercessions is still in use on Good Friday. "*Officiant*: Let us pray my dearly beloved, for the holy church of God. *Deacon*: Let us **bow the knee**. (All **kneel** and pray in silence for a while). He then tells of an Eastern scheme taken from the Alexandrian liturgy. "The deacon proclaims first: Stand to pray. (All have been 'standing at ease' or sitting on the ground for the sermon). *Then he begins*: Pray for the living, pray for the sick, pray for all away from home. Let us **bow the knee**. (All pray in silence) Let us arise. Let us **bow the knee**. Let us arise again. Let us **bow the knee**. The people say, 'Lord have mercy.'"[391]

David Trembley: "The pose we learned in childhood, **head bowed and on our knees**, also suggests *humility*. **Bowing and kneeling** have been customary postures of deference before nobility or royalty throughout human history. Paul admonishes this body language in the prayers of the faithful when 'at the *name* of Jesus **every knee should bow**, in heaven and on earth, and under the earth, and every tongue *confess* that Jesus Christ is Lord' (Philippians 2:10). Praying **on our knees with our face down on the ground** puts us in the mind of someone who knows he or she is in

390. Longfellow, Henry Wadsworth. "Sonnet," *The Treasure Chest*, San Francisco: Harper & Row, 1965, 59.

391. Webber, Robert. *Worship Old and New*. Grand Rapids: The Zondervan Corporation, 1982, 128–29.

the presence of Majesty. How could such action help but shape a *humble* prayer?"[392]

Dan Dozier: "The apostle Paul wrote it beautifully when referring to Jesus in Philippians 2:9–11: 'Therefore, God exalted Him to the highest place, and gave Him the *name* that is above every *name* that at the *name* of Jesus **every knee shall bow**, and every tongue *confess* that Jesus Christ is Lord to the glory of God the Father.' It is appropriate for us to **kneel in worship**. Almost all Christians will at least **bow their heads** in prayer, but shamefully few of us will **kneel**—get down **on our knees** in public assemblies. Why do so few of us **kneel** in public **worship**?"[393]

"Ye Servants of God"

The praises of Jesus
The angels proclaim,
Fall down on their faces,
And **worship** the Lamb.

—*Charles Wesley*

Robert Webber says that today's young people, "are a rich source for understanding what's going to be happening in the future of **worship**." He then gives examples of the technology they grew up with including television, computers, the Internet, cell phones, and cyberspace. "They are a symbol conscious generation." He tells of visiting a church service in Brandon, Tennessee and says that, "A huge roughly hewn cross was placed in the center of the **worship** space. As we sang, the young began to respond. Some raised their hands toward the tree, others came and **knelt before** it and a few **layed prostrate**."

Dr. Webber then makes some very important points. He says, "I was reminded of an early Christian prayer that speaks of the 'Life giving Tree'. We lost our relationship with God through the disobedience of man at a tree. But we have regained our relationship with God through the obedience of the second Adam on a tree. Is this tree formed into the cross just

392. Trembley, David. *Pray magazine* Colorado Springs, CO, May/June 1999, 27–28.

393. Dozier, Daniel A. "Worship is a Verb." The Church That Connects III Seminar, San Antonio, TX, August 6, 1994, Audiocassette.

an empty symbol? Or is it a life-giving symbol that energizes faith and deepens our personal spiritual commitments?"[394]

Mike Gravois: "When we **fall to our knees** in prayer we have a Savior in heaven who says, 'I know—for I was there!'"[395]

Dan Dozier uses Jesus and the apostle Paul as our examples. He said, "Jesus **knelt** in the garden of Gethsemane as He prayed to His Father (Luke 22:41). As Paul was about to leave the elders of the church of Ephesus, they all **knelt down** and prayed (Acts 20:36), as did the believers when Paul left the city of Tyre (Acts 21:5). Writing to the Ephesians, Paul said, 'For these reason I **kneel before** the Father, from whom His whole family in heaven and on earth derives its name' (Ephesians 3:14)."[396]

Jim Goll: "There is one hymn I would tweak a bit if I could. It is 'Standing on the Promises.' I would adjust that marvelous hymn 'chiropractically.'"

Kneeling, kneeling,
Kneeling on the promises of God my Savior;
Kneeling, kneeling,
Kneeling on the promises of God."[397]

—*Jim Goll*

A. Beards: "**Kneeling** is the ultimate sign of *reverence* paid to God. If we attempt to banish or downplay the posture of **kneeling,** we will be doing serious harm to an element integral to Catholic liturgy. Jesus prayed while **kneeling. Kneeling** was, from apostolic times, the general custom. In the OT and NT it is the posture of the New Covenant, when all **fall to adore** God-with-us in Christ. The gesture, as Isaiah had foretold, would greet the coming of God's Kingdom and signifies profound *adoration.*"[398]

394. Webber, Robert. "The Resurrection of the Cross as Symbol," *Worship Leader,* March/April 2001, 12.

395. Gravois, Mike. "Heavenly Housekeeping." West Erwin Church of Christ, Tyler, Texas, July 12, 1998, Audiocassette.

396. Dozier, Daniel A. *Come Let Us Adore Him.* Joplin: College Press Publishing Company, 1994, 287.

397. Goll, Jim W. *Kneeling on the Promises.* Grand Rapids: Chosen Books, 2000, 17.

398. Beards, A. "Homiletic & Pastoral Review," Accessed February 1992, Online: www.salbert.tripod.com/index-14.html.

"Napoleon Bonaparte probably gave one of the best explanations between honoring man and **worshiping** God: 'If Socrates would enter the room, we should rise and do him honor. But if Jesus Christ came into the room, we should **fall down on our knees** and **worship** Him.'"[399]

A few decades ago, it was common for people, especially men in our churches **to kneel** in public worship. Why did we stop? Could it be that we have become too sophisticated to **humble ourselves** before God by getting **down on our knees** in public **worship?** We cannot ignore what scripture says on this matter.[400]

Jack Lewis: "**Worship is bowing before** the divine king. The fact that Westerners do not **bow before** any person is perhaps a part of the cause of their failure to grasp the essence of the **worship** of God. The psalmist calls: 'O come, let us **worship and bow down**. Let us **kneel before** the Lord our Maker' (Psalm 95:6)."[401]

Max Lucado preached an excellent sermon called "Someone Prayed." He began by quoting the apostle John in Revelation: "John says, 'On the Lord's day I was in the spirit, and I heard a loud voice behind me that sounded like a trumpet.' John is old now, Peter is gone, and the apostle Paul has been buried. To envision John we need to silver his hair and stoop his shoulders. He's on an island called Patmos and with slow, sometimes unsteady steps, the aged apostle is inching his way across the beach looking for a place to **kneel**, because it's the Lord's Day. He is in the spirit. He is in the presence of God, and he wants to do on this Lord's Day what he has done ever since that first Lord's Day. On much younger legs he ran to the empty tomb."[402]

399. Gentile, Earnest B. records Napoleon Bonaparte in *Worship God*. Portland: City Bible publishing, 1994, 69.

400. Dozier, Daniel A., *Come Let Us Adore Him*, College Press Publishing Co. 1994, p. 232.

401. Lewis, Jack P. "Old Testament Word Studies in Worship." Henderson: FHU Lectures, 1994, 232.

402. Lucado, Max. "Someone Prayed." Richland Hills Church of Christ, Ft. Worth, TX, September 2, 1998, Audiocassette.

"Worthy Art Thou!"

Lift up the voice in praise and devotion,
Saints of all earth **before Him should bow.**
Angels in heaven worship Him, saying,
Worthy art Thou! Worthy art Thou!

—*Tillit S. Teddlie*

Glover Shipp, *Christian Chronicle* editor says, "In my growing-up years in western Oregon, the men of our congregation would never have thought of praying in public without **kneeling**. In our informal lifestyle of today, we would consider such a posture odd, but perhaps, they had something that we have lost. **Worshipers** in Bible times not only **knelt before** God, but even **prostrated themselves** in *reverence* before their holy creator."[403]

A. W. Tozer wrote the book, *Whatever Happened to Worship?* In it he reminds us that, "The Lord is in His holy temple—let us all **kneel** before Him."[404]

According to Professor Abraham Malherbe, confessing that "Jesus is Lord" while **on bended knee** seems to have been part of the "**worship** of the church" in the first century. After receiving the Distinguished Alumnus of the Year Award at the Christian Scholars Conference held at Pepperdine University in 1994, he gave a lecture on "Creeds and Their Uses: The New Testament." Professor Malherbe quoted Philippians 2:9–11: "Therefore, God has highly exalted him and bestowed on him the name which is above every *name*, that at the *name* of Jesus **every knee should bow**, in heaven and on earth and under the earth, and every tongue confess that Jesus is Lord, to the glory of God the Father (Phil. 2:9–11)." He then made a very profound statement: "*The confession in view here seems to be part of the **worship** of the church.*"[405]

Jeff Christian: "Once upon a time there was a man who had been a Christian for much of his life. He loved to read the Bible, go to Church,

403. Shipp, Glover. "How Shall we Approach the Lord?" *Christian Chronicle*, March 19, 1999, 22.

404. Tozer, A. W. *Whatever Happened to Worship?* Camp Hill: Christian Publications, 1985, 122.

405. Malherbe, Abraham. "Creeds and Their Uses: The New Testament," *Christian Studies*, Austin, TX, Vol. #14, 1994, 11.

attend lectures, buy books, converse with scholars and preachers about the latest trends in studying the Bible, baptism, the Lord's Supper, and elders. But, he never once **fell to his knees** in praise and thanksgiving to God. I would assert that one of our biggest downfalls in modern Christianity is that sometimes we like to talk about God so much that we actually forget to encounter Him—actually **falling to our knees**."[406]

John Scott is a popular and gifted preacher who tells us that, "James, the brother of the Master and author of the book of James, was known as such a man of prayer that he had literally developed **calluses on his knees**, and he was called 'old camel knees.' Lord, we want **calloused knees** and yet, *tender hearts*."[407]

"'Tis Midnight, and on Olive's Brow"

'Tis midnight, and for other's guilt,
The Man of Sorrows weeps in blood;
Yet he that hath in anguish **knelt**
I s not forsaken by His God.

—*William B. Tappan*

Mack Lyon is the host of the international television and radio ministry called, *In Search of the Lords Way*. In his booklet entitled, *Holy and Reverend is His Name,* he quotes a number of verses on **worship** that include **bowing the knees** from both the Old Testament and the New Testament. He then makes this observation: "Always, when people or angels are seen **worshiping** God, it is an act of **humble obeisance** with *reverence* and fear, **bowing themselves** to the ground. What we read in the Bible about **worshiping** God is a far cry from what we will find when we enter most assemblies of **worshipers** today. He then quotes Psalm 95:1–7 that includes, 'O come, let us **worship** and **bow down**: let us **kneel** before the Lord, our Maker. For He is our God; and we are the people of his pasture, and the sheep of his hand.'" Mack Lyon then reminds us that, "**Worship** is the **lowest human posture** of *humility* and *submission*." He then shares this brief story: "A young Christian friend and I visited a really old church building. As we passed down the center aisle, he noticed what

406. Christian, Jeff. "Making Theology Practical." ACU Lectures, Abilene, TX, 1997, Audiocassette.

407. Scott, John. "Bluejean Christianity." Saturn Road Church of Christ, Dallas, TX, June 16, 1996, Audiocassette.

he called the foot rests; they were padded. I said, 'No, those are **kneeling rails.**' He laughed, and thought it was funny. He didn't believe me. A few congregations still have them. Our lack of *reverence* and genuine *awe* of Him in our **worshiping** assemblies is at the very heart of the many social ills from which we suffer so today. Why not **bow with your face to the ground** in genuine *humility* and *submit* to doing His will completely?"[408]

Dan Dozier uses the apostle Paul as our example. He says, "In writing to the Ephesians, Paul said, 'For this reason, I **kneel before** the Father from whom His whole family in heaven and on earth derives His *name*.' There are other positions that the Bible talks about in terms of physical postures for prayer. But, **kneeling in our worship** services, as well as is in our private time, is deeply, Biblically established."[409]

Rick Atchley: "Jesus taught us to pray, 'Thy will be done on earth as it is in heaven.' Right now we don't see His will being done on earth as it is in heaven, but that's what we're supposed to pray for. I think things are going to stay like they are until we get leaders out of meetings and **onto their knees.** We are tempted to do supernatural work through natural power. God forgive us."[410]

"It Came Upon the Midnight Clear"

It came upon the midnight clear
That glorious song of old,
From angels **bending** near the earth,
To touch their harps of gold.

—Edmund H. Sears

Chris Dempsey: "Luke records Jesus as being in agony as He '**fell down upon His knees.**' The prayer that He prayed was from His heart. His cries stemmed from His soul."[411]

408. Lyon, Mack. *Holy and Reverend is His Name.* Huntsville: Publishing Designs, Inc., 2000, 33–38.

409. Dozier, Daniel A. "Worship is a Verb." The Church That Connects III Seminar, San Antonio, TX, August 6, 1994, Audiocassette.

410. Atchley, Rick. "Resurrecting the Power of Prayer." *Up from the Grave, Jubilee Seminar*, 1998, Audiocassette.

411. Dempsey, Chris. "Teach Us to Pray." FHU Bible Lectures, Henderson, TN, 1994, Audiocassette.

Earnest Gentile: "Paul the apostle called together the Ephesian church elders, then unashamedly '**kneeled down** and prayed with them all' (Acts 20:36). He also '**kneeled down** on the shore, and prayed' with the Christian men, women, and children of Tyre (Acts 21:5)."[412]

Jack Lewis: "The primary '**worship**' word in the OT is that of **bowing one's self** in the presence of a superior. The gesture is that of *unconditional surrender*. I think that we not only have rejected the gesture but also have rejected the **bowing of the spirit** to a larger extent in the presence of the Lord."[413]

Whitney Montgomery wrote a poem that speaks of the inward matching the outward:

I **knelt** to pray when day was done
And prayed 'O Lord bless everyone.
Let me but live another day,
And I will live the way I pray!'

—*Whitney Montgomery*

Perry Cotham has been a successful preacher for over 35 years. He was approached after services one Sunday morning by his good friend, Sherron Trimble. He asked the question, "Perry, with these declarations of 'amen,' raising hands', and 'getting **down on our knees**' for prayer songs—Is that what is meant by contemporary **worship**?" Perry Cotham responded by saying, "Well, there's nothing contemporary about saying 'amen' and getting **down on your knees** in church. I remember that men in my grandfather's generation did that every Sunday—that's very traditional. Sherron replied, 'Of course, it's traditional, and as ancient as biblical times.'"[414]

Tony Evans is a gifted public speaker and preacher who wrote about Psalm 95 and calls it, "The Invitation to **Worship and Bow Down**." He quoted Psalm 95:6 which says, "Come, let us **worship and bow down**; let us **kneel before** the Lord our Maker: For He is our God

412. Gentile, Earnest B. *Worship God*! Portland: City Bible publishing, 1994, 197.

413. Lewis, Jack. "OT Word Studies in Worship" FHU Bible Lectureship, Henderson, TN, 1994, Audiocassette.

414. Cotham, Perry C. *Ceasefire: Ending Worship Wars with Sound Theology & Plain Common Sense*. Orange: New Leaf Books, 2002, 219.

(Psalm 95:6–7a)." He then reminds us that **worship** in the Bible has a wide range of emotions: from celebration to **kneeling** in *humility*. He is convinced that, "The reason we don't **bow down** more in **worship** is that we don't remember what God has done. We don't remember what He has brought us from. The psalmist calls God 'our Maker' (Psalm 95:6). He is our Creator and our Redeemer."

Tony Evans then says, "Although Psalm 95 invites us to **worship,** it closes with a warning: 'Do not harden your hearts, as when your fathers tested Me, they tried Me, though they had seen My work (vv. 8–9). The Lord goes on to say that the people who were indifferent and rebellious toward Him would not enter into His rest (Vv. 10–11). Our problem today is that we don't take God seriously."[415]

Richard Pruitt: "**Kneeling/bowing** should not be understood as a cultural matter. It is about *humility* and the breaking down of pride. Simply put, contemporary believers are supposed to utilize **kneeling** during **worship** and prayer, just as any other people group at any other time in history. I believe that we do not utilize **kneeling** enough in our times of prayer and **worship,** and that there is something greater that we can experience in Christ as we place ourselves in a position of *humility*. May our hearts be open to the Holy Spirit as He guides us. Let us **kneel** before our God!"[416]

Lynn Anderson has recently written a very timely article titled, "**Kneeling** in Prayer! Literally?" He opens the topic by saying, "Sometimes the content of our hearts is better expressed in the *posture of our bodies* when we **worship** than in just the words we say. Generations of God's people who have come before us appreciated the importance of **worship** *posture* far better than many of us do in our day. Whether this is just another sign of our culture's lack of respect for important things, or important people, or if it is just a habit, our attention to **worship** *posture* has changed dramatically over the years." He concludes by asking, "Could our day have lost some of the sense of God's Majesty and Holiness expressed in the *posture*

415. Evans, Tony. *What Matters Most*. Moody Press, Accessed 2001 Online: http//www.fni.com/heritage/jun97/Evans.html.

416. Pruitt, Richard. Accessed May 15, 2000, Online: htpp://www.guam.net/home/richpruitt/page22.html.

of **worshippers** in former times?—Something to think about, unless we just want to *sit* there 'as a sign of nothing.'"[417]

"Angels We Have Heard of High"

Come to Bethlehem, and see Him
Whose birth the angels sing;
Come, adore **on bended knee**
Christ the Lord, the newborn King.

—*Warren M. Angell*

Charles Stanley urges us to do the following: "Surrender your will to Him, pray for understanding, and rest in His trustworthiness to see you through your valley. Only when we are driven **to our knees** can we be built up. Then, as strong, Godly followers of Christ, we will stand firm when the fiercest storms strike."[418]

Ronald Allen: "One day **every knee will bow before** the risen Christ, but, sadly, not all will **bow** in joy. But we have the opportunity now, in this life, to **worship** God. We can **cause our selves to bow down** in reverent **worship**."[419]

James Burton Coffman: "Many in all ages have **prostrated themselves before** God in **worship** and in prayers, and the admissibility of this as legitimate is plain enough in this verse. (Commentary on I Corinthians 14:25)."[420]

"Zion's Call"

On the road to the goal burdens we must bear,
But we have help from realms above;
We receive courage new when we **kneel** in prayer,
Let us list to the call of love.

—*J. R. Baxter, Jr.*

417. Anderson, Lynn. Accessed May 30, 2001, Online: http://www.heartlight.org/articles/200105/20010530_kneeling.html.

418. Stanley, Charles. "From the Pastor's Heart," *In Touch*, March 2003.

419. Allen, Ronald B. *The Wonder of Worship*. Nashville: Word Publishing, 2001, 119.

420. Coffman, James Burton. *Commentary on 1 and 2 Corinthians*. Austin: Firm Foundations, 1979, 236.

Jack Reese also uses the apostle Paul as our example. He says, "In Acts 20, Paul prays for the last time with the Ephesian elders and they pray, **down on their knees**—Paul and the elders in prayer. And in Acts 21, he makes his way to the city of Tyre, and they go to the beach—men and women and children—and Paul—**down on their knees** in prayer, because an appropriate response of **worship** is *to surrender*."[421]

In 2004, Jim Thomas tells us what it means to "**worship** in spirit and in truth." He says, "To have such an encounter with the living God, to *commune* with Him in the deepest recesses of our being, to **fall at His feet** in honor of His Lordship and **kneel before** His throne, this is what it means to **worship** in spirit and in truth."[422]

Richard Leonard is correct when he says, "Although Jesus had spoken of genuine **worship** of the Father as **worship** 'in spirit and in truth' (En pneumai kai aletheia, John 4:23). This did not mean that Christian **worship** was so spiritual that it was invisible. Within the assembly of believers, acts of **worship** were visible acts. The word translated **'worship'**, as noted above, means to **kneel, bow**, or **prostrate one's self**, and such actions must accompany the vocal expressions of praise and supplication. Paul, for one, expressed his faith in prayer, 'I **kneel before** the Father' (Eph. 3:14)."[423]

Jim Goll wrote the book called ***Kneeling** on the Promises*. In the first chapter titled, **On Bended Knee**, he asks, "Why **kneeling?**" He then explains that, "**Kneeling** is a picture of dependency. **Kneeling** is a *posture of humility* and *brokenness*. **Kneeling** is a sign of *reverence* and honor. **Kneeling** is the act of **worship** that precedes petitioning. **Kneeling** is an outward expression of an inward work of grace. In fact, Paul tells us, 'I **bow my knees before** the Father of our Lord Jesus Christ.' Isn't that awesome? Sooner or later we are all going to **kneel**. Philippians 2:9–10 portrays this picture graphically."[424]

421. Reese, Jack. Preston Road Church of Christ, Dallas, TX, January 2, 1994, Audiocassette.

422. Thomas, Jim. "Worship: the Other Fall," *Worship Leader*, Fall 2004, 11.

423. Leonard, Richard C. "New Testament Vocabulary of Worship," *The Biblical foundations of Christian Worship*, Robert E. Webber, ed. Nashville: Star Song Publishing Group, 1993,19–23.

424. Goll, Jim W. *Kneeling on the Promises*. Grand Rapids: Chosen Books, 2000, 20.

Marilyn Dowdy at Oklahoma Christian University says, "I find it interesting that many of the practices our younger members wish to initiate are things done by generations long gone. The younger ones want to **kneel** in prayer—the men in the church from the 1900's were required to **kneel** in prayer. Young ones want to raise hands in prayer. Older men, including Dr. George Benson (former president of Harding) always raised one hand in leading public prayer. Maybe we are not changing, but making a full cycle back to our roots?"[425]

A good poem to conclude with is:

"Overtones"

I heard a bird at break of day, sing from the autumn trees
A song so mystical and calm, so full of certainties.
I think one could not listen long, except **upon their knees**.
Yet this was but a simple bird, alone, among dead trees.

—*William Alexander Percy*

28. Should the congregation be *invited* to kneel?

David Dykes invited others to **kneel** by his example. The day after 9-11 in Tyler, Texas, I attended the area wide "Community Prayer Service" held at Green Acres Baptist church.

In front of a packed audience, David Dykes **kneeled down** when he began the special prayer for the victims and their families. I **kneeled** also, along with many others."[426]

As mentioned earlier, Charles Stanley, in 1991, invited "more than 2000 politicians and other notables" to **kneel** at "the annual Leadership Luncheon in the main ballroom of the Washington Hilton Hotel in 1991. He preached from James 5:16—about the need for America to *humble* itself before God. He allowed that some might not be physically able, but for the rest he said, 'Unless God does something in this nation, we are going to be humiliated in some fashion, at some time. I want to ask you if

425. Dowdy, Marilyn. A Response to "Worthy is our Worship?" *Christian Chronicle*, September 2000.

426. Dykes, David. "Facing the Future without Fear." Green Acres Baptist Church, Tyler, TX, September 12, 2001, Audiocassette.

you'll join me **on my knees.**' Gradually, chairs began shuffling, and most of the crowd followed his lead."[427]

I was privileged to be present when Scotty Ratliff, a gifted Worship Leader and Youth Minister, invited the congregation to **kneel** in Brownwood, Texas. He began by saying, "I feel very humble in the presence of our Lord this morning. I feel burdened for the needs of this congregation. When Jesus was burdened in the Garden of Gethsemane, He **kneeled** when He prayed to the Father (Luke 22:41). And the apostle Paul said, 'I **bow my knees** to the Father' (Eph. 3:14). And at the name of Jesus **every knee should bow** (Phil. 2:10). If you would allow me to, I would like to **kneel down** as we pray this morning, looking to Jesus as our example. If you are physically able, and you would like to, I invite you to join me. You can just **kneel** in front of the pew where you are sitting. If you are not physically able or would feel uncomfortable, it's O.K. You don't have to. Now, with **humble hearts**, let us go to our Heavenly Father in prayer."[428]

Mike Warner invited his congregation to "humble themselves" on Sunday evening, April 29, 2001. When I visited with Mike one week later he said, "You should have been here last Sunday night. Everybody was **on their knees.**" I ordered the audiocassette and heard Mike Warner say, "The Lord can use us when our hearts are right—when we're *humbled* before the Lord—when we're surrendered to the Lord—when we're willing to be His servants, and His instruments. Scripture says, 'The Lord resists the proud, but He gives grace to the *humble*.' I'm going to ask you to join me in humbling ourselves before the Lord, in whatever way that means for you. If you are most humbled before the Lord **on your knees**, or if that means you stand, or if that means that you sit in the pew with your head bowed, or if it means you raise your hands—whatever it means to you to humble yourself before the Lord. Harvey Grant is going to come and lead us in prayer."[429]

427. Merrill, Dean. "Whatever Happened to Kneeling?" *Christianity Today*, February 10, 1992, 24.

428. Ratliff, Scotty. Worship Leader & Youth Minister, Austin Avenue Church of Christ, Brownwood, Texas, November 29, 1992.

429. Warner, Mike. "He said, "Love One Another." Shiloh Road Church of Christ, Tyler, TX, April 22, 2001, Audiocassette

"No Higher Calling"

Down at your feet, oh Lord, is the most high place.
In your presence, Lord, We seek your face.
There is no higher calling, no greater honor,
Than to **bow and kneel** before your throne.
I'm amazed at your glory, embraced by your mercy,
Oh Lord, I live to **worship** you.

—Lenny LeBlanc, Greg Gulley

Robert Webber says, "We **dropped to our knees** as instructed and stretched our arms forward with palms directed upward as a symbol of receptivity to the Holy Spirit."[430]

Rick Atchley is an humble and dynamic preacher in Ft. Worth, Texas. When he invited his congregation to **kneel**, he said, "Why don't we sing '**On Bended Knee I Come**'? He then prayed, "Father, we know that before we can rise we have to **kneel.** That is what we do this morning. Receive this offering of our contrite spirits—This we pray in the name of the one that taught us to be servants, Jesus of Nazareth."[431]

I was present one Sunday morning at the Saturn Road Church of Christ in Garland, Texas shortly after the year 2000 began. Following an excellent sermon by John Scott, a penitent young father came forward. In his written request, he asked that the elders **kneel** with him, and pray that his relationship to God and his family be restored. I gladly joined all the other folks who **kneeled**, and I received a blessing as well.

Richard C Leonard is considered an authority on "worship words." He says, "**Worshipers** are invited to **bow down** (*kara*', Psalm 95:6; Isaiah 45:23) to the Lord, to **kneel** or **bend the knee** (*berekh*, Psalm 95:6) **before** him."[432]

Dan Dozier: "People need to be given permission to **kneel**, to say 'amen,' even to lift their hands to God, if they feel the need to express themselves to the Father in that way. Not only is this type of physical participation

430. Webber, Robert E. *Worship is a Verb*. Nashville: Star Song Publishers, 1992, 148.

431. Atchley, Rick. "If My People Will Humble Themselves." Revive Us Again #2, Richland Hills Church of Christ, Ft. Worth, TX, June 21, 1998, Audiocassette.

432. Leonard, Richard C. "Old Testament Vocabulary of Worship," *The Complete Library of Christian Worship*, Vol. 1, Robert E. Weber, ed. Nashville: Star Song Publishing Co., 1993, 5.

Biblical, it also has the practical benefit of helping people keep their attention focused on the Lord."[433]

Gary Selby wonders, "What would happen if just once, when we were about to pray, we invited any who wished—to **kneel before** the Lord?"[434]

Marvin Phillips said, "If you want to come in and get **down on your knees.** Understand there is an awesome God into whose presence we have come. Some people come out of habit with no expectation, and other people come in like one of those new choruses today: 'We place you on the highest place, for you are the great high priest. We place you high above all else, and we **bow and worship at your feet.**'—Wonderful, wonderful, marvelous song. Well, *it takes a personal encounter to bring this awe.*"[435]

In a personal communication with Jerry McChehren, he believes **kneeling** has "an impact." He recalled, "As our new member started to lead the congregation in prayer, he said, 'Where I came from, we always get **on our knees** to pray, and we haven't done that yet. Would you all mind doing that with me?' He had that whole Church **on their knees** and it really had an impact on that Church."

Roland Bowen closed his sermon by saying, "The choice is ours now. The scriptures tell us that one day **every knee will bow** and every tongue will *confess*. I encourage you today to *confess* His name. We are in His *presence* now. But He calls you to come into His *presence* and to **kneel before** Him —to **kneel** at His cross. Will you come as we stand and sing a song for your encouragement?"[436]

Mike Warner told his congregation, "If you need to **kneel** when we pray as your expression of humility before God, I would encourage you to do that. Likewise, if someone can pray more naturally seated with **bowed** head, I encourage them to do so. Do you need to lift your hands to God?

433. Dozier, Daniel A. *Come Let Us Adore Him*. Joplin: College Press Publishing Co, 1994, 244.

434. Selby, Gary. "Journey to Worship: A Personal Journey," *Image Magazine,* 1994, 32.

435. Phillips, Marvin. "Bowing Before an Awesome God." Jubilee Seminar, Nashville, TN, 1994, Audiocassette.

436. Bowen, Roland."Kneeling in His Presence." Austin Avenue Church of Christ, Brownwood, Texas, October 11, 1998, Audiocassette.

If that will help you **worship** more fervently and sincerely, then I need for you to do it."[437]

Welton Gaddy: "Often the Psalmist seems to function as the **worship** leader in a cosmic service of praise. Many of his words have the sound of a '**call to worship**' extended to a congregation made up of the whole creation. Psalm 95:6–7a says, 'O come, let us **worship and bow down**, let us **kneel before** the Lord, our Maker!'"[438]

"Our God wears the crown"

O come, let us **worship** and **bow down**:
Let us **kneel before** the Lord our maker!
For He is our God who wears the crown,
Then, let us rise to serve our great creator.

—*Ralph Rowe (From Psalm 95)*

Before Lynn Anderson began the closing prayer at the Church that Connects III Seminar, he invited everyone who wished to **kneel** to please do so. This occurred in San Antonio, Texas in August, 1994. The church auditorium was filled to capacity and I was surprised and pleased when almost everyone present responded to his invitation. It was also a pleasant experience for me, because I was into my second year of studying **kneeling in worship**, and was in the process of documenting all the **kneeling** events in the New Testament. As I **kneeled**, along with the others, I felt very *humble* with a strong assurance of the Lord's *presence*. (Personal Experience).

Robert Webber refers to **kneeling** many times in his book, *Worship is a Verb*. He told an interesting story about his friend Dan Sharp and his experience with **kneeling** at Grace Chapel in Lexington, Mass. Dan Sharp said, "One of the first Sundays that I asked everyone to **kneel** during the prayer, some people came to me with tears in their eyes, thanking me. One said, 'Now that I know Christ, **kneeling** takes on a whole new context." Dan Sharp went on to say, "In the next sanctuary we build, **kneelers** are a very obvious thing to put in."[439]

437. Warner, Mike. "Being Big People," *Shiloh Family Chronicle*, Tyler, TX, March 15, 1998, 1.

438. Gaddy, Welton C. *The Gift of Worship*. Nashville: Broadman Press, 1992, xviii.

439. Webber, Robert E. *Worship is a Verb*. Nashville: Star Song Publishing Group, 1992, 104.

When I visited the Preston Road Church of Christ in Dallas, TX, on Jan. 2, 1994, the song leader said, "You should have been here this morning. Jack Reese had **everyone on their knees**." That got my attention, and I ordered the cassette tape of the sermon that Dr. Reese preached on Psalm 95, and when he arrived at verse 6, he said, "The **worshipers** are called to a response that is also appropriate in our assemblies. The Psalmist says, 'Come, let us **worship** and **bow down**. Let us **kneel before** the Lord, our Maker.' Come in submission. Come in reverence. Come in awareness of who God is, and you see God in all of His greatness and glory, but you see yourself also."[440]

Lynn Anderson often invited his congregation to **kneel**. He once said, "I have just been delighted the last few weeks when we have literally **knelt** for prayer. I'm going to sort of put in our minds—that at the end tonight—when we are dismissed, for those who are comfortable, we would **kneel** for prayer at that time. That's one of those physical manifestations of **worship**. The act itself, says what words cannot say to God. And the act itself creates in us an experience that words themselves cannot create."[441]

Rex Humbard invited all those who wanted prayer to come and **kneel** at the altar. He said, "With every head bowed and every eye closed, how many of you want prayer? Lift your hands. Every man, woman, boy, and girl that wants prayer, lift your hands to the Lord. The Lord will see it. Everyone that lifted their hands for prayer, I have prepared a place for you to come and **kneel** at this altar while I pray for you."[442]

29. Final question: *Shall we kneel in worship*—literally?

In the May 2004 issue of *Gospel Advocate*, Phil Sanders is convinced that unity of God's people requires **bowing their knees** to the one Lord in every matter. Would that not include "**worship?**" He says, "There can never be unity when men abandon God's instructions for their own devices.

440. Reese, Jack. Preston Road Church of Christ, Dallas, TX, January 2, 1994, Audiocassette.

441. Anderson, Lynn. Preston Road Church of Christ, Dallas, TX, 1993, Audiocassette.

442. Humbard, Rex. "Born Again." January 7, 1971, Audiocassette.

Unity comes at the price of all men **bowing their knees** to the one Lord in every matter."[443]

In The *Tyler Morning Telegraph*, Sec. 10A, June 25, 2004, Mike Warner says, **"On Your Knees !** 'That at the name of Jesus **every knee should bow**, of those who are in heaven, and on earth, and under the earth' (Philippians 2:10). Read Philippians two. You will be left **on your knees before** the Lord. It's one of the most profound portions of scripture in the Bible. Paul explains (in verses 5–11) that because Jesus left heaven and came to earth as a man, and because He became a servant and gave himself up to die on a Roman cross; as a result of the perfect life and perfect sacrifice, God has declared that in the entire universe of both physical and spiritual beings, there is no one greater than His Son. In fact, God demands, that **the knee of every being, is to bow before** Jesus and acknowledge that He is 'Lord.' But notice something—something important—the acknowledgement of the Lordship of Jesus is not that He is Lord of the Cosmos or even that He is Lord of heaven and earth, it is that He is YOUR Lord! Have you got the picture? The Almighty God of Heaven says, 'This is My Son who died for you! **On your knees** before Him!'"[444]

Mike Cope: For review, he uses Mary, the sister of Lazarus to illustrate. He points out that, "When Mary is there with Jesus, she is **kneeling** at His feet. In Luke 10, she is **kneeling** at His feet soaking up His words. In John Chapter 11, she is **kneeling** at His feet sharing her grief with Him. And in John chapter 12, she is **kneeling** at His feet, and wiping her tears from His feet with her hair. Now that is not a bad place for us to be in 2004, is it—at Jesus' feet?"[445] Amen!

443. Sanders, Phil. "Then and Now," *Gospel Advocate*, May 2004, Vol. CXLVI, No. 5, 14.

444. Warner, Mike. "On Your Knees," *Tyler Morning Telegraph*, Sec. 10A, June 25, 2004.

445. Cope, Mike. "Kneeling at Jesus Feet." Highland Church of Christ, Abilene, TX, January 1, 2004, Audiocassette

"How Great Thou Art"

When Christ shall come with shout of acclimation
And take me home, what joy shall fill my heart!
Then I **shall bow in humble adoration**
And there proclaim, My God, how great Thou art!

—Stuart K. Hine

Finally, what source or testimony shall we use to answer the final question: Shall we **kneel** in **worship**—literally? After **kneeling** in prayer personally, the decision was made to have a Bible scholar answer, who also believes that the Word of God is the "Final Supreme Court of Appeal." Therefore, if anyone still has reservations about **kneeling** in **worship**, and wants a Biblical answer, Dr. Daniel A. (Dan) Dozier offers this wise counsel. He says, "I challenge you to search the Scriptures again. I am convinced I will **bow** and **kneel** and raise my hands to the Lord in heaven, and I do not want to wait until I get there to start expressing my adoration and reverence in those ways. After you re-examine Scripture, I think you will be forced to admit that these practices are found in Scripture in the form of commands, necessary inferences, and examples."[446] Amen!

"The Old Country Church"

As a small country boy, how my heart filled with joy
When I **knelt** in the old country church,
And the Savior above, by His wonderful love
Saved my soul at the old country church.

—Author unknown

446. Dozier, Daniel A. *Come Let Us Adore Him*. Joplin: College Press Publishing Co., 1994, 291.

8

Review of Study Findings—Kneeling in Worship

THIS STUDY ON **KNEELING** in **worship** was done to determine (1) if the New Testament "**worship**" word in John 4:24 includes "**bowing the knees**" or **kneeling**, literally, (2) if the **kneeling** gesture is one that our heavenly Father approves and desires in our worship, or if **kneeling** is just another prayer posture, (3) if **kneeling** is just a matter of culture, and (4) to document all the **worship** events in the NT that include a form of **bowing the knees.** This task was undertaken using the five (5) reliable sources of information or testimony. Again, for ease of recognition, the words that indicate a form of **bowing the knees** or **kneeling** are bolded.

1. <u>The Testimony of History</u>: Numerous historical facts that document **kneeling** in worship, including the OT, were mentioned in various places throughout the study. The 13 different Greek words translated as "**worship**" in the NT were discussed in chapter V. Examples of various Bible versions were displayed in a table format showing the trend toward a more literal translation of the Greek terms that should help decrease the confusion that now exists. This study revealed that the main Greek word translated as "worship" in the New Testament is *proskuneo* which is also the **worship** word used in John 4:23–24.

Which churches **kneel** routinely? In questioning the various groups, I found that the Greek Orthodox churches, the Episcopal or Anglican churches, the Catholic churches, the Lutheran churches, and some Baptist churches practice **kneeling** during their time of "**worship**." For example, Dr. David Dykes, at the Green acres Baptist Church in Tyler, Texas—**kneels** routinely during prayer. Also, a lady Physician who works at the University of Texas Health Center in Tyler, Texas said that the Baptist church where she attends, **kneels** routinely during every worship service.

Kneel literally? The Testimony of Bible Scholars

Joe E. Strickland, Monsignor and Rector of the Cathedral of the Immaculate Conception Catholic Church, in Tyler, Texas reminds us that, "**Genuflection** is the traditional **bending to one knee** that the priests and faithful are called to perform in the presence of the Eucharist (the consecrated bread and wine that we believe that Christ is truly present in)."

2. The Testimony of the Lexicons (or Greek dictionaries) documented that the two-act "*proskuneo* pattern" of worship that includes **bowing the knees** is present in the definition of the main "worship" word *proskuneo* in John 4:23–24. The findings from the eleven (11) Greek-English Lexicons are summarized in a table format as follows:

WHAT IS WORSHIP (PROSKUNEO)?

	OUTWARD ACTS		INWARD
Reference	**FIRST ACT**	**SECOND ACT**	**ATTITUDE or INTENT**
The Sum Or Combination of All Lexicons	Kneel or prostrate oneself	To (*pros* to or toward) and (*kuneo*) To kiss (hand, feet, ground, hem of garment reverently). to kiss toward, or throw a kiss toward	(Fall down and) worship Reverence, Humility, Adore, Venerate, homage, Honor, Reverence, obeisance, Unconditional subjection

The Bauer Lexicon gave the shortest summarized definition of *proskuneo* which is "(**Fall down** and) **worship.**" Obviously, that definition indicates that the act of *proskuneo* is always preceded by **bowing the knees**. In fact, all of the Lexicons except Young's Concordance included a form of **kneeling** or **prostration** in the definition.

3. The Testimony of the Translators also documented that the word *proskuneo* includes **bowing the knees**. Twenty-eight (28) of the thirty (30) Bible versions examined, translated the word *proskuneo* as a form of **bowing the knees** one or more times. Only the 1611 King James Version, and the 1901 American Standard Version translate the verb *proskuneo* as "**worship**" each time that it occurs for a total of 60 times. This indicates

that the more recent translators of the New Testament acknowledge the fact that the act of "bowing the knees" by **kneeling** or **falling prostrate** is present or included in the *proskuneo* **worship** event. For example, the 2001 Analytical-Literal Translation of the New Testament (ALT) translates the word *proskuneo* as a form of **bowing the knees** 59 times out of 60.

4. "<u>The Testimony of God", or Scripture</u> (1 Corinthians 2:1 KJV), documents that the two-act "proskuneo pattern" of worship can be demonstrated 99 times in the NT, as shown in the Worship Chart, is referred to in the following three ways: (a) 35 times by the first act, (b) 51 times by the second act, and (c) 13 times by both acts. The wise men mentioned the word worship (proskuneo: kiss toward) the first time in the NT in Matthew 2:2, and they were referring to the two-act "*proskuneo* pattern" of worship to be performed in Matthew 2:11: The wise men **fell down and worshiped** (*proskuneo*: kissed toward) the Christ child. The last command in the Bible is "worship (*proskuneo*: kiss toward) God" (Rev. 22:9). This is the angel's response to John who "**fell down** to **worship** (*proskuneo*: kiss toward)" the angel. Scripture has shown that each act in the two-act "*proskuneo* pattern" is a part of speech called a synecdoche, which means that a part can be mentioned for the whole. Thus, the act of **bowing the knees** is understood to be present in the angel's command by necessary inference or by means of a synecdoche. If the act of **bowing the knees** is not understood to be present in the angel's command, then the angel changed the subject. It is the same "worship" word Jesus and the Samaritan woman used nine (9) times in John 4:20-24.

Also, we learned that Matthew, Mark, Luke, John, Paul and Jesus all referred to the "*proskuneo* pattern" in each of the three ways. Scripture showed that Jesus and all the apostles practiced **kneeling** in **worship**. We also found that the parallel accounts of the *proskuneo* worship events supplement each other and can only be harmonized by using the words that God used—the words that He breathed into the inspired writers. The word "kiss", which is the literal translation of *proskuneo*, was required when harmonizing Philippians 2:10 with Psalms 2:12, and Romans 11:4 with the Old Testament in 1 Kings 19:18.

And finally, we learned that when the OT was translated into Greek (the Septuagint) in 270 BC that the main Hebrew "worship" word *shachah* that means to "**bow down**" was replaced with the Greek word *proskuneo* a total of 170 times.

5. The Testimony of Bible Scholars supports the act of **Kneeling** in worship and documents that the Greek "worship" word *proskuneo* used in John 4:23-24 includes **bowing the knees** by definition and by its practice. Also, the Bible scholars gave answers to 31 key questions. Some of the quotes are educational—Some are inspirational—Some are enlightening—Some are encouraging, but all the quotes are informative, and worth studying. Now, here are some questions for the readers of this study.

What are the Truthful Facts regarding the "worship" word *proskuneo* that is used in John 4:23–24?

Interestingly, a sign spotted outside the Church of Christ in Mountlake Terrace says, "God Answers **Knee-mail**."[1]

All agree that any and all acts of **worship** should be done according to the truth of God's word. John 17:17 says, "Thy word is truth" (KJV). The Greek word that Jesus said, "true worshipers" shall do "in spirit and in truth" is *proskuneo*: "But the hour cometh, and now is, when the true worshipers shall worship (*proskuneo*) the Father in spirit and in truth: for the Father seeketh such to worship (*proskuneo*) Him. God is a Spirit: and they that worship (*proskuneo*) Him must worship (*proskuneo*) Him in spirit and in truth" (John 4:23–24 KJV). The last command in the Bible is "Worship (*proskuneo*) God" (Rev. 22:9).

Spiros Zodhiates wrote *The Complete Word Study of the Old Testament*. He says that, "*proskuneo* (NT) and *shachah* (OT) were not used in the Bible for **worship** in general. He emphasizes that, "*Shachah* was not used in the general sense of worship, but specifically to **bow down, to prostrate oneself** as an act of respect before a superior being.' The equivalent' in the New Testament is '*proskuneo*.'"[2]

This study has searched the Scriptures (Acts 17:11) for the "TRUTH" regarding worship (*proskuneo*). Jimmy Clark at the Florida School of Preaching is correct when he says, "The inspired word of God is only present where the text is accurately translated."[3] So now, what do the Lexicons or Greek dictionaries say *proskuneo* means?

1. Godden, Jean. "Ballard loyalists unite," *The Seattle Times*, May 29, 2002.

2. Zodhiates, Spiros and Warren Baker. *The Complete Word Study Old Testament*: Chattanooga: AMG Publishers, 1994, 2372.

3. Clark, Jimmy.—"Expediencies in Worship"—Florida School of Preaching Lectureships, Lakeland, FL, 1998, 377.

1. A Summary of the Testimony of Lexicons regarding the "worship" word *proskuneo* that is used in John 4:20–24 *Proskuneo*: is derived from the Greek *pros*, meaning "to" or "toward," and *kuneo*, meaning "kiss"—literally "to kiss," or "kiss toward," or throw a "kiss toward" the object of worship while **kneeling** or **prostrating oneself** to express submission, reverence, **worship**, or adoration. So now, what do the Scriptures say?

2. A Summary of the Testimony of Scripture regarding the "worship" word *proskuneo* that is used in John 4:23–24.

Just for added emphasis, the ole' cowboy Texas Bix Bender has said, "Comin' as close to the truth as a man can come—without actually getting there—is comin' pretty close, but it still ain't the truth."[4]

Seeking the truthful facts about **kneeling** in **worship** was the primary reason this task was undertaken using the following five (5) reliable sources of information or testimony: Scripture, the Lexicons (or Greek dictionaries), Bible translators, history, and Bible scholars. All five testimonies supported and documented **kneeling** in **worship**, literally! So here are the TRUTHFUL FACTS found in God's word regarding the "**worship**" word *proskuneo* used in John 4:23–24:

- *Proskuneo*: is derived from the Greek *pros*, meaning "to" or "toward", and *kuneo*, meaning "kiss"—literally "to kiss", or "kiss toward", or throw a "kiss toward" the object of worship, while **kneeling** or **prostrating oneself**, to express submission, reverence, worship, or adoration.
- *Proskuneo* is the Greek verb that Jesus said "true worshipers" shall do "in spirit and in truth" (John 4:23–24) and, therefore, it excludes all other verbs.
- *Proskuneo* is the most common Greek word translated "worship" in the NT, which is a total of 60 times.
- *Proskuneo* is always the second act in the two-act "*proskuneo* pattern" that occurs in Scripture by command, example and necessary inference.
- *Proskuneo* is always done in the NT while **bowing the knees**, which is the first act in the two-act "*proskuneo* pattern" of worship.
- *Proskuneo* is never done in the NT while sitting or standing.

4. Bender, Texas Bix. *Don't Squat with your Spurs On*: Layton, UT. Published by Gibb Smith. 1994 Preface.

- (This fact was confirmed by professors at four different Christian Universities).
- *Proskuneo* never begins until the **knees bend.**
- *Proskuneo* always ends when the knees extend.
- *Proskuneo* is the only "worship" word used in the Bible in the Worship Assembly
- (1 Cor. 14:25; Acts 8:27; 24:11).
- *Proskuneo* is the only "worship" word used in the book of Revelation, and thus, around the throne in heaven.
- *Proskuneo* was never done "figuratively" or "in the heart only.
- Several worshipers in the NT performed the "*proskuneo* pattern" *in pretense* and not *in truth* because they did not rise to serve (*latreuo* Matt 4:10).
- The meaning of *proskuneo* and the "*proskuneo* pattern" never changed during the writing of the NT—from the first chapter of Matthew to the last chapter of Revelation. If the meaning of *proskuneo* changed after the New Testament was written, it was changed by men—not by God.
- *Proskuneo* never requires a *visible* presence. Example: 1 Cor. 14:25.
- "Speaking where the Bible speaks:" None of the "five acts of worship" were ever called "worship" (*proskuneo*) in the NT. That includes singing, praying, teaching, giving, and the Lord's Supper. In fact, none of the 13 Greek words translated as a form of "**worship**" in the NT were used with any of the "five acts"—even though
- they do "ascribe worth." Also, in contrast to "worship" (*proskuneo*), each of the "five acts" can be done while sitting or standing.
- *Proskuneo* (NT) and *shachah* (OT) were "not used in the general sense of worship in the Bible, but specifically to **bow down, to prostrate oneself** as an act of respect before a superior being . . . See the equivalent, *proskuneo.*"[5]
- When the Hebrew OT was translated into Greek (the Septuagint 270 BC), *proskuneo* is the Greek "**worship**" word used a total of 170 times to replace the Hebrew "**worship**" word *shachah*, which means to "**bow down.**"
- 2000 years have come and gone since the original New Testament was written, and yet, the Lexicons, the Translators, and yes, even the

5. Zodhiates, Spiros and Warren Baker. *The Complete Word Study Old Testament* Chattanooga: AMG Publishers 1994, 2372.

Kneel literally? The Testimony of Bible Scholars

Bible scholars acknowledge that the act of **bowing the knees** is present in the Greek word *proskuneo* by definition and by its practice.

Questions for Readers Only

1. All agree that we should, "speak the oracles of God" (1 Peter 4:11), which means we should "speak where the Bible speaks", and give a "thus saith the Lord." Does this study on **kneeling** in **worship**, do those things?
2. When Jesus was praying in the Garden of Gethsemane, what posture was He in when He presented His living body for a sacrificial death on the cross, for our sins? Luke 22:41–42 says, He **kneeled down** and prayed, saying, 'Father if thou be willing, remove this cup from me: nevertheless not my will, but thine be done'" (ASV). Does the church, which is His present living "body" on earth, need to present itself in the same posture as a "living sacrifice"—for sacrificial service?
3. All agree that, "any change that brings us closer to God is good." Would **kneeling** in **worship** help bring us closer to God?
4. All agree that, "we should respect the authority of Scripture." Does this study on **kneeling** in **worship** respect the authority of Scripture?
5. Most agree that "the SILENCE of Scripture limits what we are authorized to do in **worship**." Is the Scripture silent regarding **kneeling** in **worship**?
6. All agree that, "a servant of the Lord does not argue with God." Do you agree that, "**every knee should bow** . . . And that every tongue should confess that Jesus Christ is Lord, to the glory of God the Father . . . without murmurings and disputings?" (Phil. 2:10–14 KJV). The New American Standard says, "without grumbling or disputing."
7. All agree that any and all acts of **worship** should be done according to the truth of God's word. Some say that the posture of the body is not important when performing **worship** (*proskuneo*). They say that **kneeling** can be done figuratively or inwardly—in the heart only. However, the "**worship**" required of true **worshipers** in John 4:23–24, is **worship** (*proskuneo*) and is <u>always</u> done while **bowing the knees** in spirit and in truth. *Proskuneo* is <u>never</u> done while sitting

or standing. Question: For those who **kneel** figuratively, or inwardly—in their hearts only, what should we tell those who are baptized inwardly—in their hearts only?

8. The Bible scholar Sam Hester, addresses the issue of performing God's required physical acts inwardly—or in the heart only. For illustration, he gives a profound example. He said, "The Quakers refused the Lord's Supper and baptism. They claimed to observe these things inwardly."[1]
9. Since the title of this book came from Dr. David Dykes' prayer on his television program just five days after 9/11, it seems appropriate to mention briefly how the title obviously connects with his opening prayer and 2 Chronicles 7:14:

"IS 9/11 A KNEEL-DOWN-CALL TO HEAL AMERICA?"

Dr. Dykes **kneeled down** as he prayed, "Father, we have heard people say that 9/11 is a 'wake up call' for America, but we think this is a '**kneel down call**' to America. We need to get **on our knees** and on **our faces before** you, and seek your face. We know that only when we *humble* ourselves, and pray, and *seek* your face, and *turn* from our wicked ways—only then—will you *hear* from heaven, *forgive* our sin, and *heal* our land" (2 Chronicles 7:14).[2]

10. Should we **kneel** to *heal* this land?

What will happen if we don't?—Here is just another reminder:

When a nation is too proud
To **kneel** to daily pray,
It will crumble into chaos,
And descend into decay.

—*Helen Steiner Rice*[3]

1. Hester, Sam. "Acceptable Worship: Lessons From Church History," Henderson: FHU lectures, 1994, 144.

2. Dykes, David. "Facing the Future without Fear"—Green Acres Baptist Church in Tyler, TX, September 16, 2001, Videocassette

3. Helen Steiner Rice. *A Book of Prayer* Compiled by Virginia J. Reuhlmann, Administrator of The Helen Steiner Rice Foundation. This Guideposts edition is published by special arrangement with Fleming H. Revell, a division of Baker Book House Company: 1995, 94–95.

11. Revelation 14:7 says, "The time has come for Him to judge everyone."—Has it?

The apostle John wrote, "I saw another angel. This one was flying across the sky and had the eternal good news to announce to the people of every race, tribe, language, and nation on earth. The angel shouted, "**Worship** (*proskuneo*) and honor God! The time has come for Him to judge everyone. **Kneel down before** the One who created heaven and earth, the oceans, and every stream" (Revelation 14:7—Contemporary English Version).

"The King of Kings is Passing By"

On your knees! Along the street there comes,
Lord Jesus, our Savior, the Holy One.
And look at the awesome, Majestic sky.
Kneel down! The King of Kings—is passing by.

—Ralph Rowe